THE GIFT
OF BIRDS

FEATHERWORK OF NATIVE SOUTH AMERICAN PEOPLES

THE GIFT OF BIRDS

HEADDRESS OF SHAMAN

Apalaii people
(SA 771).

Contents

FIGURES

ACKNOWLEDGMENTS

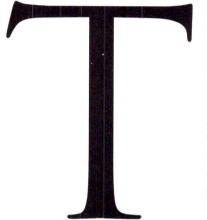There are many individuals who deserve recognition for their contributions to "The Gift of Birds" exhibition program and to this volume. I am extremely grateful and full of admiration for the talents of all the scholars, students, artists and museum professionals who participated.

In the early research phase of this project, I had the benefit of the codirection of John Lawrence, graduate student in the Department of Anthropology at the University of Pennsylvania, and the assistance of many undergraduate and graduate students in gathering and processing data and photographing collections. It soon became essential to have the participation of scholars who had lived among native peoples of the Americas and had an intimate knowledge of their language and ways of life. Ellen Basso, Kenneth Kensinger, Catherine Howard, Elizabeth Calil Zarur, and Kay Candler lent us their expertise on various South American groups, while Marianne Stoller, Dennis Lessard, and Craig Bates provided information about native groups of North America. Pamela Hearne, then Keeper of the American Section of The University Museum, was always generous with her time in helping us to survey the feathered objects of the Americas. Mark Robbins, ornithologist from the Academy of Natural Sciences in Philadelphia, examined all feathered objects and trained us in identifying feathers.

The core staff of the final exhibition project consisted, first, of the consultants for each of the areas or South American groups chosen for display—Kay Candler (Andean), Catherine Howard (Waiwai), Elizabeth Calil Zarur (Bororo), and Kenneth Kensinger (Cashinahua)—along with ornithologist Mark Robbins. These highly knowledgeable scholars assisted in planning the major themes for the didactic cases, determined which objects from the collections would

be used, and generally advised on all matters relating to their special areas. Kenneth Kensinger also undertook the coeditorship of this volume and the planning of the symposium. Kay Candler also acted as the assistant curator for the exhibition and assumed with great competence many research tasks, the coordination of installation activities, and the preparation of the text panels and labels. Connie Ledwell with great goodwill and skill served as the keeper and registrar of the collections for the exhibition. The interactive video for the exhibition would not have been possible without the dedication and proficiency of Anja Dalderup who directed the project, oversaw the research for the video and the photography of the collection, gathered other visual material, and supervised the production phases together with Glen Muschio of New Liberty Productions Company. The Museum is grateful to New Liberty Productions for their hard work and professionalism in creating a very high-quality interactive video. Irene Romano worked closely with me and assumed the coordination of many parts of the exhibit program, including grant preparation, fund-raising, and scheduling. Her constant involvement and advice made my task as curator much easier. Eleanor King served as the consultant and author for the teachers' and parents' educational guide and was vital in the earlier phases of the exhibit in the preparation of the NEH grant. To all of these key staff members I want to express my deepest and warmest appreciation.

Virginia Greene, senior conservator of the Museum, prepared the objects for display and gave of her wide technical and scholarly expertise. Tamsen Fuller assisted with testing of particular objects. The Exhibits Department, headed by John T. Murray, did an extraordinary job of designing and installing a complex exhibition. Aiding in this task were Will Bucher, Wai K. Au, Renwei Huang, Stephen Oliver, and Raymond Rorke. Christopher Ray undertook the fabrication of the model of Pachacamac, which involved a difficult trip to the site; on this he was accompanied by Edward K. Hueber. Kay Candler and Clark Erickson saw to the scholarly accuracy of the model. William Sarno deserves credit for creating the 20 remarkably lifelike and ethnographically accurate human figures and for helping to design the murals. Elizabeth Scote was of special service in preparing the models and the preliminary sketches for the murals.

I am grateful to numerous individuals for generously sharing their knowledge and time: Anne Pollard Rowe (Textile Museum, Washington, D.C.); Stephen Fabian (Hanover College); Nancy Rosoff (Museum of the American Indian, Heye Foundation); Robert Carneiro, John Hysslop, and Laila Williamson (American Museum of Natural History, New York); Vincenzo Petrullo, who shared his recollections of his 1930 expedition; Muriel Kirkpatrick; David Taicher ('88 Films, Inc.); Peter Roe (U. of Delaware); Richard Ameral; Richard Hahn (Emory U.); Helaine Silverman (U. of Illinois); Clark Erickson (Dept. of Anthropology, U. of Pennsylvania); Stephen Epstein (U. of Pennsylvania); Robert Engman (Dept. of Fine Arts, U. of Pennsylvania); Richard Chalfin (Dept. of Anthropology, Temple U.); Blenda Femenias (U. of Wisconsin); Mark Magel and Peter Lullemann, who contributed to the interactive video. The National Museum of Denmark and the Museum Aemilia Goeldi in Belém, Brazil, provided film and photographs for the video. And special thanks are owed to Charles Briggs, Michael Bernstein, William Giles, and James A. Yost for helping us to enrich our collection of feathered objects and photographic documentation.

I acknowledge with gratitude the authors who contributed to this volume: Catherine Howard, Elizabeth Calil Zarur, Kenneth Kensinger, Kay Candler, Mark Robbins, Peter Furst, Patricia Lyon, Virginia Greene, and Jon Pressman. Kenneth Kensinger deserves special thanks for his hard work in the scholarly editing of this volume.

I am deeply indebted to the many student workers and volunteers from the University of Pennsylvania and other institutions for their assistance with many aspects of this project: Julie Chinitz, Beebe Bahrami, Peter Demerath, Rafael Figueroa, Salvador Figueroa, Ida Goldstein, Laura Janke, Elizabeth Neaves, Barbara Roberts, Gertrude Russell, David Smedley, and Loa Traxler. Jon Pressman merits special recognition for his steady and excellent work in the last year and a half of the project.

Many individuals and departments in the Museum participated in the preparation of this exhibit: John Hastings volunteered his time to prepare computer programs, train staff, and care for equipment; computer specialist Philip Chase was invaluable in the planning for the interactive video; Jennifer Quick edited the exhibit text. Indispensable support was provided by Pamela Hearne, Coordinator of Museum Services; photographers Harmer Frederick Schoch and John Taggart, with expert assistance from retired Museum photographer William Clough; Gillian Wakely and Lupe Gonzalez of the Education Department, and the Volunteer Guides; archivists Douglas Haller, Alessandro Pezzati, and Colin Varga; Rebecca Buck, Janice Klein, and Chrisso Boulis of the Registrar's Office; Special Events Coordinator Patricia Goodwin; Public Information Officer Pam Kosty; Development Officer David Nelson; Associate Director Alan Waldt and his staff; superintendent Donald Fitzgerald and his staff; the Museum Shop staff; the Director's Office staff; the Museum Library staff. My special appreciation goes to Karen Vellucci and her staff in the Publications Department for overseeing the production of this book and the teachers' and parents' manual. Laurie Tiede did an outstanding job of editing the manuscripts, while the design was undertaken by Ann Bagnell and Sophie Socha.

The Museum is grateful to the following for their financial contributions to the "Gift of Birds" exhibit program: the National Endowment for the Humanities, for planning and implementation grants which made the exhibition possible; the Women's Committee of The University Museum, who provided the initial matching funds and a critical contribution toward the interactive video; CIGNA Corporation, for support of the teachers' and parents' guide; The Downs Foundation for helping to defray exhibition expenses. Generous individual gifts came from J. Garfield DeMarco for this volume; Criswell C. Gonzalez; Mr. and Mrs. Alvin P. Gutman and other friends of the Museum.

All participants in this project have earned my heartfelt thanks for a job well done. Their enthusiasm for the fundamental concepts of this exhibit and their skills and good sense made the project a pleasant learning experience for everyone involved. The Museum can take great pride in their achievement.

"The Gift of Birds" reflects the effective and constant leadership of Dr. Robert H. Dyson, Jr., Director of the Museum. His conviction that an anthropological museum can make an important teaching contribution in our present world served as a guiding principle throughout the years of planning and preparation. This exhibit is dedicated to him and to the Board of Overseers and the Women's Committee of The University Museum.

Ruben E. Reina, Curator

I. GUANA MASK OR COLLAR
(SA 968).

*From the Paraná lowlands,
Paraguay. The feathers are from the
White-necked Heron and the
Great Egret.*

FEATHER OBJECTS IN CULTURE

by Ruben E. Reina

ong ago an instructor at the University of Michigan inspired his students with descriptions of objects produced by native peoples of North and South America. The excitement was not so much about how these objects were made, but rather about the knowledge and wisdom required to control the natural elements necessary for their production. But there was more. These objects had a special place in the life of the people. Not only were they documents of their culture, he said, but they were needed in important rituals. The cosmology and myths of the people were behind many of these objects. To this anthropology instructor, the producers had become his teachers.

He spoke at great length, I remember, about the interrelationships of the natural resources and the ability of humans to manage them. We, as young students listening to this lecture, were amazed at the amount of information the teacher could extract from such silent and antiquated objects. Evidently he had learned to "read" them and the objects were like chapters in the history of mankind.

Certainly, I have forgotten specific facts from this class, but the one lesson I cannot forget is the instructor's attitude toward the objects and his respect for the people who had manufactured them. This has remained a vivid model through my professional years at the University of Pennsylvania and is responsible for my orientation as a researcher and teacher.

What was so new for many of us was that the objects brought for our examination in class were produced by "our primitive contemporaries," as they were referred to in those days. What was curious to me was that those artifacts, and many thousand more, have been placed in the midst of our industrialized society, in the custody of museums. I was beginning to learn from this instructor that much knowledge was hidden away in the galleries or in obscure museum basements awaiting the time when someone would study them, create an exhibit, or bring them to a class as a testament to people through the ages.

In the year 1947, when I was attending that anthropology class, I learned about societies around the world and particularly about those Indians whom I had known in South America. At that time I had not thought of them as "teachers," not even as good examples of a way of life. The instructor was saying instead that they may be "primitive" by our contemporary standards, but we need to understand that they, simple as they may appear, possess a complex system of beliefs, knowledge, and social organization . . . in other words, they have culture. At the end of the semester, I understood the fascination of anthropologists, particularly archaeologists, with the material world. The artifacts were true documents of unwritten knowledge, and the instructor's inspiring approach served merely as a catalyst to allow these objects to tell their own story.

This unexpected lesson from that thoughtful instructor became more important to me a decade later when, at the University of Pennsylvania, I began visiting the Museum basement. Seeing these enduring objects, I thought of the many people who had created them. The cold and silent atmosphere of the basement, hiding the products of many societies, depressed me at first. Remembering my Michigan instructor, I decided that I should incorporate artifacts when I taught introductory courses. Borrowing objects from the Museum collections, I would encourage students to feel as intimately connected as possible to people with other ways of life, culture. I must confess that the first time I had the objects spread in front of me I expected the class not to be interested; instead, the objects created more enthusiasm than I had anticipated. The producers became the students' "hidden teachers"!

Year after year, I discovered more and more about the Museum's contents and their collectors, particularly those objects from the Americas. I also began to appreciate the point of view of the keepers and conservators who meticulously look after the objects in storage. They

FIGURE P.1

Guaná mask or collar (SA 968). From the Paraná lowlands, Paraguay. The feathers are from the White-necked Heron and the Great Egret.

guarded not only objects but knowledge. The lesson in the classroom and the experience of working in a museum made me realize that *these man-made objects are the books of nonliterate people. Museums are their libraries.*

Among the many collections which had been stored in large barrels since the turn of the century were objects made of feathers. Most of them were from North and South America. Not as durable as wooden, textile, or ceramic objects, feather objects were not as favored for exhibition, but I thought perhaps someday an exhibit could be designed to display them in their own social and cultural context. They could break the silence of the storage rooms, and speak about their past and their former owners.

Creating an anthropological exhibit, to my surprise, was as complex a task (if not more so) as the preparation of a book, using data collected after many months of fieldwork. An exhibit, I began to understand, is a visual ethnographic document, and therefore it should be positioned in the context of the academic field. Since the exhibit explores an anthropological orientation, the basic concept of "culture" was the cornerstone.

Nonliterate people have complex systems of knowledge and beliefs, and there is a lesson to be gleaned for those of us who were brought up in a literary tradition. They like us, have been able to adjust to the environment, to other human beings, and have created a distinct philosophy of life. As the famous anthropologist Ruth Benedict said, "Culture is that which binds men together."

Classroom learning, curatorial work, and particularly field experiences brought me to the realization that culture is a concept closely related to human events directly experienced by members of a specific social group. As the living members cope with threatening events, they form assumptions and create principles to guide their thinking and behavior. Culture is therefore an ever-moving phenomenon with a high degree of constancy that, while uninterrupted, may continue to move and to build upon its own components and dynamics. The ecology, the people, and the daily and ceremonial activities represent the overall elements of a social drama that can be observed in the present, cannot be divorced from its past, and has all the potential for surviving into the future. Anthropologists, therefore, immerse themselves in the setting of the present to observe and to participate in this historically created phenomenon. The study of culture has been and continues to be a central concern for anthropological activities.

Anthropologists have "held up a great mirror to man and let him look at himself in his infinite variety" (Kluckhohn 1979:11). This great mirror has been uncovered by anthropologists through many years of observation and participation in the lives of people mostly left out from history.

Early in this century, Dr. Vincenzo Petrullo undertook, for The University Museum, a difficult expedition into the interior of Mato Grosso state in Brazil. In one manuscript describing his expedition he opens his account with the following reflection:

If a pot of gold or even some strange species of butterflies had lured me away from the lecture hall to the wilds of Brazil, my friends might have shown more enthusiasm about my trip. But, they wanted to know what is fascinating about naked, greased, ill-smelling savages living at the end of the world . . . ? This was a hard question to answer, but perhaps the truth of the matter lay in this: A LITTLE KNOWLEDGE OF MANKIND IS A SORT OF TREASURE ALSO. ("Uni" [Water]: A Journey to Mato Grosso. Ms., University Museum Archives, University of Pennsylvania)

The fact is that most anthropologists, whose research is intended to foster appreciation of other cultures, have to strip themselves of certain conventions in order to reach out and occasionally touch other human treasures. In this exhibit, "The Gift of Birds," we have transported certain of these treasures from their indigenous social environment to the Museum's halls, in order that some of the cultures of the native people of South America might be

*Tapirapé Mask
(89–1–1a–c). This mask,
worn during the harvest
festival, is constructed of
Scarlet Macaw and parrot
feathers affixed to a wooden
panel with beeswax. The
mask represents a spirit, and
the cord of feathers, inserted
into the frame and made to
project outward, is the spirit's
headdress. Collected in the
Mato Grosso, Tapirapé
River, Brazil, 1965.*

more fully understood. In addition to an introductory section focusing on beauty and technology, we have chosen three ethnographic scenes and one archaeological collection to provide backdrops for the feather ornaments and allow them to be seen in their social context. The three ethnographic scenes are rituals because it is during such ceremonial times that the feather ornaments play a prominent role. The fourth display presents archaeological objects from Andean cultures now extinct.

The initiation ritual in a Cashinahua village of eastern Peru is a ceremonial scene from a day-long ritual in 1965, when Professor Kenneth Kensinger lived among the people. He, as a consultant to the exhibit, has portrayed the "coming of age" for Cashinahua children with a deep understanding of the social and cultural significance. It is a dramatic moment for children and adults involved in the ritual. He notes that a sense of *oneness* is transmitted to the children as they are incorporated into the village society. For this important event the initiates wear their most beautiful feather headdresses to attract the attention of the people and of the spirits. Feathers are thought to manifest the inner radiance of the individual, the *dua*. The more beautiful the headdress, the more it enhances the *dua* of the person. This portraiture is further elaborated in this volume and in the interactive video presentation.

An intervillage visiting ritual among the Waiwai people of British Guiana constitutes the next "chapter" in the exhibit. The cultural and linguistic settings are different from those of the Cashinahua group. The feather objects were collected for The University Museum by William Farabee in 1913–14. Catherine Howard, who lived among the Waiwai in the 1980s, planned this ethnographic scene as a representation of an occasion for very formal behavior, when people wear their best feather objects. Visiting is not merely a social activity, indicates Howard; it serves to reaffirm fundamental beliefs about the world. Visiting expresses underlying concepts about beauty, self, personal rights, and obligations as human beings. The social sphere is constructed by people making themselves beautiful and attractive to

others. Beauty is not a competitive attribute as it is in Western societies; it is people's contribution to the social whole. Through this ceremonial way of creating beauty, the Waiwai people dissipate tensions and bring about social harmony in a region of culturally distinct village.

The Bororo feather objects are part of the third portrayal of another South American Indian way of life. In 1986, Dr. Elizabeth Calil Zarur, a consultant to this exhibit, witnessed the long days of funerary rituals and felt that some aspects of Bororo culture could be illustrated with a day of the funerary ceremony (Parabara). The Bororo believe that death is caused by evil spirits who, as jaguars or harpy eagles, trap the dead person's soul. Approximately 45 days of rituals are designated to help liberate the spirit and help in the transition into another world. Feather objects are important ornaments during these days, when the living people coalesce with ancestors and culture heroes.

The Bororo ideals of beauty and adornment are related to their view of themselves as social beings. Through beautiful featherwork individuals reveal membership in a specific social group (clan) and their relationship to the world of spirits and ancestors.

The final section of the exhibit displays feather artifacts from coastal Peru. A model shows the Inca Temple of the Sun at the site of Pachacamac as it might have looked around A.D. 1500. This archaeological site, excavated by Max Uhle in 1896-97, was formerly a thriving pilgrimage center. Pachacamac, a creator deity and oracle, was visited by pilgrims from diverse regions of the Andes. In A.D. 1500, this center was at the crossroads of Andean cultures, and among the commodities brought for trade and tribute were feathers from tropical birds such as parrots, toucans, and macaws. Kay Candler, as consultant, designed the layout for the

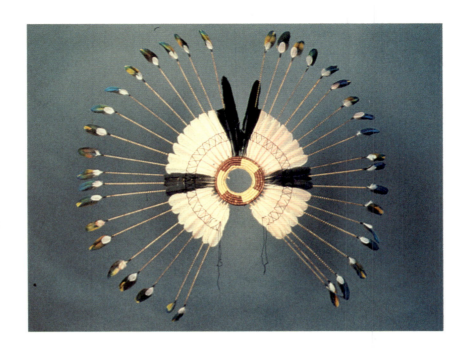

FIGURE P.3

*Karajá headdress
(89–1–3a,b). This
circular fan headdress is
called "Aheto" or "House
for the Head." The
feathers of the Roseate
Spoonbill, Scarlet
Macaw, and Black
Curassow are mounted
onto long split sticks
which have been
wrapped with plant fiber.
each stick is then topped
with smaller feathers
attached with beeswax.
Collected in Goias,
Araguaia River, Brazil,
1965.*

presentation of objects illustrating the role of feather ornamentation in Andean cultures of the past. A mural-sized photograph of a highland pilgrimage illustrates cultural continuity to the present. Despite drastic political changes since the Spanish conquest in the 16th century, certain cultural contexts of feather use have retained their importance in rituals.

The 37 groups of people represented in the exhibit transform feathers, harvested from a handful of tropical species, into ornaments of beauty. The members of each group, however, achieve this transformation through their own technological processes, creating a style by which their ancestors were known and they are recognized today. Behind these ways of life, and particularly behind feather ornaments, are many "hidden" teachers. Loren Eiseley said, "We think we learn from teachers, and we sometimes do. But the teachers are not always to be found in school or in laboratories" (1978:116).

Feather ornaments are not an invention of the recent past among people of South America, and as such they are important to the understanding of each culture. Through the feather ornaments nonliterate people transfer many basic cultural ideas such as symbolism, myths, and social identity from one generation to another. These objects serve then as important instructional vehicles for the continuity of a style of life, *culture*.

It is remarkable how residents of small villages in the tropical rainforest and in the Andes continued to build this tradition along the patterns established by their ancestors. For these contemporary South American Indians, culture deeply shared serves to reinforce their place in history, in their native habitat, and guides them into the future.

These people have searched for ways to overcome the unknown by controlling and manipulating their links to the natural world. As we shall see, for instance, birds have given some of these groups a way to escape from the present as they move along a difficult path, modernization. In myths, birds not only have created man and frequently have taught people how to behave, but have saved people from total destruction.

The transformation of natural resources into cultural adornments was and still is central among many groups in South America. The ancestors of these groups in the exhibit "The Gift of Birds" have left a legacy that remains deeply rooted in their forest tradition in spite of the modernization and destruction of the forest. What is significant is that each group manifests distinctive ornaments and unique styles, with their own symbolism and meaning. Each group's ornaments are used for different social purposes: at times in initiation and funeral rituals, other times in shamanistic practices, social visiting, expressions of group identity, and exercise of political power. These creations reveal profound aspects of people's world-view, the way humans relate to and look upon their universe.

A lesson on the nature of culture can be created with any objects, but feathers are, among traditional peoples of South America, a special and important aid to formal interaction. The overall lesson, furthermore, is that these human groups inhabiting South America with different lifestyles make their own assumptions about the purposes of their existence. They, like any other human group, including

FIGURE P.4

Apalaii wasp frame (SA 773). This frame contains the feathers of the Scarlet Macaw, the Channel-billed Toucan, and a hawk. The feathers have been glued in large blocks of color on to a basketry frame constructed in the shape of a jaguar. If a boy could not stand the pain of the wasp stings when this panel containing living wasps was pressed against his stomach, he could not become a man. Collected by William C. Farabee, 1913–1916.

our own, developed by means of a system of conventional understanding transferred from one generation to the next. In this system, they find the standards to evaluate each other. The exhibit in general is therefore an anthropological lesson to help the visitor experience and understand the traditional South American cultural systems.

The groups selected for the exhibit continue with a lifestyle of their own making. Behind the overall planning of the exhibit is the postulate that the understanding of culture provides at least some distance from values of our own. We learn here that the environment, elements in it, ornaments, producers, and their behavior form a complex web of relationships to be understood in the context of each group's social history. Culture, we learn, makes objects and actions more predictable.

It is very appropriate to end this preface with a quotation from a well-known anthropologist, Margaret Mead:

Knowledge joined to action—knowledge about what man has been and is—can protect the future . . . There is hope . . . in the shared trust that knowledge about mankind, sought in reverence for life, can bring life. (1972:296)

It is my personal hope that this exhibit, prepared by a team of dedicated scholar and technicians, will satisfy many interests among our visitors. For me, it is the fulfillment of remembrances of my early youthful days in my native South America.

Ruben E. Reina

II. Parukoto earring pendants
(SA 434a,b).

From the Apiniwau River, Brazil.

WHY FEATHERS?

by Kenneth M. Kensinger

ulture is a set of mechanisms for survival, but it provides us also with definitions of reality and codes of morality. It is the matrix into which we are born, it is the anvil upon which our persons and destinies are forged. The study of human cultures and their workings is at once a venture into the outer limits of the social universe and an inquiry into ourselves . . . The inquiry is made troublesome by the complexity of the subject matter and by the contrariness of the individual subjects, who never seem to do what they are supposed to do. But it is made doubly difficult by the faulty perceptions of both the anthropologists and the people they study, for both parties are defining their "real world" by culturally given meanings. And even when we manage to break through this wall of mutual misunderstanding we find that behind every conscious motive there is a hidden agenda, behind every social practice or institution there lies a covert and undetected rationale, and after every great plan there follows a series of wholly unintended and unanticipated consequences. We must look, then, behind the facade of appearances and the reality of common-sense experience in order to reach the organization and flow of social life that goes on beneath the surface. (Murphy 1989:14)

Objects in a museum exhibit, like those in "The Gift of Birds," have by necessity been separated from their original physical, cultural, and social context. No matter how lifelike and ethnographically accurate they are, dioramas and display cases lack the excitement and emotional intensity of the real thing. They are removed in time and space from the events depicted. They lack the sounds, the smells, the immediacy of experience. They represent a moment of time in the lives of people far removed from the halls of The University Museum. The objects were made by individuals living in particular places at specific times, individuals who shared their lives, beliefs, and aspirations with family, kin, neighbors, friends, and enemies. They were created to be used for particular activities by specific people, usually their makers, for whom they had meaning, purpose, and value. The creators of the exhibit and of the interactive video have attempted to provide information that might narrow the chasm between the viewer and the reality depicted. That chasm is more than one of time and space, however. It is one of vast cultural differences.

Although each object in the exhibit was made by a specific artisan or group of artisans, it is simultaneously a reflection of more than just the artisan's skill and creativity; it makes a statement about the physical, social, and cultural world of its maker. If we, as viewers of these objects, are to see and appreciate them as more than simply curios made by alien beings, it is necessary to examine the worlds in which the makers lived and died, worked and played, married and raised families, loved and hated, hoped and despaired. The essays in this volume are intended to serve that purpose.

The use of feathers by indigenous peoples is ubiquitous throughout South America. Mark Robbins (see Ch. 10) has identified feathers from 18 families and 48 species of birds in or on objects in The University Museum's collections. Examination of collections in other museums would undoubtedly add to this inventory. However, these birds represent only about 1.6% of the avian families and species actually present in South America. But the prevalence of birds in the habitats of the various societies does not explain either (1) how and why people use feathers, or (2) why, out of the diversity of bird families and species available to them, people choose to use the feathers of a limited number of species.

FIGURE I.1

*Cashinahua headdress (65–10–7).
This headdress was mostly commonly
worn at fertility rites, but sometimes
also at initiation ceremonies. The
white feather off to one side gives an
asymmetrical effect that is pleasing.
Restraint, sparseness, and
asymmetry give this piece beauty.
The headdress is adorned with body
feathers from the trumpeter bird.
Made by Xuliu and collected along
the Rio Curanja, Peru, 1965.*

All Amazonian peoples exploit the avian resources of their environments. For many groups, birds are a major source of food. Some species, particularly the curassows, the guans, the trumpeters, and the tinamous, are considered delicacies and are avidly hunted. Some species are hunted primarily for their feathers and may or may not be eaten; these include the parrots, the raptors, and the carrion eaters. The young of several species, particularly the parrots, curassows, and trumpeters, are stolen from their nests and raised as pets; these are never eaten although they may be used as a source of feathers. In central Brazil, harpy eagle chicks also are captured and raised; as adults they serve as a kind of village mascot and, in some cases, may be used as a source of feathers. Ruben Reina and Jon Pressman provide further data on "harvesting" feathers in Chapter 9.

The primary use of feathers in South America is in the fabrication and/or ornamentation of festive and ritual attire. In Chapter 2, Virginia Greene describes several Peruvian feathered garments and accessories from the Museum's archaeological collections; the Caudivilla headdress is a particularly splendid example. However, Patricia Lyon reminds us in Chapter 6 that although feather headdresses are the most memorable of the uses for feathers in the inventories of South American native crafts, the fletched arrow may be the most significant, if not the only, practical use of feathers. Arrows are used for hunting, a major source of food, and for protection. Even so, she notes, arrows need not be fletched in order to function properly, although feathers may in fact provide arrows with greater accuracy. She goes on to point out that there is clearly more to feathering arrows than simple functional necessity.

In my essay, Chapter 4, I report on the reasons the Cashinahua give for using feathers, i.e., their availability, their beauty, and their utility. But examination of their reasoning shows that it is not simply that the Cashinahua live in an environment in which there are lots of birds, many of which they kill for food, or that the feathers are beautiful and can be used to beautify objects and people, or even that they are a kind of medicine. Understanding why the Cashinahua use feathers requires knowledge of the ways they perceive and experience their world, a world inhabited by people and spirits, both of whom share the right to use the resources of the visible and invisible aspects of their environment.

Amazonian peoples have an intimate knowledge of their physical environment: its plants, animals, rivers, streams, seasonal changes, etc. Anthropologists who have studied the biological taxonomies in the languages of various indigenous groups have found them to be extremely thorough and accurate. So also is native peoples' knowledge of the geographic distribution, the growth patterns, and the behavior of animals and plants. But all societies go well beyond the order these taxonomies create and try to explain the irregular, the unpredictable, and the fortuitous that are an integral part of their experience of their world by creating cosmologies and mythologies. Jon Pressman's essay (Ch. 7) in this volume examines some of the myths about how birds got their colorful plumage. Thus, humans use the environment as more than just a source for food and the raw materials used to produce their houses, tools, clothes, medicine, ornaments, and ritual objects. They transform their physical world into one that is also a cultural and spiritual world, the context within which they live and work, a world of meaning and value.

We turn now to the question of how and why Amazonian peoples use feathers. I suggest that there are four major reasons: (1) feathers are beautiful, (2) they provide the wearer with an identity, (3) they allow the wearer to emulate aspects of the appearance and/or behavioral characteristics of their animal source, and (4) they provide spiritual strength and protection.[1]

Most indigenous groups of the Amazonian rainforest wear a minimum of clothing but, although they do not abhor the naked body, they universally find it necessary to place the imprint of society on the body in order to transform it into a social body through body painting, tattooing, earrings, clothing, etc. As Thomas Gregor says of the Brazilian Mehinaku:

FIGURE I.2

Mundurucú headdress (44–3–1). Birds: Scarlet Macaw, Blue-and-yellow Macaw, White-necked Heron, and toucan.

FIGURE I.3

Yawalapiti armbands (31–48–454a,b). The bands are made with Blue-and-yellow Macaw feathers. Kuluene River, Mato Grosso, Brazil. Collected by Vincenzo Petrullo, 1931.

Being naked is "being without anything" (*melatutsi*). A second word for nudity, *metalute* (literally, "without feathers" or "without earrings"), is especially interesting, since it is also used for a featherless arrow and incorporates the notion of being incomplete. To be naked is to be socially incomplete, and it is fitting only at nonpublic times and places. (1977:154)

Although feathers are usually not worn as a part of daily attire, they are a major part of the attire worn for festive and ritual occasions.

The possession of feathers and their use are intimately connected with personal and social identity in Amazonia. They are often seen as the sign of a successful hunter/provider and by extension of leadership. As a successful hunter, a man is recognized by other men as a "real man," making him desirable as an ally, a man of substance, and by women as a desirable spouse, son-in-law, or lover. Catherine Howard on the Waiwai (Ch. 5) and Elizabeth Calil Zarur on the Bororo (Ch. 3) have provided vivid illustrations of how feathers signal the wearer's social membership and/or political position. Kay Candler, in her paper on the Andean Inca empire and coast (Ch. 1), shows that feathers were imported from the Amazonian rainforest and were the possessions of persons of high political rank.

Many indigenes of the tropical rainforest wear feathers and the parts of other animals as a way of identifying with the appearance and/or behavior characteristic of various animals. According to Calil Zarur, the Bororo identify with the red-and-green macaw. She further argues that "the mythology and the rigidity of Bororo social structure were the source for Bororo feather art" (see Ch. 3). Howard has shown that a Waiwai male in his full ritual regalia does not simply identify with birds and animals; he becomes a "microcosm" of Waiwai cosmology (Ch. 5). During the Cashinahua initiation rites, women "become" turtles and birds with sharp beaks and attack men with sticks, jabbing and pinching them while imitating the sounds of the animals. Peter Furst (Ch. 8) documents the close identification between shamans and the harpy eagle and jaguar. The key to understanding why particular animals are chosen for emulation is incorporated in each society's mythology, according to which the primeval ancestors were or interacted with the socially significant birds and animals.

Finally, feathers (and other body parts of other animals) are used as a kind of spiritual medicine, a fetish or talisman. According to the Cashinahua, feathers provide protection against predatory spirits while at the same time they enhance the wearer's beauty, attracting the spirits of fertility. Calil Zarur concludes that "through the use of feathers, it is possible . . . to understand the secular and sacred messages that maintain harmony between [the Bororo] and their environment, both terrestrial and spiritual" (Ch. 3).

Despite our best efforts, the beliefs and customs of the indigenous societies and cultures of South America still may seem strange, exotic, and perhaps even a bit bizarre. But imagine for a moment trying to explain to the Cashinahua, the Waiwai, and the Bororo the feathered finery of the Philadelphia Mummers or, even more difficult, the behavior of millions of Americans who, although they have never encountered the real animals, cheer themselves hoarse in support of the Philadelphia Eagles, the Detroit Lions, the Miami Dolphins, et al.—to say nothing of the antics of the team mascots. The authors of the essays in this catalogue hope that their contributions will lead to a narrowing of the distance between the viewer/reader and the people who made and used the objects in this exhibit.

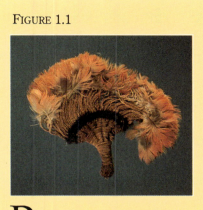

FIGURE 1.1

Plume ornament, probably worn in a headdress (CG110691–2119). Bird: Scarlet Macaw.

FIGURE 1.3

Map of sites mentioned in the text.

THE BEAUTIFUL FEATHERED OBJECTS recovered from archaeological sites, where they were preserved by the fortuitous coincidence of aridity, proper temperature, and appropriate soil characteristics, are dramatic evidence of the importance of feathers in Precolumbian times. The skill and sophistication with which these objects were made indicate that they are part of a well-developed tradition, and not just the spontaneous or whimsical addition of a few feathers to decorate an artifact. The feathered clothing from the north coast of Peru, amply discussed and illustrated in Ann Rowe's *Costumes and Featherwork of the Lords of Chimor* (1984), the objects recovered by Max Uhle at the central coast sites of Pachacamac, Caudivilla, and La Centinela, and the materials excavated on the south coast, including those collected by William Farabee in the Nazca region, are proof that this was a widespread tradition and not just a localized development. Like the textiles with which they are usually associated, archaeological feathers have been preserved almost exclusively on the coast.

It is very likely that the tradition of featherworking extended very far back in time, possibly even to the preceramic period (see the chronological chart, Fig.1.2, and map, Fig.1.3), although the perishability of the material makes it unlikely that we will ever find direct

FIGURE 1.2

		Northern Highlands	North Coast	Central Coast	South Coast	Southern Highlands
COLONIAL LATE HORIZON	1600	COLONIAL INCA	COLONIAL INCA	COLONIAL INCA	COLONIAL INCA	COLONIAL INCA
LATE INTERMEDIATE PERIOD	1400 1200 1000		CHIMU			
MIDDLE HORIZON	800 600			COASTAL WARI	COASTAL WARI	TIWANAKU
EARLY INTERMEDIATE PERIOD	400 200 AD / BC		MOCHE	Construction begins at Pachacamac	NAZCA	
EARLY HORIZON	200 400 600 800	CHAVIN			PARACAS	
	1000 1200 1400					
INITIAL PERIOD	1600 1800 1200 1400					
	1600			El Paraíso		
PRECERAMIC	1800 2000					

Chronological chart of Peruvian culture areas.

RECOLUMBIAN PERU
PLUMAGE

by Kay L. Candler

III. Plume ornament, probably worn in a headdress (CG110691–2119).

ZATIONS OF IDEAS WHICH PERHAPS WERE ONLY PRODUCED ONCE . . ." – *MAX UHLE*

FIGURE 1.4

South coast poncho with design of coastal birds. (SA 4604). Probably a condor or "vencejo," a relative of the whippoorwill.

FIGURE 1.5

Textile from Pachacamac with stylized design of birds (29595). Museum Expedition, Max Uhle, 1896.

physical evidence of this. Most archaeological feathered artifacts come from the Late Intermediate Period, Late Horizon, or Colonial Period. It is also very likely that the tradition of featherworking flourished in the Andean highlands, although, again, poor preservation conditions make it unlikely that this will ever be proved.

A complete seriation of featherwork, one which would associate any given piece with a specific culture area and time period, has not yet been constructed. One of the difficulties of such a task is the relative scarcity of feathered objects excavated by archaeologists in an absolutely secure context; a seriation cannot be based on artifacts with uncertain provenience. Even a secure provenience can sometimes be misleading, as artifacts (especially highly valued artifacts) are often found far removed in space and time from their site of original manufacture. Fortunately Andean featherwork is often attached to textiles, and there is a steadily growing body of information on textile seriation. For example, the pieces illustrated in Figures 1.25 and 1.26 were probably manufactured by Chimú people because of the distinctive weave of the textiles (A. Rowe 1984), although they were both excavated by Uhle at Pachacamac.

Max Uhle was a meticulous excavator, and he made notes of where he found things. Although this is now considered essential in archaeological practice, it was unusual in 1896, when Uhle recovered the pieces in The University Museum's collections. Unfortunately the collection made by William Farabee is not as well documented. Farabee became seriously ill during his work on the south coast, and never fully regained his health. Although he excavated at several locations in the Nazca area, most of the textiles he collected were apparently purchased, and presumably the feathered pieces also. Furthermore, he seems to have purchased items in Arequipa and Lima, as well as the Nazca region, which makes even general provenience somewhat difficult to establish.

Several themes (the role of birds and the relationship between birds and featherwork, the production of feathered cloth, the meanings of feathered dress, the ritual value of feathers, and aesthetic observations) will be discussed, using comparative information from Andean coastal archaeology, ethnohistory, and contemporary ethnography. The importance of establishing the cultural and temporal origin of a feathered artifact becomes clear through a comparison to the ethnographic contexts of featherwork in the tropical forest. Simply put, the Waiwai, Cashinahua, and Bororo are very different from each other, and no generalization can be made from one group to the next. The Precolumbian cultures of coastal Peru varied both through time and through space, and it is misleading to attempt to generalize about the role and meaning of featherwork among these diverse peoples. Nevertheless, some preliminary generalizations may be useful in identifying areas for further research.

The most important supplementary archaeological material will be the iconographic representations of birds, feathers, and feathered clothes and ornaments from various Precolumbian cultures. The major sources of ethnohistorical information are the chronicles written by the colonial Spanish conquerors, administrators, and priests after the conquest of Peru in 1532 (Cobo 1979, 1990 [1653]; Arriaga 1968 [1617]; Betanzos 1987 [1551]; Avila [1598?]). A few were written by the sons of Spanish men and indigenous women (Guaman Poma 1980 [1583–1615]; Garcilaso 1987 [1609]), and even fewer by indigenous men taught to write by the Spaniards (Santacruz Pachacuti Yamqui 1950 [1613]). Contemporary ethnography, especially in relation to the Waiwai, Bororo, and Cashinahua, is used to suggest different perspectives which might be helpful in understanding the archaeological material. This is not to say that there are necessarily any direct parallels

FIGURE 1.6

Textile with design combining human and bird features (CG840312–4549).

FIGURE 1.7

Design from a Moche ceramic combining human and bird features (39–20–48). Drawing by Virginia Greene.

FIGURE 1.8

South coast textile design combining human and bird features. (SA 3523).

between the ancient coastal Peruvians and the modern tropical forest dwellers. All of these comparisons are offered as points of departure, possibilities to be corroborated or discarded as further archaeological information becomes available.

The ubiquity of bird designs through space and time indicates that birds played an important role in the world-view of the Precolumbian Andean peoples, but it is much more difficult to discover exactly what that role was. The majority of naturalistic bird representations in coastal ceramics, textiles, gold, wood, architecture, shell, and other media are of species commonly found on the coast (Fig. 1.4). Representations so stylized that the species is not identifiable are almost as common, especially on the central coast (Fig. 1.5). A third type of representation combines human and bird elements, sometimes with elements of other animals (Fig. 1.6).

The ceramics of the Moche people are renowned for their realistic depictions and for their presentation of complex scenes. Christopher Donnan (1978) has shown how a thematic approach to Moche art, starting with one figure and studying how it is represented in conjunction with various other figures in a variety of scenes, can provide insight into the meaning of that figure. He has also used ethnographic information gained from a north coast shaman, Eduardo Calderón (Sharon 1978), to suggest ideas which Precolumbian peoples may have associated with their iconography. Moche birds are depicted primarily in two different ways: either in naturalistic scenes of ecological relationships (for example, seabirds eating fish), or as anthropomorphized figures in scenes showing social interactions. Human figures, apparently men, are shown with a variety of bird heads, wings, and tails, including hummingbirds, Muscovy ducks, and eagles (Fig. 1.7). The figures, which have human torsos, legs, and arms, carry weapons and shields. They are usually called "bird warriors" by Moche scholars, but, as Donnan (1978:132) notes, a shaman is considered a "warrior" as he does battle with the spirits of the invisible otherworld (see Furst, Ch. 8). Donnan records several shamanic associations with birds: the hummingbird, which sucks nectar, is like the shaman who sucks a sorcerer's poison darts from a victim; eagles are associated with intelligence, vision, and the soul's magical flight during hallucinogenic trances; and the owl, which can see in the dark, is helpful in discovering the causes of sorcery, but is also dangerously close to corpses, cemeteries, and spirits of the dead (Donnan 1978:124–32). An owl-person, apparently a woman shaman, is often depicted in a scene that appears to be a curing ceremony.

Bird-people are also depicted on south coast ceramics and textiles, but usually not in complex scenes (Fig. 1.8). Instead, the figures themselves are very complex combinations of a wide variety of elements such as falcon eyespots, killer-whale mouths, protruding tongues which contain small human figures or fishes, and trophy heads. Feathered wings and tails are commonly seen on these creatures, but, as in Moche art, it is not always easy to determine whether they are intended to represent actual appendages on a supernatural body or an elaborate costume on a human body. Posture, especially the horizontal or vertical position of a figure and the orientation of the head to the spinal column, is useful in distinguishing among human beings (including those wearing masks or costumes), nonhuman aspects or "doubles" of human beings, truly "mythic beings," and shamanic figures (Peters n.d.; Paul and Turpin 1986).

Two aspects of south coast iconography are especially pertinent to the theme of featherwork and its meaning to Precolumbian peoples. The first is the frequent use of "kenning," a kind of visual punning or metaphor first suggested by John Rowe (1967). Rowe observed that hair was often depicted as snakes in Chavin art, and he suggested that there might have been an underlying linguistic or

FIGURE 1.10

FIGURE 1.9

Design from a south coast ceramic bowl (SA 3045). This flying figure with a snake headdress, falcon eyespots, and a trophy head on the wing is a typical south coast composite figure. Note the small faces on the tips of the wings and tail feathers. Drawing by Raymond Rorke.

South coast ceramic bowl (SA 3163). This feather motif, with two "eyes" and a "mouth" at the tip, is sometimes called "snake feathers." There seem to have been visual puns made on representations of hair, snakes, feathers in south coast art.

FIGURE 1.12

FIGURE 1.11

South coast gold mask (46–24–1). The elements projecting from the face might represent snakes, feathers, hairs or the sun's rays.

FIGURE 1.13

Feathers of the Scarlet Macaw are braided into human hair (SA 4374b). Mummies of south coast people often have elaborately braided hairstyles.

South coast textile (SA 3586). This figure holds a staff in one hand and a fan in the other.

FIGURE 1.14

Wooden staff (29460) decorated with unidentified white feathers.

FIGURE 1.15

Max Uhle uncovered this staff (29460) and mummy bundle (26626) at the site of Pachacamac.

ideological association between snakes and hair. In south coast art, feathers are often "animated" by giving them eyes and mouths, so that they look like snakes (Fig. 1.9). These "snakes" are clearly feathers when they are found on the wings of birds (Fig. 1.10), but their meaning is less obvious when they project from the head, where they may be either feathers or hair. In fact, there appears to have been a close association between hair and feathers, as feathers have been found braided into human hair (Fig. 1.11). The associations with both snakes and hair have intriguing parallels in the tropical forest, as the Cashinahua use the same word for both "hair" and "feather," and a Waiwai myth (which is one version of a very widespread narrative) attributes the birds' brightly colored feathers to the blood of the anaconda. A fourth association is suggested by the gold mask, one of several from the south coast, which appears to represent the sun (Fig. 1.12). Are those snakes, feathers, hair, or the sun's rays projecting from the face? Perhaps the intention of the artist was not to restrict the meaning to any one of these elements but to convey certain associations among all of them. Again the Cashinahua provide a provocative comparison, as the sun's rays are given as an example of *dua*, a concept intimately related to featherwork (see Kensinger, Ch. 4).

Another theme common in south coast iconography involves feathered ornaments. A figure is frequently depicted, usually in an upright "human" posture or a curved "shamanic" position, holding a staff in one hand and a feather fan in the other (Fig. 1.13). The staff is often decorated with what appear to be "animated" feathers. The feather fan has sometimes been identified as a *tumi*, a crescent-shaped ceremonial knife commonly found at north coast and Inca sites, but the south coast knife is not shaped like a *tumi* (or fan). On the north coast, Moche iconography clearly shows elaborate feather "fans" as headdress ornaments, not held in the hand.

The elaborate feather fans of the south coast may be compared to the fire fans of many tropical forest peoples. Most fire fans are made from woven palm leaves, not feathers, but they often have symbolic associations with the spirit world. During ritual dances in which Bororo men embody their spirit ancestors, women fan them with fire fans and compare this activity to the mythical fanning of the celestial fires into the heavens (Elizabeth Calil Zarur, personal communication). Cashinahua fire fans are made of feathers. Everyday fans are made from curassow feathers, while fans for ritual occasions are made from harpy eagle, macaw, and yellow oriole feathers (Rabineau 1975:159).

On the Peruvian coast, the feather fan seems mainly confined to the southern traditions, but the wooden staff is more widespread, both iconographically and ethnographically. Staffs, both with and without feathers, are depicted in the artistic traditions from Chavín de Huantar, Moche, and Chimú in the north to Paracas, Wari, Tiwanaku, and Nazca in the south, in both highlands and coast, and from early to late time periods. The decorated wooden staff in the University Museum collection was recovered by Uhle at the site of Pachacamac, where he found it associated with a mummy bundle (Figs. 1.14, 1.15). Donnan compares the carved staffs found in a Moche tomb to the staffs used by Eduardo Calderón in his curing ceremonies. The *sunturpaucar*, a feathered staff, was one of the royal insignias of the Inca ruler.

> The *sunturpaucar* was a staff, a little shorter than a pike, all covered and adorned from top to bottom with short feathers of various colors which were placed with such skill that they made an elegant effect, and to finish it off, the tips of three large feathers rose up from the top. (Cobo 1979 [1653]:246)

When highlanders today dress up and perform dances imitating tropical forest peoples, such as the "Chuncho" dancers of

FIGURE 1.16

Pilgrims to the glacier of Qoyllur Rit'i. The ornaments made from the feathers of tropical forest birds and the wooden staff are the costume of dancers who represent tropical forest people. Photograph by Dinorah Marquez.

FIGURE 1.17

Design from a Moche stirrup-spout vessel (39–20–46). The warrior's headdress combines an animal effigy in front with a plume ornament in the back. Drawing by Virginia Greene.

FIGURE 1.19

Bird effigy (representing a parrot), probably worn in a headdress (SA 3981).

FIGURE 1.20

Pair of small plume ornaments, probably worn in a headdress (CG852611–6434a,b). Birds: Blue-and-yellow Macaw, Scarlet Macaw, and probably Toucan.

FIGURE 1.18

Central coast textile with scene including animals, fish, and birds (CG852611–6459). The central figure wears a headdress with double-bird effigies.

FIGURE 1.21

Wooden bowl (33916). This shallow bowl in the shape of a bird has the distinctive head and beak of a parrot.

the Qoyllur Rit'i pilgrimage in Peru (Sallnow 1988; see Fig. 1.16) and the "Yumbo" dancers of Ecuador (Salomon 1980), a wooden staff is an important part of their costume. The Yumbo dancers associate their wooden staffs with the shamanic potency originating in the tropical forest. In many Quechua communities today, a decorated staff is emblematic of political leadership. It is possible that the two separate roles associated with staffs today, community leadership and ritual power, were more closely intertwined in Precolumbian times.

The iconography of the north and central coast clearly depicts the use of feathers and birds in headdresses. Moche iconography presents an especially varied array of elaborate headdresses, often combining effigies of birds and animal heads with complex feather plume ornaments. (Fig. 1.17). A spectacular headdress on display at the American Museum of Natural History in New York, an effigy of a fox head, is covered with yellow feathers.[1] This suggests that even when other animals were represented, feathers were the favored material used for headdresses. Animal effigies on headdresses are less common in other traditions, but a double-bird headdress is not uncommon (Fig. 1.18). Although we do not know the provenience of the bird effigies and small ornaments shown in Figures 1.19 and 1.20, their size and construction make it likely that they were used to decorate headdresses.

Tropical forest birds such as parrots, macaws, and toucans are depicted in coastal iconography with such clear detail that the artists must have been familiar with living birds of these species (Fig. 1.21). The remains of parrots, sometimes carefully wrapped in miniature mummy bundles, have been recovered from Pachacamac and other central and south coast sites. The Precolumbian coastal peoples must have obtained live birds, and not just plucked feathers, from tropical forest peoples. It is especially interesting that the overwhelming majority of feathered artifacts were made from tropical forest species that are easily tamed, rather than from local or tropical forest species that are killed in the hunt (Mark Robbins, personal communication). Among the Cashinahua, feather use is largely opportunistic, that is, birds are hunted primarily for food, and the Cashinahua make use of whatever feathers they happen to have at hand (see Kensinger, Ch. 4). This was clearly not the case on the coast, as the feathers of local game birds were rarely used on the artifacts. A. Rowe (1984) suggests that an increase in the use of local species indicates Colonial Period manufacture, after the Spanish had disrupted the traditional trade networks between the coastal and tropical forest peoples. Some trade networks between Andean highlanders and tropical forest peoples are still used today; they are the source of the feather ornaments used in the Ecuadorian Yumbo dances and the Cambas dances in Copacabana, Bolivia (Salomon 1980; Richard Ameral, personal communication; see Fig. 1.22). In both of these cases, however, the feathered pieces are manufactured in the tropical forest, unlike the Precolumbian artifacts, which were manufactured by coastal peoples.

Although the chronicles written shortly after the Spanish conquest of Peru occasionally mention the spectacular feathered clothes and headdresses worn by high-ranking indigenous people, they rarely mention the types of birds used or details of their production. The account of myths and rituals of Huarochirí, 25 miles east of Lima, provides the most interesting information about the Precolumbian people of the central coast. The material collected by Francisco de Avila, a Spanish priest in the late 16th and early 17th centuries, describes the cults of the sacred places, called *huacas*, and the mythical exploits of the personified *huacas*.

Paria Caca (a snow-covered peak) was the principal *huaca*. One tale relates how, before Paria Caca and his brothers were born from falcon eggs, there was a *huaca* named Huallallo Caruincho. At that time there were many beautifully colored macaws, red,

FIGURE 1.22

*Modern shoulder
ornament from
Copacabana, Bolivia
(87–10–1). Worn during
the Cambas dances in the
highlands, this ornament
was originally made by
tropical forest people.
Birds: Blue-and-yellow
Macaw, Scarlet Macaw,
Cotinga, Tanager,
Amazon Parrot, and
Trogon or Quetzal.*

yellow, and blue, on the coast. They were later expelled, with Huallallo Caruincho, to the tropical forest. When Paria Caca appeared,

> one [of his brothers] penetrated the place we called Mullo Cocha and turned it into a lake, Huallallo flew away like a bird. Then he entered a mountain, a mountain called Caqui Yoca [*caqui* = toucan or macaw].[2] This mountain was a gigantic rocky escarpment. Huallallo Caruincho got inside the cliff and hid there. Paria Caca, in the form of lightning, blasted it again and again; he and his five brothers shot lightning bolts so violently they almost demolished that rocky mountain, and from there they once again forced Huallallo Caruincho to flee. Then Huallallo Caruincho turned loose a huge snake called the Amaru, a two-headed snake, thinking, "This'll bring misfortune on Paria Caca!" When he saw it Paria Caca furiously stabbed it in the middle of its back with his golden staff. At that very moment, the snake froze stiff. It turned into stone . . . Then, clambering up a mountain called Puma Rauca, Huallallo thought, "From here I'll fence Paria Caca in so he can't pass through." He set against him a certain kind of parrot called a *caqui* or toucan and made it brandish its wing points. But Paria Caca effortlessly broke one of its wings, turned the toucan to stone, and climbed right over it. Once Paria Caca stepped over it Huallallo Caruincho had no power left, so he fled toward the Anti lowlands. (after Salomon and Urioste 1991:92–93)

After defeating Huallallo Caruincho, Paria Caca set about converting the communities of Huarochirí to his cult. As he won each community, he instructed them in the celebrations they were to hold, choosing a member of each lineage to direct and perform the rituals. These ritual specialists were given the title *huacsa*. During the celebrations in April, June, and November, the *huacsas* performed dances, some of which lasted for five days. Apparently they wore a variety of ornaments, but only a few are mentioned specifically: macaw wings, llama skins, the tails of animals trapped in a ritual hunt. One of the dances, performed for the *huaca* Chaupi Ñamca, was named Casa Yaco, perhaps referring to a colorful bird or ornament called *casa* (probably a macaw or its feathers). Chaupi Ñamca was the daughter of a rich *huaca*, whose house was covered with red and yellow feathers called *casa* and *cancho*. She was given in marriage to a poor man who, with Paria Caca's help, succeeded in curing her father of a devastating illness. Chaupi Ñamca's brother, angry that his sister was married to a poor man, challenged him to a series of five contests. The first competition was to see who could dance and drink the most, and the second was to see who could dress the most splendidly in *casa* and *cancho* feathers. The poor man defeated his rich brother-in-law in all five contests.

These accounts of the ritual dances of the *huacsas* and the mythological exploits of the *huacas* provide tantalizing glimpses, hints of how important tropical forest birds and feathered costumes were to the people of ancient Huarochirí. We have more information from the highlands, especially around the area of the Incaic capital, Cuzco. These accounts hardly reflect the situation of pre-Incaic coastal peoples, although many Incaic practices originated among non-Inca peoples. For example, archaeologists Conrad and Demarest (1984) suggest that the elaborate cult of the ancestors can be traced to coastal traditions.

Betanzos (1987 [1551]) mentions that one or two "falcon" feathers were worn by all of the descendants of one of the Inca rulers. Garcilaso describes in detail the Inca's use of *coriquenque* feathers.

> The Inca wore on his head two of the outer wing feathers of a bird called corequenqe . . . the feathers have black and white bands and

FIGURE 1.23

LASETIMACOIA
IPAVACOMAMAMA
CHI

*Inca "queen" with parrot,
macaw, and monkey. After
a drawing by Guaman
Poma.*

are about as big as those of a hen sparrow-hawk: They are required to be one of a pair, one from each wing . . . the birds from which they are taken are found in the desert of Villcanuta, 32 leagues from the city of Cuzco, on a small lake there, at the foot of that inaccessible snow-covered range. Those who have seen them state that only two are seen, one male and one female: if they are always unique, and where they come from or breed is not known, nor, according to the Indians, have any others but these been seen in all Peru . . . It was because only this pair of birds was to be found, and there was no news of any others in the world that the Incas wore their plumes, and esteemed them so highly that no one else was allowed to wear them under any circumstances, not even the heir to the throne. They declared that these two birds, in their uniqueness, resembled their parents, the first Incas, who were only two, man and woman . . . In order to obtain the plumes the birds were taken as gently as possible, and when the two plumes had been removed, were released. Whenever a new Inca inherited the throne, they were caught again and had the feathers removed. The heir always took new insignia and never used the same as his father, since on the latter's death his body was embalmed and buried with the same imperial insignias he had used during his lifetime. (1987 [1609]:375)

The feathers of specifically tropical forest birds are mentioned only in the chronicle of Arriaga (1968 [1617]) and the dictionary of Gonzalez Holguín (1952 [1608]). Arriaga notes that the feathers of macaws were called *astop tucto*, as *asto* is the Quechua name of the macaw, and "*tucto* means plume, or something that sprouts" (Arriaga 1968 [1617]:45). Gonzalez Holguín (1952 [1608]) does not indicate the species, but says that *pillco* is a red bird of the tropical forest which is valued for its plumage. Other chroniclers state that the Inca received birds as gifts or tribute from various groups in the tropical forest and several describe "brightly colored feathers" without mentioning a tropical forest origin. Garcilaso (1987 [1609]) and Betanzos (1987 [1551]) are among those who specifically mention parrots and macaws, as well as monkeys and other wild animals, as gifts from the conquered people to the Inca lord. Cobo relates an incident wherein the Inca requested a tropical forest chief to send him "certain birds that are found in that land, to be kept in cages" (1979 [1653]:121). When the chief replied that he had no such birds for the use of the Inca, the Inca sent military troops to the region and installed his own brother as governor of the province. His brother sent him "a thousand cages of birds . . . and many strange animals" (ibid.).

The wonderfully illustrated account of Guaman Poma (1980 [1583–1615]) mentions two Inca queens who had a special fondness for tropical forest birds as pets (Fig. 1.23). This suggests that although the Inca ruler may have used military force to obtain the birds, their care was primarily in the hands of women. The contents of a tomb at Pachacamac recorded by E. G. Squier (1967) support the suggestion that women cared for the tropical forest birds. In the tomb were the remains of five people, which Squier interpreted (probably correctly) as a family: an infant, a young boy, a young woman, an older woman, and a man. Associated with the mummy of the younger woman was a mummified parrot, as well as weaving implements, gold and silver jewelry, and a feather fan. The older woman's mummy was associated with another feather fan, shell ornaments, a spindle, and some cotton. The boy and man were found with only rustic fishing implements and no fancy ornaments. The difference between the artifacts found with the women and those of the man and boy supports the idea of parallel inheritance, that is, a daughter inherited her rank from her mother, and a son from his father.[3] It also suggests the high value placed on women who were skilled textile artisans.

Much has been written about the extraordinary weaving traditions of the Andes, which continue, in part, to this day (on the functions of Inca cloth see especially Murra 1962). The Spaniards' overwhelming interest in gold and silver did not completely blind them to the fact that *cumpi*, the most finely woven cloths, were equally valued by the Incas. *Cumpi* is prominently featured on any list of precious objects given as tribute or used in ritual sacrifices. When feathered cloths are specifically mentioned, they are generally named with *cumpi*. Guaman Poma refers to "*cumpi* of feathers" (1980 [1583–1615]:183), and Cobo states that one type of cloth "was made with colored feathers woven into and fixed over the *cumbi*" (1990 [1653]:225). He further describes the sumptuous cloth:

> The feather cloths were the most esteemed and valued, and this was quite reasonable because the ones that I have seen would be highly regarded anywhere. They were made on the *cumbi* itself, but in such a way that the feathers stand out on the wool and cover it like velvet. The material that they had for this kind of cloth was extensive because incredible numbers and varieties of birds are found in this land with such excellent colors that it is beyond belief. They used only very small, fine feathers. These they fastened on the cloth with a fine, wool thread, laying them to one side, and making with them the same patterns and figures found in their handsome *cumbis*. The gloss, splendor, and sheen of this feather cloth was of such exceptional beauty that it must be seen to be appreciated. Upon entering this land, the Spaniards found the storehouses of the Incas well supplied with many things; one of the most important ones was an abundant supply of valuable feathers for these textiles. Almost all of the feathers were iridescent, with an admirable sheen which looked like very fine gold. Another kind was an iridescent golden green. And there was an immense amount of those tiny feathers which are found on the chest of the little birds that we call *tominejo* [hummingbird], in a small patch about the size of a fingernail. (ibid.: 225–26)

It is likely that the production of feathered cloth was associated with the production of *cumpi*.[4] The most skilled weavers in the Inca empire were gathered in special buildings, *aclla wasi* or "houses of the selected women," to produce the exquisite textiles. Each *aclla wasi* was associated with the Inca Temple of the Sun. The *aclla wasi* in Cuzco was restricted to women of the royal divine lineage of the Inca ruler, who was considered a direct descendant of the sun. The *cumpi* produced by those "selected women" was also imbued with divinity and could only be used as a sacrificial offering to the sun or his divine descendants, the mummies of the Inca rulers, or else worn by the living Inca himself. The women in a provincial *aclla wasi*, such as the one at Pachacamac, were the most talented local weavers or Inca women of nonroyal lineages. They were often related to high-ranking local lords, but it was possible for a skilled woman of undistinguished lineage to enter a provincial *aclla wasi*. They produced *cumpi* for the Inca, who used it in sacrifices and gave it as gifts to nonroyal leaders.

> The Inca distributed his goods and royal income in the following order. What was brought for him to his court came there before the fiesta of *Raymi* [the solstitial celebration in June] and commonly they brought him a large quantity of animals, clothing, and other necessary things . . . The finest and most valuable things, such as gold, silver, precious stones, feathers, exquisite clothing, and other

FIGURE 1.24

Panel of blue and yellow feathered cloth (46–24–5). This large panel was found in a large cache of special objects in the Department of Arequipa, Peru. Bird: Blue-and-yellow Macaw.

things of this kind, were normally brought to the Inca by the *cacique* [leader] of each province himself . . . the Inca would also give the bearer some of the exquisite clothing . . . In the sacrifices made by order of the Inca in the ordinary and special fiestas, a large part of the income and tributes was burned and consumed . . . The Inca ordered that of the exquisite clothing and other precious objects from each province, a certain amount was to be given to lords, *curacas* [leaders], and important people of the area, according to the social status and rank of each one. Although it is true that the women and Indian servants . . . made clothing for them, it was ordinary and coarse . . . but the magnificent clothing made of fine *cumbi* worn by the *caciques* and lords could be made only for the Inca, and he handed it out to these lords. (Cobo 1979 [1653]:220)

Just as the production and distribution of fine *cumpi* cloth were strictly controlled, the production and distribution of the beautiful feathered textiles and ornaments must also have been regulated. The provincial *aclla wasi* provided an effective way to control the production of sumptuous *cumpi*, as it ensured that the most adept weavers wove only for the Inca. The concentration of feathered-cloth production in the *aclla wasi* would also have provided a simple means to control the distribution of those marks of favor, since feathers could be worn only by certain high-ranking local rulers by special permission of the Inca. The Inca's concern in limiting feathered clothes and ornaments to certain privileged individuals indicates that those ornaments must have been very potent symbols of power.

The use of feathered cloths, and sometimes just feathers (Arriaga 1968 [1617]), in sacrifices also reflects their symbolic potency. During Inca times, sacrifices were made to the sun, the royal mummies, and a number of sacred places and stones. Women also made sacrifices to the moon, and common people made sacrifices to the mummies of their own ancestors. An overwhelming amount of valuable goods was burned, buried, or thrown in rivers during these rituals. Apparently only the Inca had the right to sacrifice the feathered cloths and feathers, as he alone had the right to sacrifice the finest *cumpi* cloths.

The brilliant blue and yellow feathered cloth (Fig. 1.24) in The University Museum's collection was found in a context which indicates that it was part of a large sacrificial offering. A Peruvian newspaper article described the discovery:

A Precolumbian tomb was discovered, with mud and stone walls in three concentric rings. The first extended one meter above ground, and the other two were subterranean. In the outer ring, eight large portrait jars, one meter high and two meters in circumference around the widest part, were discovered. Each one of the eight contained twelve feathered panels made by ancient Peruvians. Inside the second ring the following objects were found: three small vessels of silver, a small llama of gold, two silver idols, three artistically carved wooden cups, three shawl-pins of silver, a small cloth of alpaca wool with forty-two silver discs, a small multicolor llama wool poncho, an aryballoid bottle and other ceramic plates. All of these objects have the unmistakable marks of classic Incaic style. The innermost circle was not excavated. (Bernedo Malaga 1950)

Of the 96 feathered cloths, 44 were placed in an archaeological museum in Arequipa, and several others are in museum collections here in the United States.

Although featherworking on the coast was probably less restricted in pre-Inca times, it is difficult to assess how tightly it might have been controlled. Much work has yet to be done in identifying the exact nature of sociopolitical control in the various coastal

FIGURE 1.25

FIGURE 1.25

Feather crown (28549).
Found by Max Uhle at
Pachacamac with the
same mummy as the
feather panel (28550) in
Figure 1.26. Birds: Blue-
and-yellow Macaw, Scarlet
Macaw, and Tanager.

FIGURE 1.26

Feather panel (28550).
One of a matched pair
found with the same
mummy as the crown
(28549) in Figure 1.25.
Both the crown and pair of
panels are made with cloth
woven in the north coast
Chimú style. Birds:
macaw, tanager, and
unidentified.

polities, but the degree of control probably varied extensively, and presumably the common people's access to exotic goods, such as feathered ornaments, varied in a similar manner. Although the Inca's bureaucratic organization of the empire is often emphasized, it must be remembered that he was the supreme ritual leader, as the living descendant of the divine sun, as well as savvy political leader. The superficial observation that feathered ornaments were associated with political status in the Inca empire, but apparently signified shamanistic or ritual status in non-Inca cultures, ignores the possibility that political and ritual status might have been linked in non-Inca cultures, as they were in Inca times.

The Inca also controlled the style of dress that the conquered peoples of the Inca empire wore, especially the headgear.

> The men and women of each nation and province had their insignias and emblems by which they could be identified, and they could not go around without this identification or exchange their insignias for those of another nation, or they would be severely punished. They had this insignia on their clothes with different stripes and colors, and the men wore their most distinguishing insignia on their heads; each nation was identified by the headdress. (Cobo 1979 [1653]:196)

This information can be used to interpret one of Uhle's finds at Pachacamac. The beautiful feathered "crown" and a matched pair of feathered panels (Figs. 1.25, 1.26) were found with one mummy, apparently a very important man. The iconography on the panels and the weave of the fabric have been identified as a style distinctive of the north coast Chimú people (A. Rowe 1984), contemporaneous with the Inca. Since no one else would have been allowed to wear the insignias of Chimú, this mummy interred at Pachacamac must have been a distinguished man from the north coast.

During Inca times, feathered clothing and ornaments were not worn every day, but are mentioned in association with special events. Cobo informs us that the Incas wore their finery

> . . . when they went to war and in their celebrations and solemn festivals. The majority of these ornaments were made of feathers which came in a variety of attractive colors. Above the forehead they put a large diadem of feathers standing up high in the form of a crown or garland; it was called *pilcocata*. They wore another string of the same feathers around the neck like a Vandyke collar, and still another across the chest like a gorget which ended at the shoulder. Hanging from the *llauto* [a thick wool cord wrapped around the forehead] they had several flowers and other finely made feather decorations . . . For their most solemn festivals, they had very bright garments made of feathers, which were their richest and most esteemed apparel. (Cobo 1990 [1653]:187)

The calendrical festivals celebrated in fancy dress include the monthly "first day of the moon" (Garcilaso 1987 [1609]:394); the month of December, when boys were initiated (Sharon 1976); February, when virgin land was plowed for cultivation (Guaman Poma 1980 [1583–1615]:213, 1031); June, December, and the time of harvesting corn (Arriaga 1968 [1617]:50; Arriaga uses the Catholic calendar to refer to dates and his "Corpus Christi" and "Christmastime" probably refer to important solstitial celebrations). Garcilaso describes the ritual plowing of the fields in August:

> The last land to be cultivated was that assigned to the king. It was tilled communally. All the Indians went out together to the fields of the Inca and of the Sun with great rejoicing and satisfaction. They

wore the clothes and adornments they kept for their greatest festivities, covered with gold and silver plates and with feather headdresses. As they ploughed (which was the work that gave them most pleasure) they sang many songs composed in praise of the Incas: their labor thus became a matter for festivity and joy because it was performed in the service of their god and kings. (1987 [1609]: 244)

The principal noncalendrical celebration associated with feathers was the sanctification ritual upon the death of the Inca. The Incas were not the first Andean people to preserve and honor the bodies of their dead ancestors. The tradition probably began on the coast where the dry sands inhibited decay, as evidenced by a multitude of astonishingly well-preserved mummies. The mummies of the Incas were all destroyed by the Spaniards in their campaign to "extirpate idolatry" in Peru. We do not know exactly what methods were used to preserve them, but Garcilaso's opinion was that the bodies were taken above the snow line and left there to dry, in a way similar to making *charki*, dried meat.

Betanzos (1987 [1551]) provides the most detailed information on Incaic mummification. He credits Inca Yupanque, the tenth Inca,[5] as the originator of most of the cult's basic elements, beginning with the construction of the Temple of the Sun in Cuzco. When this was done he ordered that a *bulto* ("bundle," the same term used for mummy bundles) be made to represent the sun. This sacred bundle was revered in place of the actual sun. Later, when his father died, Inca Yupanque had his father's body preserved and made into a bundle. This bundle was paraded before the public, and sacrifices were offered to it. Inca Yupanque ordered that more bundles be made, one for each of the previous Inca rulers. They were all placed together with the bundle of his father and that of the sun in the Temple of the Sun, seated on benches decorated with elaborate feather mosaics.

Before Inca Yupanque died he gave instructions for the rituals to be conducted after his death. These included periods of fasting and restrictions on wearing finely made or decorated clothes, or any ornament such as featherwork. Elaborate and costly sacrifices of precious goods and children were performed simultaneously throughout the Inca empire. One year after the Inca's death was the most important observance, which lasted an entire month. Betanzos states that the rituals and costumes were too numerous for him to describe all of them, but he does mention one in which four men, completely disguised by their feathered costumes, came out to the plaza, and another in which a squadron of women wore men's clothes, with men's headdresses and feathers. The month ended with more sacrifices, of children, animals, clothes, and other goods. The body of the Inca, sanctified by these rituals, was then buried in a house built for that purpose outside of Cuzco. Above the burial was placed a bundle with a golden image, which was revered and cared for by his descendants. Another bundle was made containing his hair and nail clippings, and this was sent to Cuzco, where it was cared for by his heir. Offerings were made to all the bundles, and the ones in Cuzco were dressed in sumptuous clothes and paraded around the city on special occasions (Fig. 1.27). Cobo witnessed a reenactment of such a parade, performed to celebrate the beatification of St. Ignatius in 1610.

. . . the representation of their former kings in a great and splendid display, which included the eleven kings of Cuzco, looking very majestic on their litters, which were highly decorated with feathers of diverse colors and carried by Indians on their shoulders. The kings were wearing the same mantles and adornments that the kings themselves used to use; dressed in fine *cumbe*, which was their brocade and finest cloth, holding a scepter, each one had his royal insignia and attendants dressed according to their custom and an

FIGURE 1.27

Inca procession of a mummy bundle. After a drawing by Guaman Poma.

FIGURE 1.28

Feathered garment from Pachacamac (28639). This cloth was probably tied around the waist with the flap either in the front or back. Birds: Red-and-green Macaw, Blue-and-yellow Macaw, and unidentified.

FIGURE 1.29

Feathered headdress from the central coast site of Caudivilla (33887).

officer by his side who carried a sunshade of attractive feathers . . . (1979 [1653]:101)

The spectacular pageantry and sumptuous costumes of the Inca celebrations must have been as beautiful to the Andean peoples as they were to Cobo. The people who made the wonderful artifacts in the University Museum collections cannot explain to us how they evaluated beauty, but perhaps a consideration of a few of the aesthetic values of the Waiwai, Cashinahua, and Bororo will allow us to appreciate these objects in a new way.

The Waiwai's great preference for red is not reflected in the examples of coastal featherwork. Blue and yellow appear to be the favored colors, with red used primarily as an accent. Red was an important color in Precolumbian times, but the precious red spondylus shell and an abundance of red textile dyes may have satisfied the Andean peoples' desire for that hue. The brilliant blue of macaw feathers is certainly unique, and the bright, nonfading yellow of feathers is more difficult to produce with textile dyes.

The Cashinahua's sophisticated aesthetic of sparseness, and the delicacy of Waiwai feather creations, are lacking in the Andean pieces. The feathers are massed together as blocks of color, so that their individual textures and shapes are secondary to the shape and design of the piece as a whole. This is clearly seen in the feather mosaics applied to textile panels (Figs. 1.25, 1.26, 1.28), and also in the feather whisks or plumes (Fig. 1.1). On the textile pieces, the feathers are used not as separate decorations on an artifact, but as the medium with which the artifact is colored. This use of feathers as a surface treatment is similar to the Bororo style of creating patterns with blocks of colored feathers.

While the Bororo use feathers to cover hard objects, such as wood, Andean feather mosaics were usually applied to flexible cloth. The Cashinahua interest in the movement of feathers, which displays the sheen and subtle iridescence found in some species, was apparently also important to the coastal Peruvians. The feathers on the plumes for headdress ornaments were not held in place rigidly, but were attached so that they would move easily. The complex techniques used in the manufacture of the spectacular blue headdress from Caudivilla (Fig. 1.29; see Greene, Ch. 2 and Figs. 2.1 and 2.2) seem to be designed to emphasize beauty in motion, perhaps the motion of dance.

Our appreciation for these examples of ancient plumage can be enhanced by a deeper knowledge of the contexts of their production and use. Although we will never approach a complete understanding of what these artifacts meant to the vanished Precolumbian peoples who made and wore them, they are the evidence that their world was rich in meaning and beauty.

by Virginia Greene

IV. *Feathered textile with mosaic pattern (CG852611–6381).*

"THERE IS THUS NOTHING IN THE TYPES OF CIVILIZATIONS WHICH IS NOT CAPABLE C

HEADDRESS

FIGURE 2.1

*S*ide and front views of an
Andean headdress (33887).
Height from edge of cap to top of
crest, 9¼". This is an example of
an unusual early style and use of
feathers. Birds: Blue-and-yellow
Macaw, and Scarlet Macaw.
From Caudivilla.

WHILE EXCAVATING AT THE SITE of Pachacamac in 1896, Dr. Max Uhle also purchased archaeological collections from other sites. One of these pieces is a unique example of ancient Andean featherwork: a headdress decorated with a crest of blue feathers and a red and blue feather mosaic (Figs. 2.1, 2.2). Three different techniques have been used to attach the feathers to the textile, each carefully chosen to produce a different visual effect.

The headdress was reported to have come from the site of Caudivilla, in the Chillon Valley (Fig. 1.2). Its age is uncertain, as we have no archaeological context with associated objects, but it is different in both construction and style from the Inca Period headdresses known from documents and figurines as well as surviving examples.[1]

A careful study of technique can tell us more than just how the object was made. Detailed examination of this object and other feathered textiles has provided information on the social context in which they were produced, and possibly even their age. The use of feathers from tropical forest birds indicates a time period when trade across the Andes was flourishing; the Caudivilla headdress may be earlier in date than the late Inca Period examples, which are made primarily with feathers from coastal species of birds. Comparison of the methods used to attach feathers to a variety of textiles reveals techniques that were shared widely over time and space, as well as others of more limited distribution. The presence of more than one system of knots and stitches on a single piece suggests that more than one person was involved in the manufacture. Feathered pieces, therefore, may have been made in the same kind of special workshop that produced the most elaborate and technically sophisticated Andean textiles (Candler, Ch. 1).

THROWING LIGHT ON THE CHARACTER AND ANCESTRY OF CIVILIZATIONS . . ." – *MAX UHLE*

FIGURE 2.3

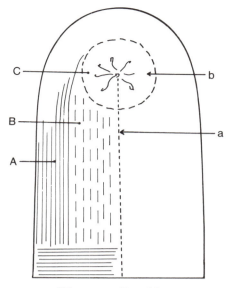

Diagram of headdress construction (33887). Drawing by the author.

A. *Feather mosaic*
B. *Back panel*
C. *Crest*
a. *center seam*
b. *fabric pad*

FIGURE 2.4

Closeup of scroll design on headdress (33887).

FIGURE 2.2

Front view of an Andean headdress (33887). Height from edge of cap to top of crest, 9¼". This is an example of an unusual early style and use of feathers. Birds: Blue-and-yellow Macaw, and Scarlet Macaw.

WORKMANSHIP OF THE HEADDRESS

The foundation of the Caudivilla headdress is a plain-weave cotton textile. The weaving is loose and somewhat uneven, and the yarns are variable in thickness and degree of twist. The thread count also varies, 23–24 warps/in. x 16–19 wefts/in. The warps are Z-spun, 2S-plied; the wefts Z-spun and unplied.

The cap and back flap were made from a single four-selvage rectangle of fabric (Fig. 2.3). This was folded crosswise and seamed along one long edge, the seam running down the center of the back. At the fold, the fabric was gathered, forming the cap. Round pads of similar fabric were stitched to the interior and exterior of the cap, concealing the gathers. On the exterior, this pad is the foundation for the feather crest. On the interior, a heavy cord of plant fiber[2] has been stitched from side to side across the interior pad. At present, the ends of the cord are broken about two inches below the edge of the cap. The cord may originally have tied under the chin.

In addition to the feather crest on top of the cap, the front of the cap and the edges of the back flap are decorated with a feather mosaic scroll in blue and red. The central part of the back flap, between the scroll borders, has a series of long vertical feather strings, six on each side of the center seam. The red feathers come from the scarlet macaw (*Ara macao*), the blue feathers from the blue-and-yellow macaw (*Ara ararauna*). The feathers used for the mosaic are body feathers; those on the back of the flap and the crest are wing coverts. There are 240 feathers in the crest. When the headdress was complete, there were approximately 300 feathers in the back panel, and 1400–1600 body feathers used in the mosaic border.

The scroll design is formed by the standard technique for Andean feathered textiles: long strings of small body feathers are sewn in overlapping rows onto the fabric (Figs. 2.4, 2.5A). Three cords are used, all cotton, spun and plied like the weaving yarns: (a) a carrier cord, over which the feather shafts are bent; (b) a tying cord, which secures the bent shaft and holds the feathers onto the string; and (c) a sewing cord attaching the string to the fabric.[3] The feathers lie flat against the fabric. At the top and bottom of the scroll band, the strings of

FIGURE 2.5A

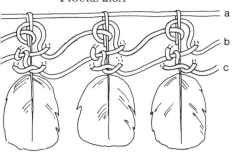

*Drawing of feather string
for mosaic (33887).
Drawing by the author.*

FIGURE 2.5B

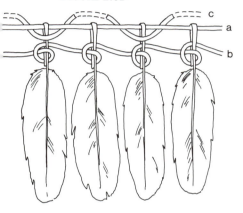

*Drawing of feather string
for back panel (33887).
Drawing by the author.*

FIGURE 2.6

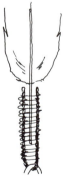

*Drawing of crest feather
attachment (33887).
Drawing by the author.*

red or blue feathers run completely around the front and side edges of the headdress, or across the back edge. The scrolls themselves are formed with short sections of feather string, and the shape of the scroll was enhanced by the way in which the feathers were trimmed after they were sewn into place. By using this system rather than strings with different-colored feathers in precisely measured sections, strings could be prepared in advance and stockpiled for use on a variety of feathered textiles.

The long strings of feathers on the central part of the back flap are constructed using the same system of cords and knots as the strings for the mosaic. These cords are also cotton, but four-ply (Z–2S–4Z). Unlike the mosaic, however, the sewing stitch only loosely secures every other feather to the fabric (Fig. 2.5B). When the headdress was worn, the feathers would have stood out at an angle from the fabric, free to move with the slightest motion of the wearer. The entire back section of the headdress, therefore, would have appeared as a shimmering panel of iridescent blue.

The crest feathers are attached using a shaft-extension technique which causes the feathers to stand straight out from the cap (Fig. 2.6). A short length of heavy plant-fiber cord was inserted through one yarn of the fabric pad on the cap, and the ends of this cord were tightly bound to the feather shaft with fine cotton thread. Some movement of the feathers, especially those at the edges, probably occurred when the headdress was worn, but the stiff binding of the shafts would have helped the crest to hold its shape.

COMPARABLE ARTIFACTS

Similar headdresses illustrated by Ann Rowe in *Costumes and Featherwork of the Lords of Chimor* (1984:179, 181–82) all have a cap and long back flap with feather mosaics, and a feather crest on the cap. However, the lower back edge is finished with a row of long (wing or tail) feathers, and with one exception, the crest is an inverted cone above a smaller plume. No information is available on the knots or stitches used to make the feather strings and attach them to the fabric.[4] Three are made entirely, and the others partially, of Chimú plain-weave fabric (with paired warps), and the featherwork shows Chimú iconography. Unlike the Caudivilla headdress, they are constructed in sections: the back flap, and two narrow panels which hang on either side, are separate pieces sewn to the edge of the cap (Ann Rowe, personal communication).

The most notable difference, however, is in the feathers. Rowe's examples are predominantly brown and white, from coastal species such as the Muscovy duck, with only occasional use of tropical forest birds such as parrot or macaw. Rowe suggests that the brown and white feathered headdresses (and tabards of similar style) may be very late, "made after trade over the Andes had been disrupted" (1984:178–79). As this trade was still active during the Inca Period, the disruption would have been caused by the Spanish conquest, and the surviving headdresses would therefore date from the Colonial Period.

The Caudivilla headdress, made entirely with feathers from tropical forest birds, may therefore be an early version of these Inca Period feathered headdresses. The different construction may also be exclusively time-related; without a body of comparative material it is difficult to know whether it also represents a local style.

Ten additional pieces from the collection of The University Museum were also examined to determine the type of fabric, and the system of knots and sewing stitches used on the feather strings. These included two feather strings and a pouch (all of uncertain provenience, possibly the south coast, collected by William Farabee), five feathered textiles excavated by Max Uhle at Pachacamac and La Centinela, one excavated fragment of uncertain provenience, and a purchased piece from the south coast. These objects are illustrated in Figures 2.7–17, along with diagrams of the feather strings. Full details are in the Appendix.[5]

The system of knots and stitches varies slightly from textile to textile, with a very limited number of knots used in different combinations. Two pieces, the "miniature tabard" (Fig. 2.13) and the blue and yellow feathered panel (Fig. 2.17), have distinctive stitching patterns, but the construction of the feather strings follows the same pattern as the other objects.

The extensive literature on the technology of ancient Andean textiles is not matched by similar studies of featherwork, including feathered textiles. We know, for example, that fabrics with characteristic Chimú paired warps were used for feathered as well as other textiles, but there is little comparative material available on knotting systems for the production of the feather strings. A few diagrams of knots have been published, but with the exception of the excavated textiles from the site of Las Avispas, it is not clear to which objects the diagrams refer.[6]

Several of the knotting systems, including one from Las Avispas, are duplicated in the central coast material from The University Museum. The second system from Las Avispas has a more complex sewing stitch, which is found on the Caudivilla headdress, although it is associated with a different knot on the tying cord.[7] The basic knots used to make feather strings and attach them to fabrics appear to have been used throughout the Peruvian coastal area. It is not possible to tell at this point whether certain distinctive stitches will turn out to have a more restricted distribution.

We know from the Spanish chronicles that during the Inca Period the most elaborate and beautiful textiles were produced by women in special workshops. It seems likely that the feathered cloths were also made in these workshops (Candler, Ch.1).

On three of the objects, the tabard (Fig. 2.11), the blue and yellow panel (Fig. 2.17), and a small (and badly deteriorated) fragment which may be part of another tabard (Fig. 2.16), the knots used on the feather strings vary within a single object. On the small fragment and the panel, different systems are associated with different colors of feathers. This suggests that more than one person made the strings. It seems likely that the strings were produced in quantity in advance, and used as needed. One of the strings collected by Farabee (Fig. 2.7) was found wrapped around a short piece of wood; this may have been a method for keeping prepared strings from becoming tangled before they were used.

Because of the deteriorated condition of the yarns, and the fact that the sewing cord is usually knotted very close to the tying cord, it is often difficult to see the exact structure of the knots, even under the microscope. In addition, the fragility of the feathers and yarns makes it impossible to uncover more than a few of the knots for adequate examination. It is likely, therefore, that some of the textiles which appear to have one system of knots actually have more.

Detailed examination of a larger sample of Andean feathered textiles may eventually enable us to place the Caudivilla headdress in its proper geographic and chronological context. For the present, it remains a superb example of the technical skill and artistic creativity of the ancient people of the Andes.

FIGURE 2.7A

Feather strings prepared for sewing onto a textile (SA 3794).

FIGURE 2.7B

Feather strings wrapped around wooden stick (SA 3794).

FIGURE 2.7C

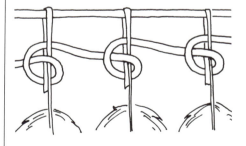

Knots on string (SA 3794). Drawing by the author.

1. Feather strings (SA3974; Fig. 2.7). Provenience: South(?) coast. Purchased by Dr. Wm. C. Farabee, 1922–23. Prepared for sewing onto a textile. The larger piece is 37" long, of which 26" has feathers. The feathers diminish in size toward one end of the string. The shorter piece (which also has smaller feathers) is 13" long, 9" with feathers. Both have bare cord at each end, suggesting that they are complete strings. Cotton cords, Z-spun, 2S-plied. Small

pink feathers (possibly flamingo), with two feathers tied together. The feather strings were found wrapped around a short piece of wood (5¾" long, 1⅜" diam.).

FIGURE 2.8A

Closeup of feather string (SA 3978).

FIGURE 2.8B

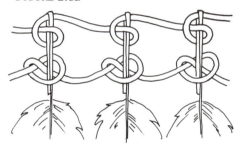

Knots on feather string (SA 3978). Drawing by the author.

2. Feather string (SA3978; Fig. 2.8). Provenience: South(?) coast. Purchased by Dr. Wm. C. Farabee, 1922–23. Prepared for sewing onto a textile. Present length 46", with the cords on both ends broken very close to the last feather. Cotton cords, Z-spun, 2S-plied, very variable in thickness and degree of twist. Single blue feathers from the blue-and-yellow macaw (*Ara ararauna*).

FIGURE 2.9

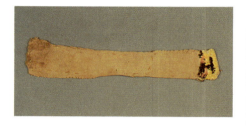

Pouch (SA 3979).

3. Pouch? (SA3979; Fig. 2.9). Provenience: South(?) coast. Purchased by Dr. Wm. C. Farabee, 1922–23. Length 18½", width at bottom 3⅛". Made of three separate pieces of fabric, all of which are cotton, plain weave, 36–42 warps/in. x 24 wefts/in. The yarns are S-spun, unplied, variable in thickness and degree of twist. The front is a single piece; the back is made in two sections. At the point where the two pieces of fabric join, the pouch is sewn completely closed through all three layers of fabric. All of the edges of the fabric, including the selvedge along one side of the front, are overcast; some edges were turned under first. All seams are sewn with an irregular running stitch. The thread used for the overcast and running stitches is an unidentified plant fiber. The carrier, tying, and sewing cords for the feathers are cotton. The first two are all S-spun, 2Z-plied; the sewing cords included S-2Z and Z-2S yarns. On the front of the pouch, the bottom 2" is decorated with a feather mosaic design in pink, yellow, and black (with iridescent blue tips). The feathers are at present unidentified. The system of knots is identical to that on the pink feather string, SA3974. Also as on this string, the feathers are extremely small and all but a few of the black feathers are tied in bunches of two. The sewing stitch is a simple whipstitch, which goes over the cords between bunches of feathers. The sewing stitch, therefore, most closely resembles that used on 46–24–5 (No. 10, below), which has a definite south coast provenience.

FIGURE 2.10

Tabard (32823). This feathered textile may be part of a tunic. Tunics were constructed as two panels, sewn together up the middle with a space left for the head.

4. Half of a tabard (32823, Uhle #2175; Figs. 2.10, 2.12A). Provenience: La Centinela. Excavated by Dr. Max Uhle, 1896. Cotton, plain weave, 56" x 22". Full loom width 28", with 3" turned under on each side. Warps Z-spun, 2S-plied, 28/in. in tightly woven sections, 20–22/in. in looser areas. Wefts Z-spun, unplied, 22/in. in tighter sections, 20–22/in. in more loosely woven areas. Yarns vary greatly in thickness and degree of twist. The fabric is covered with feather strings, except for a narrow strip at the shoulder (3½"–4" wide). Yellow ground, band of yellow and blue scrolls bordered with red and blue stripes. Red feathers from the scarlet macaw (*Ara macao*); yellow and blue from the blue-and-yellow macaw (*Ara ararauna*). Cotton cords, Z-spun, 2S-plied; some Z-2S-2Z using very fine two-ply yarns. One system of knots and stitches positively identified; the same as one of the systems found on 32824 (see Fig. 2.12A).

FIGURE 2.11A

Tabard fragment (32824A).

FIGURE 2.11B

Tabard fragment (32824B).

FIGURE 2.11C

Tabard fragment (32824C).

5. Half of a tabard (32824A–C, Uhle #2175; Figs. 2.11, 2.12B). Provenience: La Centinela. Excavated by Dr. Max Uhle, 1896. Three fragments of a feathered tabard. The two larger pieces, B and C, seem to be part of the same object; A may or may not belong to this piece. The fabric of all three is identical: cotton, plain weave with paired warps ("Chimú weave"). The warps are Z-spun, 40–44 pairs/in.; single wefts, S-spun, 30–34/in.

Fragment A (Figs. 2.11A, 2.12B): Height 8", width 10½". The lower edge has four heading cords, S-spun, 8Z-plied. Yellow ground, single border row of blue, two small areas of indigo at the upper edge. Blue and yellow feathers from the blue-and-yellow macaw (*Ara ararauna*); indigo feathers from a jay (*Cyanocorax* sp.). Along the lower edge of the fragment is a row of long pink feathers (unidentifiable, possibly flamingo). The absence of the scroll design found on fragment B, and the presence close to the edge of indigo feathers, indicate that this piece does not join to the lower edge of B. It may be from the other edge of the tabard, if the border design on the front and back was not identical. The carrier, tying, and sewing cords are all cotton; some are Z-spun, 2S-plied; others are S-spun, 2Z-plied. The large feathers at the lower edge are sewn with two strands of S-2Z cords.

Fragment B (Figs. 2.11B, 2.12A–C): Height 40", width 14½". The knots are illustrated in Figures 2.12A–C. The lower edge has three heading cords, S-spun, 8Z-plied as on fragment A. The tying and sewing cords are S-spun, Z-plied, with two or three plies. The design has a yellow ground, and a band of blue and yellow scrolls with a single border row of blue. The lower edge has a row of long pink feathers, of which only a few remain. On the opposite end from the finished edge are the remains of a step design, red with indigo borders. The shoulder area, which is not covered with feathers, is 1½"–1¾" wide.

Fragment C (Figs. 2.11C, 2.12A–C): Height 28", width 21½". The cords are all cotton, and include Z-spun, 2S-plied; S-spun, 2Z-plied; and S-spun, 3Z-plied. Yellow ground, with a step design as on B. The position of the design and undecorated shoulder area are in alignment with fragment B.

FIGURE 2.12A

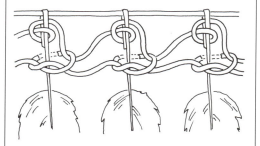

*Knot-stitch systems on tabards 32823
and 32824B,C.*

FIGURE 2.12B

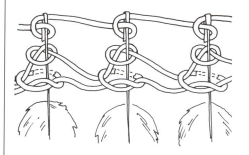

*Knot-stitch systems on tabard
fragments 32824A–C.*

FIGURE 2.12C

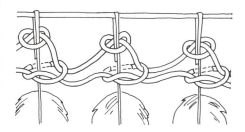

*Knot-stitch systems on tabard
fragments 32824B,C. Drawings by the
author.*

FIGURE 2.13A

Miniature tabard (28642).

FIGURE 2.13B

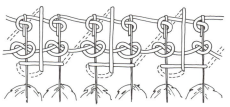

*Knots and stitches on miniature
tabard (28642). Drawing by the
author.*

6. "Miniature tabard" (28642, Uhle #1758; Fig. 2.13). Provenience: Pachacamac, Gravefield I. Excavated by Dr. Max Uhle, 1896. Height 18", width 8½". Cotton, plain weave. Both warp and weft yarns are S-spun, unplied, 28/in. x 22/in. This is a small rectangle of fabric, which was folded in half. One side has four rows of long feathers (wing coverts), with a bottom row of small body feathers. All these are from the scarlet macaw (*Ara macao*). The other side has a multicolor feather mosaic: a central scallop in green with a red border, on a blue ground. The green feathers are parrot (*Amazona* sp.), the red and blue are scarlet macaw. The selvedges are on the sides; the edge on the side with blue feathers is hemmed, the other is incomplete. Like the large feathered tabards, there is an undecorated strip across the shoulders, about 1" wide. A vertical neck slit has been cut at the center of the shoulder area, extending down into the upper rows of feathers. The edges of this slit are unfinished. The cords are cotton, S-spun, 4Z-plied. The sewing system is distinctive and is used on both sides, though the spacing of the stitches on the multicolor side is difficult to determine. The sides of the "tabard" are not sewn, but on the observer's right facing the blue side, the selvedges near the shoulder have been caught together by a single stitch, in the same yarn used to tie and sew the feathers. The piece will therefore not lie flat.

FIGURE 2.14A

Garment (28639).

FIGURE 2.14B

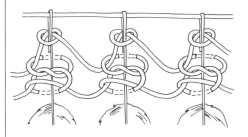

Knots and stitches on garment (28639). Drawing by the author.

7. Garment (28639, Uhle #2012; Fig. 2.14). Provenience: Pachacamac, Gravefield I. Excavated by Dr. Max Uhle, 1896. Height 21", width of garment 9", length of waistband 47". The textile is a rectangle of heavy cotton fabric, plain weave. All the yarns are Z-spun, 2S-plied, 45 warps/in. x 24 wefts/in. A selvedge is on the observer's right; the bottom and left side are hemmed on the front. The waistband is made of a folded piece of very loosely woven cotton, stitched to the upper edge of the rectangle. The garment has two wide bands of red feathers and one of blue, with a red and blue scroll design near the bottom. Along the lower edge is a row of long yellow and black feathers. The red feathers are from the red-and-green macaw (*Ara chloroptera*); the blue feathers from the blue-and-yellow macaw (*Ara ararauna*); the yellow feathers are probably scarlet macaw (*Ara macao*); the black ones are unidentifiable. The cords are cotton, Z-spun, 2S-plied; some of the sewing cords are doubled.

FIGURE 2.15

Feather textile (CG852611–6381).

8. Fragment of feathered textile (CG 852611–6381; Fig. 2.15). Provenience unknown. Height 14", width 17½". Cotton, plain weave, with paired warps and single wefts (Chimú weave). The yarns are S-spun; 60 paired warps/in. x 20 wefts/in. There is a selvedge on the observer's left. The bottom edge looks naturally frayed; the other two edges were clearly cut after excavation to make a neat rectangle. Blue ground, with a band of blue and yellow scrolls. The feathers are from the blue-and-yellow macaw (*Ara ararauna*). The tying and sewing cords are cotton, S-spun, 3Z-plied. See Figure 2.12C for knots and sewing stitches.

FIGURE 2.16A

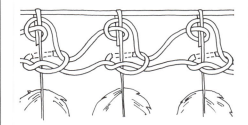

Knots and stitches used for the blue feather strings (28640).

FIGURE 2.16B

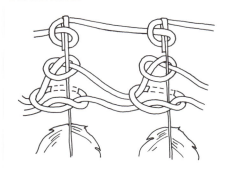

FIGURE 2.16C

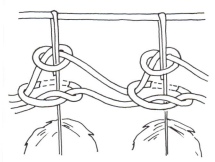

Two different systems of knots and stitches used for the red and yellow feather strings (28640). Drawings by the author.

9. Fragment of a feathered textile (28640, Uhle #1482x; fragment not illustrated; for knots see Fig. 2.16). Height 15½", width 14½". Provenience: Pachacamac, Gravefield II. Cotton, plain weave. The yarns are Z-spun, 2S-plied; 29–34 warps/in. x 24 wefts/in. Blue ground, with a band of yellow and red of unknown design. Almost all the feathers are missing; those remaining appear to be macaw (*Ara* sp.). Cotton cords. The carrier and tying cords all appear to be S-spun, 2Z-plied, the opposite of the weaving yarns. Some of the sewing cords follow the weaving yarns, others are like the tying cords. Some of the Z-2S sewing cords—but not the others—are doubled.

FIGURE 2.17A

*Detail of feather panel (46–24–5).
(See Fig. 1.24 for complete object)*

FIGURE 2.17B

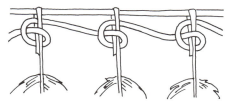

*Knots on blue feather strings
(46–24–5).*

FIGURE 2.17C

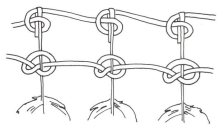

*Knots on yellow feather strings
(46–24–5). Drawings by the author.*

10. Feather panel (46–24–5; Fig. 2.17). Provenience: South coast, Department of Arequipa, Ocona Valley. Purchased by The University Museum in 1946. One of 96 similar pieces found in a series of large jars, together with a variety of other objects. Height 27", width 78". The panel is a four-selvedge rectangle with the warp horizontal. Cotton, plain weave, 78 warps/in. x 34 wefts/in. The yarns are Z-spun, 2S-plied; two four-ply heading cords at the left and right edges (Z-2S-2Z). Sewn along the upper front edge is a narrow fabric tape. This tape is plain weave, 90 warps/in. x 30 wefts/in. The warps are camelid fiber, Z-spun, 2S-plied. The wefts could not be observed. Sewn to each of the upper corners is a braided cord, 23"–24" long, also camelid fiber. The panel is quartered in yellow and blue. The yellow strings are made on cotton cords, Z-spun, 2S-plied, like the

weaving yarns. The blue strings, however, are made with a plant fiber (unidentified at present), S-spun, 2Z-plied, and with a different combination of knots. Although the fabric and the feather strings are well made, the sewing stitch is very crude and does not follow a regular pattern of one stitch for each feather. The strings are sewn using an irregular backstitch, which passes over the feathers as often as over the knots. Whether this is a function of time or geography—or urgency in assembling the panels for a ceremony—cannot be determined.

Acknowledgment

I would like to thank Kay Candler, who patiently read several preliminary drafts of this paper and made many helpful suggestions.

FIGURE 3.1

Hairpin (L-24-131). *This hair ornament is made from the feathers of various Parrot species, the Scarlet Macaw, and the Red-and-green Macaw.*

FIGURE 3.2

Map of Brazil with area of greatest Bororo expansion, circa 1850. From Albisetti and Venturelli 1962:0.25–0.26.

ONE OF THE MAJOR CHARACTERISTICS OF human beings is their need to express and communicate feelings and emotions through symbols. The environment and the beliefs of a society dictate the development of a visual language through individual and group creative processes. Art is the visual communication of ideas, concepts, and attitudes by members of a society in an attempt to document and preserve moral and philosophical values. Art also is for enjoyment, and it serves as a means of elevating viewers and artists to a new sphere of experience. Through the study of artistic expression within a society, we are better able to understand the society's organization and cultural concepts as well as their perception and interpretation of the universe.

Feathers and birds are outstanding inspirational artistic sources for many ancient and modern cultures. In some societies, feather art tends to be the most important cultural manifestation documenting artistic expression, social, political, and religious structures. Feather art is often a striking aesthetic and cultural manifestation in lowland South American cultures and in particular among the Bororo of central Brazil. Featherwork is the principal mode by which the Bororo artistically express and document their social and political structures, as well as their beliefs. Artistic expression is also fundamental to the Bororo's sense of identity as superior beings. For example, my informants recounted a myth about the unification of two native groups whose members wore ornaments or simple decorated fibers. Their great chief Birimodu valued the individuals who were decorated and killed the ones without ornaments. The decorated people were called Boe,[1] which means "the real people," and they were tribally organized. The use of ornaments and the appreciation for decoration distinguish the Boe as superior beings in relation to other people and animals.

FIGURE 3.3

Present Bororo reservations in central Brazil. The studied village of Córrego Grande is located in the Indigenous Area of Gomes Carneiro. Source: Ivair Luiz V. Busatto and Murílio Pereira Barcellos, unpublished research, Cuiabá, Mato Grosso, Brazil, 1985.

LANGUAGES OF FEATHER ART
CENTRAL BRAZIL

by Elizabeth Netto Calil Zarur

v. Hairpin (L-24-131).

...AT BEAR WITNESS TO THE INEXHAUSTIBLE CREATIVITY OF THE HUMAN MIND." — *CLAUDE LEVI-STRAUSS*

FIGURE 3.4

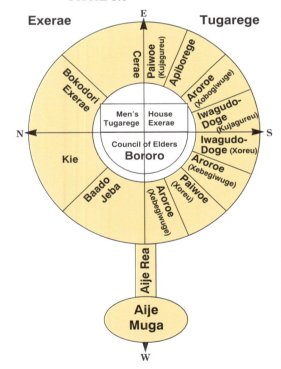

LEGEND

■ Standing Structure
▢ Fallen Structure
=== Dirt Road
--- Trail
▦ Garden
▨ Orange Grove
◙ Wooded

N

0   100m

*Village of Koreguedu Paru,
Córrego Grande, in the
Indigenous Reservation of
Gomes Carneiro, Mato
Grosso, Brazil, 1986.*

FIGURE 3.5

Exerae   **Tugarege**

E

Cerae Paiwoe (Kujagureu) Apiborege

Bokodori Exerae Aroroe (Xobogiwuge)

Iwagudo-Doge (Kujagureu)

Men's House Tugarege | House Exerae

N ← Council of Elders **Bororo** → S

Iwagudo-Doge (Xoreu)

Kie Aroroe (Xebegiwuge)

Baado Jeba Paiwoe (Xoreu)

Aroroe (Xebegiwuge)

Aije Rea

Aije Muga

W

*Diagram of ideal plan of
Bororo village. The outer
circle of houses is labeled
with the names of the
Bororo clans, located as
dictated by the ideal plan.
Based on José Américo's
information. Córrego
Grande, Mato Grosso,
Brazil, 1986.*

BORORO CULTURE

Historical Influences

The environment played an important role in developing and establishing Bororo artistic endeavors and beliefs. The Bororo ancestors had access to an abundance of raw materials in the rich central Brazilian lowland environment, the homeland of the Bororo for centuries. This territory covered an extensive region in the central plateau of Mato Grosso, Brazil (Fig. 3.2). It is characterized by flat fields, tropical savannah, a large central plateau with underlying sandy soils, and a multilevel vegetation, less densely forested than the Amazon Basin. A great variety of flora and fauna and the largest bird sanctuary in all South America are still found there.

Early Bororo society was based primarily on hunting and gathering with small agricultural plots. Women were responsible for manioc gardening; men hunted and fished. This system of subsistence persists today, but the Bororo no longer relocate their villages in the dry season as they did before the arrival of the Euro-Brazilians.

After the first contact with Euro-Brazilians early in the 18th century, the Bororo were split into two groups, geographically divided by the Paraguai-Cuiabá River. The Bororo located on the western side of the river were characterized by their docile nature, whereas the groups on the eastern side of the river were characterized as hostile. The western groups were soon subjugated by the new settlers, and their disappearance was inevitable. The surviving eastern groups, the Orarimugu-doge, which in Bororo language means "speckled-fish eaters," lived on a forested plateau between the São Lourenço and Vermelho rivers and along the tributaries of the Araguaia (Fig. 3.3). The most culturally conservative of the surviving Bororo villages, Córrego Grande, is located in the indigenous reservation of Gomes Carneiro on the western edge of the lower São Lourenço River (Fig. 3.4).[2]

Dual Social Structure

The stylistic development of Bororo art is directly associated with the organization of their society and their system of beliefs. To better appreciate Bororo feather art it is necessary to understand their social and political organizations, the system of belief, the meaning and use of colors and feathers and, foremost, the symbolism involving birds. The physical layout of the village displays the Bororo's laws and regulations coordinating social, religious, and aesthetic expressions. The layout was established, according to mythological sources, by the two Bororo culture heroes, Bakoróro and Itubóre. Bororo villages are believed to be replicas of their ancestral village located in the "upper world." This layout is based on an idealistic plan which is recognized and followed as closely as possible by all Bororo as a fundamental expression of their social and religious values and relations.

Topography is essential in the selection of the village's location. The Bororo believe the ancestors' village is located close to a main river where the waters run from east to west. And they assume that the eastern area of the village is located on a higher slope than the western area. Most of the Bororo's villages were and are built near the São Lourenço River and its tributaries, which flow from east to west for

FIGURE 3.6

Interior of men's house on a ceremonial day. Córrego Grande, Mato Grosso, Brazil, 1986.

FIGURE 3.7

View of the bororo *on a ceremonial day with burial in center.*

most of their length (see Figs. 3.3, 3.4).

The ideal layout consists of a circular arrangement of huts, built side by side, facing a larger central house (Fig. 3.5). The circle of houses is the domain of females and their offspring, whereas the central house, known as the men's house or *baito*, is the residence of the males. The *baito* functions as temple, school, workshop, social club, and living quarters for initiated boys, adult men, and visitors. This house, forbidden to the women for most occasions, is also where most Bororo secret rituals are performed (Fig. 3.6). The public rituals are held in a semicircular plaza, called the *bororo*, adjacent to the exterior western wall of the *baito* (Fig. 3.7). The area between the *baito* and the *bororo* is occupied by the council of elders (Fig. 3.8). The central plaza is connected to another circular plaza, *aije muga,* outside the circle of houses by a long pathway called *aije rea* (Figs. 3.9, 3.10). *Aije muga,* also forbidden to women, is located on the western end of the east-west pathway of the sun. The final preparations for a ritual take place in this area.

The female circle of houses is divided by the east-west path of the sun into two equal halves, moieties (see Fig. 3.5). The houses located in the northern half are called Exerae, whereas the houses in the southern half are called Tugarege. The men's house, also divided by the same axis, shows an internal division opposite to the females' exterior arrangement of moieties. The Tugarege men occupy the northern half of the house, whereas the Exerae men are limited to the southern half.

Each moiety is composed of four clans, which are themselves divided into two or three units with members of distinct households in each one (Fig. 3.11). The households located on the western area of each clan are called the *xebegiwuge* or *xoreu,* respectively "lower slope" and "black." The units located in the eastern area are called the *xobogiwuge* (*cerae*) or *kujagureu,* meaning "upper slope" and "red." A few clans have a third division, the *boe-e-iadadawuge*.[3] The "upper" and "lower" slope terms are related to the topography of the terrain whereas "red" and "black" have physical and mythological explanations.

The east and west sections of the village have additional physical and spiritual associations. The west of the village is associated with the moon, black, death, night, and male. It is also the habitat of the Bororo's most important hero, Bakoróro, who is represented by the color black, wide red and black body-painting stripes, and powerful elements such as feathers of the harpy eagle and the turquoise-fronted parrot and jaguar skin. On the other hand, the east is associated with the sun, brilliant red, fertility, daytime, and female. Itubóre, the other mythological hero, is associated with this section of the village. The feather colors associated with Itubóre are red and yellow and his body is painted with thin red and black stripes. These religious and cosmological associations are well symbolized in the Bororo's featherwork designs.

Besides the distinct dual physical arrangement of houses just described, strict rules and regulations link the Bororo moieties together through social and religious reciprocity. For example, marriage is between members of opposite moieties. Post-marital residence is preferentially with the wife's family or kin group. Social harmony is promoted by the distribution of material and spiritual belongings among the clans. The Bororo believe that all physical things have another being, called *aroe*, etymologically derived from *aro*, which means feather or anything light as a feather (spirit or ghost); this is also the word used for small wing feathers (Albisetti and Venturelli 1962:99). The Bororo explained the meaning of *aroe* as *alma*, a Portuguese word for the Christian concept of spirit. To the Bororo, *aroe* is the immortal spirit existing in all objects and living beings. The Bororo's culture heroes and ancestors, living in the village of the dead, are *aroe*.

FIGURE 3.8

Council of elders after a ritual. Córrego Grande, Mato Grosso, Brazil, 1986.

FIGURE 3.9

Aije muga *on a ceremonial day. Córrego Grande, Mato Grosso, Brazil, 1986.*

FIGURE 3.10

Aije rea *on a ceremonial day. Córrego Grande, Mato Grosso, Brazil, 1986.*

FIGURE 3.11

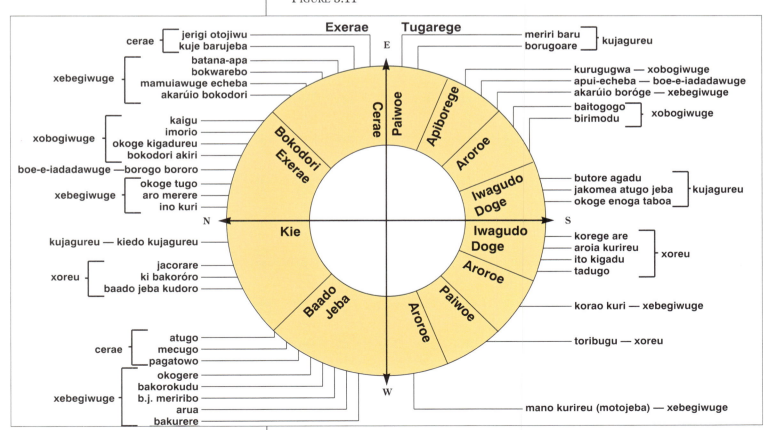

Diagram of Bororo ideal plan with clans, subclans, and lineages. Córrego Grande, Mato Grosso, Brazil, 1986.

Each one of the eight clans of the village has prior claim to a set of *aroe*, which were first claimed by an ancestor of the clan who first came in contact with a being or thing or who first created an object. For example, a member of the clan Kie saw the great tapir and claimed it for the clan's members. Subsequently, personal names and ornaments were derived and created from the tapir's behavior, as well as from its physical and spiritual characteristics. Another clan, the Bokodori Exerae, received its clan name, personal names, and ornaments after a clan ancestor claimed the right to use the great armadillo's physical and spiritual characteristics (Fig. 3.12). The word Bokodori consists of *bo* for carapace, *kodo* for basket, and *ri* for grandeur, resulting in "animal with carapace like a great basket." No clan has ownership over the animals and objects, but each has an exclusive right to use their materials and represent them. The animal of one clan can be killed and eaten by any Bororo without harming the clan's priority over the animal's *aroe*, but the hunter is not allowed to use the animal's name and body parts for an ornament.

The legendary heroes, Bakoróro and Itubóre, created ritual objects for all the clans and lineages of the village, depending upon each clan's ancestral heritage and social ranking. Bororo material and spiritual possessions consist of a set of rituals, objects, dances, chants, body-painting designs, personal names, etc. The members of each clan or lineage are easily recognized by the names they bear and the ornaments they wear. Color combinations, materials, and shapes are a tangible, symbolic language for clan and lineage affiliations, social status, spiritual and material seniority, *aroe*. Furthermore, every clan has a set of ritual and social obligations fundamental to the village's harmony and guidelines for religious and social interactions between the moieties. In addition, the Bororo's ideal village layout provides a complex and well-defined system of control for social and religious interactions among the lineages and, consequently, between the two moieties. The eradication of a Bororo village layout would result in total cultural breakdown; this tactic was intentionally used in the past for missionary and political controls.

THE MEANING AND IMPORTANCE OF COLOR

The most important source of color in the Bororo aesthetic representation is feathers. The most widely used colors in Bororo artistic pieces, whether feathers or pigment, are red, black, white, yellow, and blue. Conceptually, the two most important colors are black and red; their significance is revealed through analysis of myths and symbols.

The most readily available pigments used for coloring and body designs are black and red. Black pigment is derived from the fruit of the genipap tree (*Genipa americana*) and from a charcoal powder; red pigment is extracted from the plentiful annatto or *urucu* tree (*Bixa orellana*).[4] The Bororo term for black is *xoreu*, and for bigger and larger, *kurireu*. These two terms are often used together. Black is associated with the western section of the village, Bakoróro, and wide-striped patterns characteristic of Bakoróro's body painting. Likewise, the term for red is *kujagureu*, and for small and thinner, *kugurireu*; these are associated with the eastern side of the village, Itubóre, and small and delicate striped patterns, which are the characteristics of Itubóre's body decoration. Black is also associated with death and the spiritual realm, whereas red is associated with fertility, life, and the physical world. In a

FIGURE 3.12

Necklace ornament representing a bird, made from the front claws of the great armadillo. Zarur/Giles collection, Córrego Grande, Mato Grosso, Brazil, 1986.

FIGURE 3.13

Body-painting representation of aroe. *Córrego Grande, Mato Grosso, Brazil, 1986.*

FIGURE 3.14

Representation of Aije *(*Parabara *ritual). Córrego Grande, Mato Grosso, Brazil, 1986.*

sense, the symbolism of both colors is analogous to the fire that burns and dies out leaving only black coals. The west (black)—habitat of the ancestors—is also where the sun sets, giving way to darkness, whereas the east (red) is the birthplace of the sun and light.

Because black feathers are associated with high ranking, beauty, and the power of Bakoróro, the black and white striped feathers of the harpy eagle, *aroe eceba*, are symbols of power, beauty, and death. Only the highest lineages are allowed to use such a powerful element in their ornaments because the harpy eagle is believed to be one of the animals responsible for a Bororo's death. The charcoal powder used for body painting is believed to repel bad spirits and snakebites and to transform the wearers into representatives of spirits. During funerary rituals, the adult male Bororo represent some of their *aroe* by covering their bodies with the brilliant red annatto paste, and their extremities—the head, hands, and feet—with the opaque black charcoal powder (Fig. 3.13). The brilliance of the red stands out, whereas the black-pigmented extremities distract the viewers from the most human aspects of the performer. The women may use the brilliant red annatto and black genipap dye for body and facial paintings, but they are not allowed to use the dull charcoal powder on their bodies because of its spiritual power.

The red feathers of the macaw are symbols of goodness, power, and fertility. Every member of the village may use these feathers because the Bororo believe they are in essence red-and-green macaws themselves. Red feathers and annatto paste are used in rituals as a sign of vitality and transcendent beauty, whereas black is associated with the spiritual life and things related to life after death.

White is widely used in Bororo ornaments, but it is of less importance than red and black. The meaning of this color depends upon its source material. The white pigment from a regional sedimentary clay, known as *noa*, is associated with death. The Bororo believe that this type of soil is the habitat of the ferocious *Aije*, a spiritual monster associated with death, who frightens women and uninitiated boys (Fig. 3.14). White down from birds is associated with birth and life. The dull, white clay contrasts with the shiny and fluffy white down. The white clay represents a dangerous underwater monster and death, whereas the white down such as that of the newborn macaw represents rebirth and life.

The blue-and-yellow macaw is the main source of feathers for yellow and blue colors (Fig. 3.15). Yellow feathers also come from the crested oropendola. Yellow is associated with the brightness of the *paratudo's* flower. This regional tree (*Tecoma caraiba*) is often found around rocky mountains that hold great symbolic importance for the Bororo. Rocky mountains were the Bororo's burial grounds before the arrival of Europeans, who looted their sacred burial grounds in search of gold ornaments. According to Bororo mythology, the mythical chief Baipóro decided to beautify the fins and scales of the *okóge*, a large regional dorado fish. To this end, he picked yellow flowers and threw them onto the surface of the river. Suddenly, the scales of the *okóge* became yellow like the flowers. Therefore, this yellow flower is symbolically and mythologically associated with the magical power of beautification.

Besides color itself, the chromatic intensity plays an important part in the selection of artistic materials. I have already discussed the difference between the brightness of the shiny genipap salve and the dullness of the black charcoal powder. The red paste of the annatto is available in two intensities, light and deep red, depending on the variety of seeds from which it is extracted. The deep red denotes more spiritual power than the light orange shade. The red macaw feathers are associated with power, whereas the red feathers of the vermilion flycatcher are considered harmful because the vermilion represents Meri, the bad spirit. The iridescent yellow of the crested oropendola's rectrices is superior to the light and less deep tone of the yellow feathers and the down of the blue-and-yellow macaw. The deep, dark blue of the indigo macaw is used in the ornaments of only one clan, whereas the celestial and brilliant blue of the blue-and-yellow macaw may be used in the ornaments of every clan.

Differences in color, material, and composition represent social ranking within the hierarchy of lineages. Individuals with more material possessions and responsibility over the other members of the clan are often designated "elder brothers"; the other members are identified as "younger brothers." The ornaments of all the "elder brothers" display similar chromatic combinations, purity of elements, and special selection of feathers and other materials. The major feather-mosaic combinations used in the ritual pieces of the higher-ranked lineages are black and red, and the materials include feathers from birds, such as the harpy eagle, ornate hawk-eagle, turquoise-fronted parrot, and crested oropendola, as well as jaguar skin. The more red used with black, the lower the social rank. The use of yellow with black or red indicates an even lower rank. Because "elder brothers" are the owners of the most powerful spiritual properties, they are associated with the color black. In addition, the most brilliant and iridescent feathers have higher rank. For example, the light yellow feathers of the blue-and-yellow macaw indicate lower-status lineages, whereas the bright yellow from the crested oropendola's rectrices indicates high-ranked lineages. The lineages located in the west section of the village, regardless of their social status, display mosaics with larger patterns, whereas the lineages located in the east section use thinner and more delicate patterns in their techniques. Those are the characteristics of the two cultural heroes' body-painting designs.

SYMBOLIC VALUE AND FUNCTION OF FEATHERS

The Bororo are very proud of their appearance and therefore take great care with the construction and maintenance of their ornaments. Ritual pieces are harmonically proportioned to the parts of the human body where they are worn. Technically, the pieces are characterized by extreme attention to detail, especially in the finishing process (Fig. 3.16). The major design considerations are symmetrical shape and chromatic balance. This same sense of symmetry and balance is reflected in the physical structure of the village. Thus, both the physical structure of the village and the physical appearance of the feather pieces reflect the Bororo's aesthetic concepts, whereas the symbolism reflects their religious concepts.

A great variety of objects such as crowns, diadems, headbands, facial paintings, lip plugs, earrings, bracelets, necklaces, pectoral pieces, musical instruments, children's toys, armbands, and legbands are associated with individual clans (Calil Zarur 1989:246–309). Although there are many designs common to all members of the village, the varieties of patterns created by each clan and lineage reveal their social identity. Each clan's ritual objects are created mainly with feathers from different birds in colorful mosaics, supplemented by details of plaited compositions, different types of fibers, human hair, shells, animal skin, metal, porcupine needles, waxed or painted fibers, and cotton. The chromatic and material combinations and shapes symbolize

FIGURE 3.15

Blue-and-yellow Macaw. Córrego Grande, Mato Grosso, Brazil, 1986.

FIGURE 3.16

Boe (Bororo) José Américo finishing a headdress, pariko. *Córrego Grande, Mato Grosso, Brazil, 1986.*

FIGURE 3.19

Traditional hairstyle. Córrego Grande, Mato Grosso, Brazil, 1986.

FIGURE 3.20

Burial site in the center of the bororo *on a ceremonial day. Córrego Grande, Mato Grosso, Brazil, 1986.*

FIGURE 3.17

Hairpins of the Paiwoe clan. The color combination indicates the clan's priority over the Red-and-yellow Macaw and the design represents their priority over the dorado fish. Zarur/Giles collection, Córrego Grande, Mato Grosso, Brazil, 1986.

FIGURE 3.18

Ceremonial feathered cap
(boe et-ao kejewu).
Córrego Grande, Mato
Grosso, Brazil, 1986.

the *aroe* of each clan and the social ranking of each individual. For example, the Tugarege clan of Paiwoe has prior claim over the blue-and-yellow macaw, which is shown by the extensive and unique use of these two colors combined into feather mosaics by the clan members (Fig. 3.17).

Because the Bororo are a matrilineal society, the symbolism of an individual's ritual pieces reflects the mother's lineage for most of the individual's life. A child can use the father's matrilineal design until initiation, then adopts the mother's pattern, but the father's facial painting persists. However, a feathered cap, whose patterns can be from the mother's or the father's lineage, or even a combination of both, remains the same from birth to death (Fig. 3.18). This feathered cap is like a wig, imitating the Bororo's hairstyle. Both males and females have long hair in the back, straight bangs on the forehead, and hair over their ears, cut just below the earlobes (Fig. 3.19). The feathered cap is composed of a half-moon piece covering most of the head, two lateral bands on the temple, and a bandlike fringe glued to the forehead.

The major background material used for the feathered cap is red macaw down, with thin stripes and bands identifying the lineage of the wearer. For example, an Apiborege feathered cap is decorated with thin black and white stripes, indicating the clan's right over the harpy eagle. This cap is worn during special occasions, such as by the recipient in a name-giving ceremony (the moment of recognition of the individual as Boe), or by a person who has just recuperated from an almost fatal accident or illness, and by the deceased during the temporary burial. Later, the feathered cap is glued on the clean skull for the permanent burial ceremony. In all these events, the piece reflects birth and rebirth into a new life.

Members of each clan are extremely watchful over their material and spiritual privileges and rights and are extremely protective of their properties. Each clan's priority rights are negotiable and transferable from one member to another in exchange for social and religious services. Reciprocal exchange between clans and moieties is present in all aspects of Bororo lives, but mainly during the rites of passage. The funeral, the most elaborate of these rites, consists of a laborious set of public and secret rituals, as well as hunting and fishing expeditions. Burial takes place in two stages: the temporary and the permanent. The temporary burial, which happens immediately after death, consists of wrapping the deceased's body in a woven fiber mat and entombing it in a shallow, uncovered grave in the middle of the plaza (see Fig. 3.7). During this period of approximately 35 to 40 days, or until the flesh of the deceased is almost completely decayed, the most elaborate public rituals are performed in the main plaza (Fig. 3.20). The rituals dramatizing the realms of *aroe* are portrayed to help the deceased on his or her journey to the other world. The clans with rights over a specific *aroe* ritual give permission to a member of the opposite moiety to perform their ritual. For example, a Tugarege funeral ritual is always performed by members of the Exerae moiety and vice versa. Similarly, the feathered pieces belonging to members of one clan can be worn only by members of the opposite moiety.[5] The permanent burial takes place after the body is exhumed from the temporary site and the bones are cleaned and decorated with annatto paste and feather mosaics.

Reciprocity between the two moieties also occurs during a ceremony called Mori, a term that means revenge, retribution, payment, or compensation for the death of a Bororo. The Bororo believe that death is caused by a bad spirit, *bope*, best represented by the jaguar. The revenge for a person's death is completed by the killing of a jaguar or harpy eagle, or less often a fox, by a male from the moiety opposite that of the deceased. The hunter becomes the representation of the dead person, *aroe maiwu*, meaning new soul, or *iadu*, partner.

FIGURE 3.21

Jaguar skin used in the Mori *ceremony. Córrego Grande, Mato Grosso, Brazil, 1986.*

The skin of the jaguar killed by a hunter of the opposite moiety, *iadu*, is given to the grandson of the deceased on the mother's side (Fig. 3.21). The receiver of the jaguar skin repays the hunter by transferring to him rights to use and manufacture some ritual pieces belonging to the receiver's clan. The public ceremony transmitting the material rights takes place during the night. At this time, the hunter is instructed about the materials, design, symbolism, and technology used in the fabrication of each piece. This instruction is done in such a way that the whole village becomes aware of the transfer of material property and knowledge from one clan to the *iadu*. The wearing of the ritual pieces by the *iadu* brings great honor to the deceased's relatives. Symbolically, this transference of property rights from one clan to a member of the opposite moiety fulfills the obligation of reciprocity and strengthens harmony among the village members.

THE SPIRITUAL POWER OF BIRDS AND FEATHERS

Besides their functional and social aspects, feathers and birds are fundamental components of Bororo cosmology. Birds are believed to be messengers between the terrestrial world and the unknown upper world, the habitat of the Bororo's ancestors and heroes. Thus, the importance of feathers depends not only on their chromatic diversity but also on the fact that birds, and only birds, have feathers and the capability of flight.

The most important flight feathers are the wing and the tail feathers. The Bororo consider these feathers priceless and use them at the ends of objects, whereas down feathers are usually glued into mosaics in the central section of pieces. The placement of the wing and tail feathers on the objects must follow the same order as on the bird's body (Fig. 3.22). The two central feathers of the bird's tail must be placed in the center of the object. If more than one feather is required, the right side of the object must be decorated with feathers from the right side of the bird's tail or wing, with feathers from the left side on the left side of the object.

The Bororo have macaws, parrots, and ducks as pets. The two most important birds in Bororo mythology are the harpy eagle, *aroe eceba*, and the red-and-green macaw, *nabure*. The harpy eagle is a powerful animal believed to be responsible for the killing of many Bororo. As with the jaguar, the killing of the harpy eagle is used for the revenge ceremony. The killing of this bird of prey is reason for happiness and rejoicing because it brings freedom to a Bororo's soul. The dead bird is offered to the family of the deceased; the members of the Apiborege, the clan with prior claim over the animal, are responsible for the plucking of the feathers and the burying of the featherless body covered with annatto salve behind the clan's hut. The distribution of the *aroe eceba's* feathers follows very strict rules according to the social and political ranking of the lineages in the society and the hierarchical classification of the bird's feathers. The killing of this mighty bird and the use of its feathers denote attributes of power used mainly by the "older brothers" of each clan.

Macaws, especially, have major symbolic significance. The Bororo recognize four species of macaws; they are classified according to the different colors found on the reverse side of the feathers and by their habitats. The "yellow" macaw is called *kuido* (blue-and-yellow macaw, *Ara ararauna*), the "black" macaw is *kudoro* (hyacinthine macaw, *Anodorhynchus hyacinthinus*), the "scarlet" macaw is *cibae* (scarlet macaw, *Ara macao*), and the "red" macaw is *nabure* (red-and-green macaw, *Ara chloroptera*). Each macaw is an important *aroe* of a different clan, and the right of the clan's members over it is symbolically represented by the profuse use of each bird's feathers in their ornaments.

The Bororo understand and appreciate the ecological interdependence of the physical environment and its biological diversity. The significance of certain animals, such as the macaws, is based on their natural habitat, social organization, sexual and hunting behaviors, nesting sites, types of calls for different occasions, and food habits. The habitat of these birds is essential to the Bororo for two main reasons: it supplies the Bororo with materials and fruits essential for their survival; and the nesting sites of some of these species are believed to be the spiritual residences of Bororo ancestors.

The macaws are often obtained by removing a newborn bird from its nest. The bird receives a Bororo name and it belongs to the women. The Bororo themselves are said to "be" red macaws (*nabure*). The Bororo believe that the *aroe* of their relatives temporarily return to the terrestrial world embodied in a macaw to visit and eat nuts and other foods appreciated by the Bororo. Macaws, especially the red macaws, are never killed because they are the favored dwelling places for Bororo ancestors. The death of a pet macaw causes great sadness and its featherless body, pasted with annatto, is wrapped in a woven fiber mat and buried behind the owner's house. The most important macaws in Bororo beliefs are the red and the scarlet. These two birds have similar habitats, nesting sites, and food habits, and their feathers are predominantly red. Their main habitat is the gallery forests, but they also nest in caves on rocky mountains and cliffs, the same caves and rocky mountains that were the dwellings of Bororo ancestors and their main burial places until their desecration by Euro-Brazilians. The macaw's diet is also important to the Bororo because they believe the bird's food is good for people.

The importance of the red macaw is threefold: first, the body of the macaw is a possible habitat for an ancestor's soul; second, it holds a preeminent place in the Bororo myth-history; and last, but equally important, its red feathers are the prime material used for Bororo ceremonial objects and curing ceremonies. These birds are also seen as messengers of good hunting and forecasters of weather changes.

The symbolism of *nabure* follows the individual throughout his life and after death as well. The two most important Bororo rites of passage are metaphors of a spiritual bond that exists between the Bororo and *nabure*. In the naming ceremony, the infant, decorated like a newborn macaw, first receives public recognition as a member of Bororo society. The chanting during the naming ceremony invokes the similarities between *nabure's* baby bird and the Bororo infant. In this chanting, the newborn child is introduced to the great culture hero Bakoróro, and protection is sought over some parts of the child's body, such as the nose, penis, ears, and mouth. These are the body parts that serve as openings between the interior part of the body and the exterior world. At the end of each verse in the chant, reference is made to a rocky mountain where the baby came from, *aworo jatori to*. The metaphorical link between the bird and the Bororo is reinforced by recalling the

FIGURE 3.22

Headdress showing arrangement of feathers. Córrego Grande, Mato Grosso, Brazil, 1986.

common birthplace of the child and bird, a nest in a rocky mountain. At the same time, the analogy between the evoked parts of the child's body and the rocky mountain caves symbolizes the link between interior and exterior worlds and realms.

The relationship between the Bororo and the nesting sites of birds is again proclaimed in the burial ritual. Just after death, the body of the deceased is taken from the house of his or her lineage (the mother's house) to the *baito* to be decorated in the same way as in the newborn's naming ceremony. The procession between the mother's house and the men's house is accompanied by chanting that recalls the relationship between the rocky mountain and the men's house. This chant is called Cibae E-iari, which stands for the name of one of the rocky mountains that was the traditional Bororo's burial ground. Cibae is also the Bororo name for the scarlet macaw. At this moment, the men's house becomes a metaphor for the rocky mountain burial site and the nesting site of macaws.

For the permanent burial ritual, the cleaned bones of the deceased are taken to the men's house to be pasted with annatto and decorated with feathers in the patterns of the deceased's lineage. Once again, the analogy between the men's house and the macaw's nesting site is emphasized by the chantings. The rocky mountain symbolizes the "Village of the Dead" from where all things are governed, whereas the men's house governs the terrestrial world and serves as the link between the physical and the spiritual realms, the terrestrial and the ancestral worlds. The relationship between the macaw, the Bororo, and the harpy eagle is illustrated in the following:

Macaw	Bororo	Harpy Eagle
Rocky mountain	Men's house	Outside village
Positive spiritual realm	Physical realm	Negative spiritual realm
Ancestral world	Terrestrial world	Underworld
Red	Red and black	Black

Another link between the spiritual and the terrestrial worlds is through the representation of spiritual power by small gourds decorated with macaw feathers. The hanging of these gourds on the central post of the men's house during the Mori ceremony means that the ancestors are the governing force. The men's house, at this moment, is referred to as Cibae E-iari, symbolizing the presence of Bororo ancestors and heroes in the rituals. Furthermore, the two major birds in Bororo mythology, the red macaw and the harpy eagle, epitomize the metaphors of life and death, and their primary colors—red and black—are the two most important colors in Bororo cosmology.

CONCLUSIONS

The ritual feathered pieces symbolize Bororo social and spiritual beliefs, unify their way of viewing their terrestrial and spiritual world, and create a physical and spiritual balance. Birds and feathers are aesthetic elements of power and magic. Through the use of feathers, it is possible not only to document and identify each individual Bororo and his or her kin affiliation, but also to understand the secular and sacred messages that maintain harmony between the Bororo and their environment, both terrestrial and spiritual. It is through artistic expressions that harmony between physical and spiritual concepts is acquired in a system of reciprocity.

In essence, the Bororo culture is an example of a society where aesthetics plays a profound role in the integration and communication of social, political, and religious organization and beliefs. These artistic and cultural relationships are not unique to the Bororo people; many cultures remain to be studied in this manner. When we explore cultural ideas, such as the Bororo's "thinking with feathers," we learn to view the artistic expressions of traditional preindustrial societies with greater admiration and respect. Understanding these artistic expressions in relation to their cultural values enables us to appreciate and recognize the power of symbols, art, and, above all, respect for the people and culture.

Acknowledgment

I am very thankful to my husband, Bill Giles, for his support and for all of the photographic material. Financial support for the field work and the doctoral studies abroad was sponsored by the Conselho Nacional de Pesquisa e Tecnologia *(CNPQ) Brazilian Nacional Council of Research and Technology. I would like to thank the University of Pennsylvania Museum staff and mainly Dr. Ruben Reina for the invitation to be part of such an important project. I would also like to thank Dr. Stephen A. Kowalewski for his support, Gisela Weis for the cartographic work, and Dr. June Cooley for assisting in the editing and revisions.*

THE MEANING OF CASHINAHUA
FEATHERS MAKE

by Kenneth M. Kensinger

VI. *Cashinahua headdress (65–10–10).*

"ANTHROPOLOGY HOLDS UP A GREAT MIRROR TO MAN AND LETS HI

JS BEAUTIFUL

Cashinahua headdress (65–10–10). This is a trumpeter bird body-feather headdress, called nea dani mati. Headdresses of this type are worn primarily at fertility rites but also for other ceremonies. Birds: Pale-winged Trumpeter, and Blue-and-yellow Macaw. Made by Awadetsati and collected on the Rio Curanja, Peru, 1965.

PUBLIC RITUALS ARE FESTIVE OCCASIONS for the Peruvian Cashinahua and, as befits such occasions, they adorn themselves with festive attire, the most colorful and striking of which are feather headdresses.[1] Feathers are used either as a primary ingredient or as added adornments on most headdresses. This paper examines the reasons the Cashinahua give for using feathers,[2] namely availability, beauty, and utility.

The Cashinahua, in 1965, lived in seven villages along the Curanja and Purus rivers of southeastern Peru (Fig. 4.2). Each village consisted of two or more extended families, linked by consanguinity and/or affinity. Each person's social identity is provided by a name or set of names[3] and membership in a moiety and marriage section.[4] Within some but not all rituals, moiety and/or marriage section membership determines the groups that interact, as for example in the fertility ritual and the initiation rites. The interaction between the opposite moieties and the paired marriage sections is generally characterized by bawdy joking, tinged with hostility. Both within and outside the ritual context, a man is expected to try to gross out his brother-in-law to the amusement of all. And during the fertility rites he may try to do the same to his mother-in-law with impunity; outside the ritual context, he must treat his mother-in-law with great deference and respect, rarely if ever addressing her directly. The moieties and marriage sections are virtually invisible in the everyday life of the community, when one is reminded of their existence largely by the designs, indicating their social identity, which people paint on their bodies (Fig. 4.3).

Outside the ritual context, it is the extended families and their component nuclear or polygynous families that are most obvious because they are the basic units of the economic system. They are the groups responsible for food production and distribution. Gardening and hunting, supplemented by fishing and gathering, are the basic subsistence activities. Men are responsible for hunting, for cutting and burning the forest to clear a garden, and for

FIGURE 4.2

Map showing the location of Cashinahua villages. Courtesy of the author.

FIGURE 4.3

Body painting demonstrating moiety patterns. Photograph by the author.

planting most of the crops. Women plant some of the crops but harvest most of them, gather and carry firewood, carry water, cook the food, and care for children. Both men and women fish and gather wild plants and fruits. Against this background, we can now examine how and why the Cashinahua obtain and use feathers.

WHY DO THE CASHINAHUA USE FEATHERS?

Although the Cashinahua use feathers for such practical purposes as fletching two types of arrows and making fire fans, the most frequent use of them is for making objects to adorn the body, such as headdresses, ear and nose ornaments, and for decorating artifacts used in rituals. This paper will focus on such ornamental use of feathers.

For the most part, the Cashinahua found my questions about why they used feathers silly. After all, any fool can see that feathers are beautiful and enhance the beauty of their wearer. But the Cashinahua indulged me and with great patience answered my silly questions. Their answers roughly fall into three categories: feathers are available, they are beautiful, and they are useful.

Feathers Are Available

Men frequently told me that the reason they used feathers is because they hunt birds. Only men gave me this answer for only men hunt, and for them hunting is the primary element in their identity. A man is first and foremost a hunter. Women are not permitted to enter the forest beyond the gardens except in the company of a male kinsman, and even then never while they are menstruating. Men say that the smell of female genitalia not only drives the animals deep into the forest, but also attracts spirits who might attack the women, injuring or killing them. Men thus arrogate to themselves the task of providing what is considered by all Cashinahua to be the most valued part of the diet, meat. However, no meal is complete without garden produce and up to 65% of the diet comes from the gardens.

Men hunt and kill a wide range of bird species, both large and small, as part of the food quest. Some species, such as curassows, guans, and doves, are highly valued as food, but the Cashinahua will kill most birds, no matter how small, for meat. They also kill carrion eaters (the vultures) and raptors (the harpy eagle and the hawks) for their feathers, but never eat them since their flesh is considered to be dirty and smelly. After shooting and killing a bird, a hunter plucks the feathers or, in the case of small birds like the tanagers, skins them. He then carefully stores the feathers and dried bird skins for later use.

By using some of the feathers of the birds they eat and most of the feathers of the raptors and carrion eaters, the Cashinahua minimize waste, an important consideration since they believe they share the resources of the forest with the spirits. Birds, animals, and all living things have a visible (physical) and an invisible (spiritual) component. Humans have the right to use the visible component of natural resources while spirits use the invisible. If people needlessly waste these resources, they place in jeopardy harmonious relationships with the spirits, whose activities can bring them health or illness, fertility or barrenness, joy or sadness, life or death. My informants explained that they know that the spirits use the same forest resources that they use because they have seen the spirits when they go into unconsciousness, when they dream, and when they drink the hallucinogenic beverage *nishi pae*, a brew made from the vine *Baniteriopsis caapi* and leaves of several species of the shrub *Psychotria*. The spirits, like humans, wear feather headdresses and other feather ornaments. If humans waste forest resources, the spirits might retaliate in a variety of ways, most particularly by leading the birds and animals deep into the forest, making hunting more difficult than it already is and greatly restricting the supply of meat. Men fear this fate not simply because it means hunger for meat but because it would threaten their sense of their adequacy as hunters and thus as men.

Feathers Are Beautiful

All informants said that they used feathers because they are beautiful. Birds are the most colorful and visually arresting part of the Cashinahua environment. Flowers, which may also be brightly colored, are for the most part hidden high in the forest canopy, visible only when their petals fall to the ground or if a tree is felled, which is rarely done when trees are in bloom. The Cashinahua cut down certain trees for their fruit, but only when the blooming season is long past. Thus, birds' feathers are the only constant naturally occurring source of color other than the greens and browns of the forest. Also, feathers are almost imperishable if cared for properly and thus a potentially permanent source of visual stimulation.

The Cashinahua say of feathers that they have good *dua*. *Dua* is a difficult word to translate. A freshly bathed and oiled baby that is chubby, cheerful, and asleep or nursing is said to have good *dua*. A nubile girl with firm breasts, in good health and with no skin blemishes, also has good *dua*, as does a vigorous adolescent male with firm muscles and lively step. A perfectly and fully developed ear of corn also has good *dua*. The rays of the sun filtering through the clouds are its *dua*. A live macaw flying overhead has good *dua* but when it has been shot it has bad *dua*; it has lost its life. But, when the macaw has been plucked, its feathers have good *dua*. A well-made feather headdress also has good *dua*. Those qualities that result in someone's or something's being said to have good *dua* are beauty, radiance, luster, sheen, and vitality.

What specifically are the characteristics of feathers that have good *dua*? To answer this question it is necessary to examine the Cashinahua classification of feathers because the criteria for determining if a feather has good *dua* depend on the kind of feather it is.

The Cashinahua recognize three major classes of feathers: *pei*, the wing flight feathers; *hina*, tail feathers; *dani*, body feathers (including the coverts of the wings and legs; the word also refers to human body hair). *Dani* may be further subdivided according to the part of the body from which they come, but for our purposes here the more general category will suffice. *Pei* have good *dua* if their edges are not frayed, their tips are not broken or worn, and their coloration is normal and vibrant. *Hina* with good *dua* are straight with minimal fraying along their entire length, no breakage of the tip, and unfaded color. Both *pei* and *hina* are supposed to be *kuxi*, strong, i.e., they are supposed to look durable. *Pei* are expected to be relatively rigid throughout their length as are the *hina* of most birds; the *hina* of the macaws should be somewhat flexible for the distal quarter of their length. *Dani*, in contrast, should give a sense of lightness, filminess, and airiness. Because they are small relative to either *pei* or *hina*, there is less concern about the perfection of their edges, so long as they have not lost their luster. In general, feathers from birds that are nesting or have recently hatched a

FIGURE 4.4

Cashinahua wing-feather headdress (65–10–14). This headdress (called a pei mati*) is often worn at fertility rites and can also be used in the initiation rites for the headman of a village. Birds: Blue-and-yellow Macaw, Scarlet Macaw, and Toucan. Collected on the Rio Curanja, Peru, 1965.*

FIGURES 4.5A–D

Components of Chidín *dance leader's costume. The headman initiates the* chidín *ritual to ease tensions between the men in the village. Any adult man who knows the ritual chants may put on this costume and lead the ritual. Made by Awadetsati (headman) and collected on the Rio Curanja, Peru, 1965.*

FIGURE 4.5A

Cashinahua Scarlet Macaw tail-feather headdress (65–10–1b). Scarlet Macaw feathers are the primary element in this type of headdress, called xawan hina maiti. *The feathers are attached to a ring of vine. This is the most elaborate and spectacular of all Cashinahua headdresses. Birds: Scarlet Macaw, Blue-and-yellow Macaw, Harpy Eagle, Razor-billed Curassow, and King Vulture.*

FIGURE 4.5B

Weighted tail feather (65–10–1b). Extra feathers may be glued to the tip of the tail feather with a mixture of beeswax and chicle. The additional weight causes the feather on the headdress to bob up and down when the wearer dances.

brood or from birds that are about to molt or are molting have bad *dua*, while the fully grown feathers from birds that have recently molted always have good *dua*.

Feathers Are Useful

Although the Cashinahua use feathers for ornamenting diverse objects, they use them primarily for making or ornamenting five major classes of headdresses: *pei maiti*, wing-feather headdress; *dani maiti*, body-feather headdress; *xawan hina maiti*, scarlet macaw tail-feather headdress; *paka maiti*, bamboo headdress; and *yushin maiti*, spirit headdress. In the first three classes, the type of feather used is the defining characteristic. In the last two classes, feathers are used only as decoration.

Wing-feather headdresses are characterized by a three-quarter fan of wing feathers, *pei*, constructed on an open ring of vine, either rigidly tied (*kedex*) between two strips of vine or tied onto a length of cotton string. If they are tied rigidly between strips of vine, the strips with the attached feathers are formed into a ring and are attached above a decorative vine ring to which are attached one or more tiers of *dani*, preferably black and usually the covert feathers from the wings or the feathers from the legs of the birds (Fig. 4.4). The decorative ring is attached to the primary ring so that it covers the base of the wing feathers. If the *pei* are tied on a string, the string with the feathers is attached at several points to the decorative ring. An optional strip of vine larger than that of the primary ring is usually attached at the back of the headdress where the component strip or strips are fastened together to form the ring. It holds the *pei* erect, but not rigid. One or more tail feathers, *hina*, of macaws or occasionally of a harpy eagle or a hawk may be rigidly attached at the same place, producing an erect tail, *hina biden*. Alternatively, one or more composite tails, made by tying *dani* on a string, and/or bird skins may be attached to the back of the ring and allowed to dangle down the back of the wearer's neck, *hina pania*.[5]

In addition to their use in headdresses, *pei* of macaws, curassows, harpy eagles, vultures, and certain hawks are also used to fletch arrows. Harpy eagle wing feathers also are used in the construction of the large backrack that is worn as part of the lead dancer's costume in *chidín*, the headman's dance (Fig. 4.5c).

Hina, tail feathers, are used primarily as ornamentation, except in the *xawan hina maiti*, the red macaw tail-feather headdress, where scarlet macaw feathers are the primary element (Fig. 4.5A). Depending on how many are available, between 20 and 100 *xawan hina* are attached more or less perpendicularly around a ring of thick vine that is covered with a strip of woven cotton fabric or is tightly wrapped with heavy cotton string. They may be either unadorned or adorned at their base by two or more tail feathers from small birds or with one inch of the tip of a curassow tail feather. Two oriole tail feathers or a single one-inch tip of a curassow tail feather may be glued to the tip of the macaw tail feather with a mixture of beeswax and chicle (Fig. 4.5B). The weight of this addition causes the feather to bob up and down as the wearer dances. In addition five to 20 white plumes, made of a cornhusk around which harpy eagle or king vulture leg or body feathers are tied, may be attached to the headdress base. *Xawan hina maiti* may also be ornamented by strings of clam or snail shells, baby tapir hooves, and turtle toenails. This is by far the most spectacular headdress made by the Cashinahua and only one is made at a time for use as part of the costume of the lead dancer for *chidín*, the headman's dance.

The headman initiates the *chidín* ritual when tensions between men threaten the tranquility of community life. The men

FIGURE 4.5c

Backrack (65–10–1a). This is formed with a large circular wooden frame with bark weaving on the inside. The feathers are attached to the bark and a piece of wood holds the quills upright and together. There are 24 strings of multicolor feathers. Birds: Harpy Eagle, Parrot, Yellow-rumped Cacique, Scarlet Macaw, and Blue-and-yellow Macaw.

FIGURE 4.5d

Seven-tier frontlet (65–10–1c). This train is worn tied around the neck and hangs down in front of the body. The frame is formed by seven wooden bars fastened to each other with split quills and black cotton thread. Bird: Harpy Eagle. (See Fig. 8.15).

FIGURE 4.6

Cashinahua body-feather headdress (65–10–12). This type of headdress, made with the body feathers (dani) of the trumpeter bird, is called nea dani maiti. The effect of this headdress is one of lightness, and when the wearer moves the feathers appear to shimmer. It is worn during fertility rites. Birds: Pale-winged Trumpeter, Scarlet Macaw, and Parrot. Made by Bidixu and collected along the Rio Curanja, Peru, 1965.

FIGURE 4.7

Cashinahua Harpy Eagle headdress (65–10–8). The frame for this piece is made from palm leaf rib covered by blue and white cotton cloth. It is worn during fertility and initiation rites. Birds: Harpy Eagle, Scarlet Macaw, Blue-and-yellow Macaw. Made by Soldado and collected along the Rio Curanja, Peru, 1965.

FIGURE 4.8

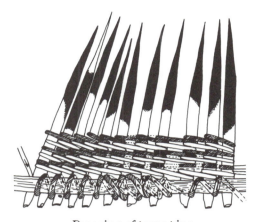

Drawing of porcupine-quill headdress. Courtesy of the author.

FIGURE 4.9

Detail of strings of feathers attached to backrack (65–10–1a). (See Figure 4.5C).

all contribute feathers from their personal supplies and jointly make the headdress, backrack (Fig. 4.5C), and feather train (Fig. 4.5D) worn by the chant leader. Any adult male who knows the chant may put on the costume and lead the ritual. As he chants, he bends forward slightly with arms and hands extended slightly from the sides of his body and dances backward in a slow shuffle step. He is guided by two men who hold his extended hands as he moves back and forth in the village plaza or within one of the houses. *Chidín*, which emphasizes male unity, is usually followed by the fertility rituals during which male-female antagonisms are acted out.

Macaw tail feathers are also used as *hina biden* (rigid tail) ornament for four kinds of headdresses—*pei maiti, dani maiti, paka maiti,* and *yushin maiti.* They are also used for men's ear and nose ornaments, and to decorate masks and spears for ritual use. A tiered train made of harpy eagle tail feathers is worn around the neck and hangs down the chest to the ground as part of the lead dancer's costume for *chidín.*

Dani, body hair/feathers, are the defining component of three species-specific types of body-feather headdress: *nea dani maiti,* trumpeter bird body-feather headdress; *nawan tete dani maiti,* harpy eagle body-feather headdress; and *isa dani maiti,* porcupine-quill headdress (Fig. 4.6). The unmodified term *dani maiti* generally refers to *nea dani maiti,* the most frequently made and used of the three types. It consists of one to four flattened strips of vine to which trumpeter bird body feathers in bunches of up to six black feathers are tied at intervals of approximately 0.5–1 centimeter; by slightly overlapping and varying the length of the feathers, added body is given to the headdress. The ends of the feathered strips are overlapped and tied so that approximately two-thirds to three-quarters of the ring is covered with feathers thrusting forward. Tiny red, yellow, and/or green leg, under-wing, and neck feathers, mainly from macaws and parrots, may be glued to the distal ends of the black feathers using beeswax-chicle adhesive. The effect is one of lightness and airiness and when the wearer moves the feathers appear to shimmer. Some men use the body feathers of the curassow and various other bird species in place of those of the trumpeter bird, *nea.* In this case the name of the headdress is changed to reflect the type of feathers used.

Harpy eagle body-feather headdresses are made in the same manner as the rigid headdresses made with wing feathers (Fig. 4.7). Harpy eagle feathers are highly valued because of their scarcity due to the great difficulties involved in the birds' capture and because of the beauty of their fluffy white breast feathers. Therefore, *nawan tete dani maiti* are the most highly prized and admired of all headdresses. As is the case with trumpeter body-feather headdresses, the body feathers of herons and other birds with long filmy breast feathers may be substituted for harpy eagle body feathers, with a consequent change of name reflecting the kind of body feather used.

Isa dani maiti is made of porcupine quills (hair), (Fig. 4.8). The bases of the quills are tied between vine strips using a technique similar to that used in the rigid *pei maiti* and the harpy eagle breast-feather headdress. However, the porcupine-quill headdress is never trimmed with *dani* but rather is trimmed by four to six strands of black, white, blue, red, and/or purple string that wraps each quill in a simple loop stitch, keeping the quills properly spaced and rigid. Tails of body feathers, feather pelts, and snail shells may be attached to the back of the headdress and allowed to dangle down the nape of the wearer's neck and back. Baubles made of short pieces of arrow cane decorated with small red and/or yellow feathers, or of short strings of Job's tears and other items, may be tied at various intervals to the vine strips so that they hang in front of the wearer's forehead.

FIGURE 4.10

*Cashinahua bamboo headdress (65–10–4). This type of headdress (*paka maiti*) is constructed from sheets of bamboo. The ends overlap and are sewn together with cotton thread. The seam is always worn in the back. The bamboo on this headdress has been painted with a design in red achiote. This headdress is worn by men during fertility rites. Birds: Blue-and-yellow Macaw, Great Egret, and Raptor. Made by Soldado and collected along the Rio Curanja, Peru, 1965.*

FIGURE 4.11

Cashinahua wearing a paka maiti daniya hinayabi, *a bamboo headdress with body and tail feathers. Photograph by the author.*

FIGURE 4.12

Dancers in fertility rites wearing yushin maiti, *spirit headdresses made of palm leaves. Photograph by the author.*

Dani from a wide variety of birds are used as a decorative element on a diverse array of both ritual and nonritual objects in addition to other types of headdresses. Long tails, made by tying *dani* from a variety of birds to lengths of spun cotton string, are attached to the harpy eagle wing-feather backrack as part of the costume of the lead dancer in *chidín* (Fig. 4.9).

Paka maiti are made from lengths of bamboo from which the tough outer bark has been shaved, leaving only a thin inner shell which, when slit lengthwise and held in the heat of the cookfire, can be opened up into a thin, flat sheet (Figs. 4.10, 4.11). The ends of the sheet are overlapped to form a crown and sewn together using spun cotton thread. *Paka maiti*, which is always worn with the seam at the back of the head, may be decorated by inserting at the seam a single erect macaw tail feather, plain or weighted with the tip of a curassow tail feather inserted into the seam, or by attaching a dangling tail or tails of *dani* feathers of assorted colors from a variety of birds, and/or shells, and/or feather pelts. In some cases, *dani* may be glued onto the crown, covering the entire outer surface (Fig. 4.15).

Yuxin maiti, spirit headdress, is made of a section of palm frond which has not yet opened and is therefore pale yellow rather than green (Fig. 4.12). The leaf is unfurled and the ends of the frond are overlapped and tied with vine to form a shaggy crown. A single erect macaw feather, plain or weighted, may be inserted at the back of the crown.

Feathers are useful not only because they are beautiful and give beauty, both to the objects on which they are used and to the user or wearer of those objects, but also because they are kinds of medicine, *dau*. The Cashinahua classify as medicine any substance or object used to decorate the body and other objects. Thus, feathers used to decorate a headdress, rather than those that are an essential ingredient in its construction, are its *dau*, as are body paint, headdresses, necklaces, ear ornaments, etc., when worn by people. They enhance the *dua* of persons and objects, giving them increased endurance, toughness, and stamina. *Dau* is always used in rituals to attract the attention of the spirits of fertility, and may also be used in daily life but not always for spiritual purposes. For example, if a man wishes to impress a potential lover he

FIGURE 4.13

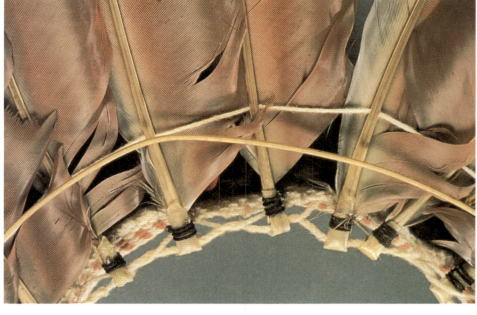

Detail of construction technique of wing-feather headdress (65–10–14). (See Figure 4.4).

FIGURE 4.14

Detail of construction technique of feather frontlet (65–10–1c). (See Figure 4.5D).

may adorn himself with body paint, a headdress, a lip plug, etc., all forms of *dau*. He has a secular goal, the seduction of the female, but by using *dau*, he is trying to enlist the aid of the spirits in his amorous quest. *Dau* has supernatural qualities that enhance his *dua*, making him attractive to the spirits of fertility. The combination of his *dua* and the spirits, attracted by the *dau* and his *dua*, is believed to make him sexually more attractive. In addition to enhancing a person's *dua*, feathers and feathered objects as *dau* provide protection against attacks by hostile spirits.

Feathers are also useful because they give visible representation to the normally invisible aspects of a person's *yuda bake yushin*, an aura which encases the body of each living person. Under normal circumstances, one's *dua* is all that others see of this aura. A person's shadow or reflection in water or in a mirror is another aspect of one's *yuda bake yushin*. But, while under the influence of the hallucinogenic beverage *nishi pae*, a man sees the *yuda bake yushin* as a black aura that encases the bodies of all human beings, out of which bright colors streak, radiate, and sparkle, particularly about the head. It is this vision that the Cashinahua attempt to replicate in the feather headdresses. Men who are adept at using *nishi pae* are said to have the clearest vision of this aura and, therefore, are the ones who usually make the headdresses with the best *dua*. Women neither drink *nishi pae* nor make feather headdresses.

The headdresses considered by the Cashinahua to be the most aesthetically pleasing, i.e., that have a lot of good *dua*, have four characteristic traits. First, they are well made. The elements used in their construction are of the best quality and they are carefully put together (Figs. 4.13, 4.14). Second, the elements are well balanced without being symmetrical. Third, they are not overwrought with too many elements or excessive decorative frills; simplicity without bareness is elegant. Fourth, they are unique, i.e., they are not exactly like any other headdress although they all share common elements. The Cashinahua say that this uniqueness of vision comes from the hallucinogenic experiences of the maker.

Although there is undoubtedly some significance in the choice of feathers used, the Cashinahua never referred to it when I asked them why they used feathers. And, although birds are present in mythology, ritual, and cosmology, their role is relatively minor and does not provide an adequate explanation for the extensive use of feathers in ritual attire. Nor do the Cashinahua say that they use feathers as a way of living in harmony with the spirits. Yet, their answers all point to this element. Feathers are used because they are available as a result of hunting and not to use them could be seen by the spirits as wasting shared resources (Fig. 4.15). They use feathers because feathers are beautiful and make them beautiful; they enhance *dua*, thus making their wearer attractive to the spirits of fertility, spirits whose assistance is needed to assure the fertility of the gardens and of women. Finally, they use feathers because they are good *dau*; as adornments to the human body they give endurance, toughness, and stamina as well as protection from spirit predation.

FIGURE 4.15

Cashinahua headdress (65–10–5). The cane dangles, tipped with colorful feathers, are the headdress's dau. *This bamboo headdress is worn with the long feather tassel hanging down the back. Birds: Blue-and-yellow Macaw, Scarlet Macaw, and Great Egret. Made by Bidixu and collected along the Rio Curanja, Peru, 1965.*

FRAGMENTS OF

FEATHERED BIPEDS

FIGURE 5.1

Waiwai woman feeding flock of green parrots, which are taught to speak. Kaxmi village, Federal Territory of Roraima, Brazil, 1986. Photograph by the author.

ONE HOT DAY DURING MY FIELDWORK AMONG THE Waiwai Indians, I was surprised to hear my next-door neighbor Tuyakawa's door slam as I passed by on my way to the river to bathe. Doors are rarely closed (and certainly never slammed) except at night or when the owners are absent. "Sister!" I called out. "What's the matter?" The only answer I received was laughter. I approached the door and repeated the question, getting only more giggles and protests of "Nothing!" "Well then, let me in!" "No, I can't!" Finally I persuaded her to open the door. Nothing seemed unusual inside. Like many others, Tuyakawa was feeding manioc bread to a flock of fledgling parrots she and her husband had fetched from the forest to raise, train to speak, and trade to other villages. She explained that she had slammed the door because she was embarrassed to let anyone see her "naked parrots." They were still too young to have grown any feathers; "unclothed" and ugly, they were unacceptable for "social" exposure.

I later observed that Waiwai pets were treated like children in numerous ways. Both were ornamented, painted, befeathered, or otherwise "dressed" by those responsible for their care and "socialization." Their growth was not considered automatic or "natural," but the result of deliberate and continuous acts of "nurture" applied by owners/parents (see Fig. 5.1). For example, the Waiwai said that puppies must have their skin stretched by their masters or else it will be too small to fit them as they mature. A naked parrot seen in public—like a naked child—reflected badly on its caretakers, as if they nurtured neither its physical nor social growth. Hence the slammed door.

Such was only one of many serendipitous lessons I stumbled across during my time with the Waiwai (Fig. 5.2). I could never take anything for granted but always had to question my assumptions—about seemingly straightforward issues like why feathers grow, up to complex conceptual bundles like what "beauty" represents. Waiwai artifacts may strike us as eminently beautiful, but we may not mean the same thing as they do when they assess objects as "beautiful." It is this topic—beauty—and its relation to featherwork—the cultural reconstruction of feathers into ornaments—that I address in this paper.

The use of featherwork to enhance the body provides one key to understanding central Waiwai concepts and values. Using methods of symbolic analysis, I will demonstrate that in converting "raw" feathers into "cultural" ornaments, the Waiwai are engaging in a form of "socializing" nature. This process parallels the transformation of the "natural," naked individual into a genuinely "social" actor when ornaments of beauty are donned (Fig. 5.3). Furthermore, since beauty is

"WE . . . BECOME THE ETHNOLOGISTS OF OUR OWN SOCIETY IF WE SE

THE HEAVENS

by *Catherine V. Howard*

VII. Waiwai headdress (SA 239).

URSELVES AT A DISTANCE FROM IT." – *MAURICE MERLEAU-PONTY*

FIGURE 5.2

Map showing locations of Waiwai villages in 1986.

FIGURE 5.3

Waiwai woman wearing toucan feather and shell earrings. Kaxmi village, Brazil. 1986. Photograph by the author.

considered by the Waiwai to be inherently a social attribute, adornments are part of public occasions when community members dramatize how their society itself is created out of resources drawn from its surroundings.

This paper will be an exercise in interpretation based on evidence about how the Waiwai use and discuss featherwork. Of necessity, it will also draw on data from many other aspects of Waiwai life. The anthropologist's attempt to understand what things "mean" from another culture's perspective requires some detective work. Members of the culture are not always verbally explicit about the many symbols and meanings that permeate their lives, since to them these significations are part of the cultural assumptions about the world that they take for granted. Often the reasons for why they do things in a certain way seem so obvious to them that no explanation is necessary; other times, the reasons are so complex that no explanation is possible, and can be represented only symbolically in ritual, myth, artifacts, and everyday activities. Jens Yde, an anthropologist who visited the Waiwai in the 1950s, was often frustrated when he asked the Waiwai for the "meanings" of certain designs, rituals, or ornaments. He hoped to hear exegetical explanations or references to the "sacred." Instead, he received reasons such as "It makes us happy," "It is beautiful"—so he concluded that there was "no particular meaning" (Yde 1965:154–55). But longer familiarity with the Waiwai would have convinced him that these are highly meaningful explanations. His attitude was typical of the Western notion of symbolism that sees meaning as static and referential, like the dictionary sense of meaning as definition. But meanings are much more than definitions; they form part of the rich fabric of everyday life with which the people of a culture make sense of the world. We could come closer to understanding the indigenous perspective on topics like featherwork if we explore the broader contexts within which the objects are made, used, and incorporated into social activities. The process of transforming raw materials into a cultural artifact is at the same time a process of constructing the "meaning" that the object has for the people who use it.[1]

To ferret out the tacit meanings that lie behind Waiwai notions of beauty, adornment, and featherwork, I will explore in this paper patterns that are echoed repeatedly in different registers of their culture: in the arrangement of featherwork on the body; in their conceptualization of the cosmos; in the division of labor between the sexes; and in social and political relations exercised in daily practice and represented in myth. These patterns suggest that the fully ornamented body becomes a metaphorical map of the "social body" and, indeed, of the cosmos. In the cosmological schema, birds are symbolically associated with spiritual and natural powers from "distant" places: the deep forest far from the socialized sphere of the village, and the celestial realms far above, both being the locales from which hunters fetch birds. I intend to demonstrate that in transforming feathers into ornaments, the Waiwai symbolically "capture" the distant powers embodied in the different species of birds and rechannel them to social ends. The array of feather ornaments worn in collective rituals thus visually testifies to the ability of Waiwai society to exercise control over its natural surroundings and to reinvigorate itself with powers assimilated from them. Moreover, a village holding a festival attempts to exercise persuasive control over its social surroundings by inviting other villages to attend. The spectacularly befeathered sponsors of such festivals graphically display their expanded influence over the region in the medium of adornments. The body beautiful is thus the visual counterpart of social and political influence, since both beauty and influence involve the ability to attract valued resources and persons. In sum, I will argue that as a vehicle of beauty, the enhanced body represents the integration of various domains in the cosmos into a whole, and at the same time articulates the links between key social and political roles. By exploring patterns that the Waiwai take for granted in their everyday lives and comparing them with occasions when they use or discuss featherwork, birds, and adornments, I hope to reveal dimensions of social meaning in feathers that we may not even have suspected from the outside looking in.

THE WAIWAI AND THE UNIVERSITY MUSEUM EXPEDITION

The Waiwai are a Carib-speaking group living in the forests to the north and the south of the Acarai Mountains that form the border of Guyana and Brazil, in the western portion of the region known as the Guianas (see map Fig. 5.2). They now number about 1200 people, including assimilated groups from the surrounding region with whom they have interacted for several centuries through trade, marriage, festivals, and occasionally warfare. The name "Waiwai," meaning "Tapioca People," originated from the neighboring Wapixana, who were impressed with the huge quantities of tapioca drinks the Waiwai would serve at intertribal feasts. They had little direct contact with non-Indians until the 1950s, when evangelical Protestant missionaries moved in, and the 1970s, when the Brazilian colonial frontier began to encroach, both wreaking extensive changes in the native culture.

The Waiwai's remoteness, spectacular material culture, and peaceful character attracted several scientific expeditions in the 19th and 20th centuries. The extensive collection at The University Museum of the University of Pennsylvania was the fruit of an arduous expedition conducted in 1913–16 by William C. Farabee, a widely-travelled and indefatigable anthropologist and archaeologist, with assistance from John Ogilvie, an adventurous jack-of-all-trades from Scotland who worked for several decades alongside the Indians of British Guiana (Guyana). During their expedition, they collected information on many of the Guiana groups that have since joined or intermarried into the composite "Waiwai" villages (Waiwai, Parukwoto, Mawayana, Taruma, Katuena, Cikyana, Wapixana, Tiriyó, etc.). Farabee published *The Central Arawaks* in 1918 on the Arawak-speaking groups of this region, but tragically, he died in 1923 of a chronic disease he had contracted during his Amazon expedition before he could finish his second book on the Carib-speakers (including the Waiwai), so The University Museum incorporated the rest of his fieldnotes to publish *The Central Caribs* (Pezzati n.d.:11). Ogilvie wrote several unpublished manuscripts, based on his long familiarity with native life, that are now located in the Museum's archives. Farabee and Ogilvie's collection of material culture is part of The University Museum's "The Gift of Birds" featherwork exhibit, which is the occasion for this paper.

The most elaborate use of ornaments among the Waiwai (including featherwork, beadwork, body paintings, oils, and so on) occurs during periodic festivals that stress the collective integration of household production and consumption units. Farabee and Ogilvie witnessed a Xorowiko feast when a village invited another for many days of feasting and drinking, dancing and singing, wrestling and ritual games, trade and romantic trysts (Fig. 5.4).[2] Nowadays, with such large, concentrated settlements, festivals draw together different "neighborhoods" (functioning much as villages used to) for the weeks of Christmas, Easter, and the beginning of the dry season, with features selected from both Christian and indigenous traditions.

FIGURE 5.4

Women in a line dance at an intervillage Xorowiko *festival. Brazil, 1913–14. Photograph by William Farabee. (*The Central Caribs *, pl. XII–f).*

53

These festivals, I would suggest, portray through performance how various external resources and powers (represented by animals, plants, spirits, trade goods, songs, news, knowledge, people, etc.) are successfully drawn in and assimilated by the Waiwai to rejuvenate their society. Through the ritual, the Waiwai socialize these powers and organize them into a sociological and cosmological whole. As a result, the society realigns itself in the "center" of the natural and social world. In word and deed, the Waiwai celebrate the "beauty" and "joyfulness" of these festivals, values that for them epitomize the height of sociability, reciprocity, and collective existence. In the very act of preparing for and holding a festival, they reactivate the ties that make up the society and renew its basic organizing principles. The ornaments they use to beautify themselves at these festivals are not so much static objects of aesthetic contemplation (how we tend to view them) as they are, rather, visual counterparts of processes—of attracting, influencing, acquiring, and assimilating. John Ogilvie found this out personally when he tried to obtain feather headdresses from the Waiwai:

> I now found I had something to learn in the art and especially in the speed of bartering . . . I was now subjected [to] the history of the hat itself! These crowns are made of feathers from a number of birds— powis, toucan, green parrots, macaws, eagles and others. I was taken on a verbal hunt after each bird, just who was at the hunt, how and where it was shot, and countless long-winded details . . . it was a slow, tiresome job.
>
> By noon, after some five hours' work, I had successfully purchased two crowns . . . I made a little better speed by being rude, and . . . insisting that the old chief reduce his information to a minimum. Even so, . . . [he] came along after dark for an hour or two, to recount some more hunts and feather history which he had had to omit previously owing to my insistence, and I dropped asleep to the steady drone of their [the Indians'] voices. (n.d.:163–64)

From the Waiwai's viewpoint, they were parting with not merely a material "artifact," but a meaning-laden "text." Every object comes to epitomize a "cultural biography" (Kopytoff 1986) that recapitulates the narrative of where its raw materials came from, how it was made, through whose hands it passed, when it was used, and whose personalities were infused in it. It is we who have to learn how to "read" these objects which are, as Mauss (1967:11) put it, "to some extent parts of persons" who in turn "behave in some measure as if they were things."

BEAUTY AND TRANSFORMATION

For the Waiwai, beauty is preeminently a social quality. Nature is not considered innately "beautiful" until reassembled, humanized, and transformed by society. For instance, the myth of the first Xorowiko festival (Fock 1963:56–67) tells how certain animals who attended took on human form but still could not hide their ugliness until they donned costumes painted with abstract animal designs and adorned themselves *like* the species they represented—nature translated into artifice. The bird people who were truly beautiful were those who had human souls (*ekatî*). But they did not become "proper" birds until they bathed in a river of blood and someone bespelled them. As they slowly sprouted wings and tails, they got caught in a rainstorm that changed their colors; they then experimented with each other's feathers until they achieved a pleasing appearance. Thus, not even the beauty of birds is "natural" or original, but the result of complex conversions that follow a meaningful sociocultural logic.

At best, the beauty found in nature exists as a potential to be actualized by human action. Most myths recount the origin of beautiful things (and cultural items generally) by narrating how the characters acquired various potencies residing in nature, either by imitating creatures that exercised those powers, wresting control of items that embodied them, or bringing manifestations of those powers into new contexts; usually the characters made several failed attempts (often involving death and regeneration) until the cultural model was just right. The weaving designs that beautify basketry and beadwork, for instance, are said to have been copied from the skin of a giant snake monster slain by a man whom the creature had swallowed and regurgitated, leaving the man's skin imprinted with its designs (Fig. 5.5; Fock 1963:91–92; Roe 1989b:23–26; Howard n.d.:3–10). Beauty is a cultural victory in the painstaking task of constructing meaning out of the givens of nature, epitomizing what Weiner (1983) meant when she said "the world of made is not the world of born."

Accordingly, let us explore the stages of making feather ornaments and see what we can infer about the process of making something "beautiful." When a Waiwai man goes out to hunt, he leaves the safe, socialized sphere of the village and ventures out into the forest, which the Waiwai say is a "wild" place filled with many dangers and powers. The various species of birds are found in the different forest canopies, each of which is associated with certain potencies that are incarnated in the species that inhabit it. Armed with his weapons and his skills, the hunter conquers the bird and then transports it from the forest back into the village. There he detaches its feathers and reassembles them into a "new" object of beauty that follows socially relevant principles of design. Its full potential as a "beautiful" article is not consummated, however, until it is arranged upon a person's body in harmony with the complete set of ornaments and, at yet a higher level, conjoined with dance and song in harmony with other social actors in the context of ritual performance (Fig. 5.6). The ornaments, the wearers, and the society as a whole can then truly be considered *cenporem*, "pleasing to behold." Such visual beauty is but one component of the social sentiment of *tahwore*, "joyfulness," which characterizes intervillage festivals. Through music, jokes, laughter, dance, feasting, drink, games, flirtation, and gift exchanges, Waiwai society transcends the everyday ties of kinship and affinity to momentarily regenerate the fundamental principles of its social life with fresh infusions of energies and external potencies. Dominant among these principles are those based on hierarchy (levels of control), complementarity (reciprocal interdependence), and concentricity (center and periphery relations). These principles, we will see, inform the social relations between men and women, leaders and followers, hosts and visitors, dominant and subordinate in-laws. Furthermore, these principles are mapped out in the vertical and horizontal arrangement of resources, both tangible and symbolic, that society acquires from its milieu. Thus, in the process of transforming the feathers of "wild" birds into "socialized" adornments, the Waiwai are touching on themes that reverberate throughout their culture.

FIGURE 5.5

A weaver making a basket with the xohri *(sloth) design, one of many originally obtained from the skin of the mythical snake monster. Kaxmi village, Brazil. 1986. Photograph by the author.*

FIGURE 5.6

Ornamented men dancing at festival and playing flutes and turtleshell resonator to generate joyfulness. Kaxmi village, Brazil. 1986. Photograph by the author.

FIGURE 5.7

*The Waiwai leader
Kiwinik in full ceremonial
dress, British Guiana,
1910. Photograph by John
Ogilvie (*University
Museum Journal *1913,
cover and p. 11)*

FIGURE 5.8

*Habitats of eagle, macaw
and toucan, and curassow
in the ecological system.
Drawing by Raymond
Rorke.*

THE ARRANGEMENT OF CEREMONIAL ATTIRE

With these general observations, let us look more specifically at the steps involved in dressing and donning ornaments to construct a "beautiful" persona. Ogilvie's 1910 photograph of the Waiwai chief Kiwinik (Fig. 5.7) is an excellent point of departure. His description (n.d.:135–42, 212–13) of the lengthy process of this stately leader's personal toilet is revealing. Normal attire would involve bathing; putting on loinstrings and an everyday loincloth; binding his hair with twine to form a long ponytail and inserting it into a simple bamboo hairtube; coating his skin with red paint; winding bead strands around his joints and putting on unadorned shell earrings, thick bead necklaces, Brazil-nut bracelets, and a bark wristguard. Preparations for ceremonial attire, however, would be much more complicated. In addition to the above steps, Kiwinik would pluck all body and facial hairs, including eyebrows and eyelashes (considered too natural and animalistic), then prepare his coiffure with oils and a special beaded hairtube with a huge pendant feather tassel; he would put on a new loincloth and belts of beads, jaguar skin or teeth, then paint delicate red designs on his face and broader black patterns on his body; after that, he would put on bark bandoleers and special necklaces, bracelets, and pendants of beads and toucan feathers. When he heard someone call out the ritual invitation to come feast, he would put on the final touches by assembling his upper-arm ornaments, composed of feathers extending from below his knees to high above his head; inserting feather ornaments into perforations in his earlobes, nose, cheeks, and/or lower lip; covering his hair and face paints with eagle down, and topping it all off with a "magnificent feather crown." Ogilvie summarized the effect:

> [When] his toilet was complete . . . a greater transformation you could scarcely imagine. From a rather drab, light-hued Indian, he was transformed into a dignified Chief, glittering in the now rising sun with paint and powder and his body almost hidden in the fluttering feathers that hung everywhere around him . . . Few, if any, of these Indians I have ever met could approach Kiwinik in decoration and dress. He was the Beau Brummell of the tribe and wore his feathers and paint with a grace and dignity that could only be imitated. (n.d.:141–42)

Peter Roe (1989a) has perceptively pointed out how the vertical arrangement of the feathers in Kiwinik's attire replicates the cosmological levels from which each of the birds comes. Towering above his head are the white feathers of the harpy eagle from the upper skies; dominating the ornaments of the middle body are the red or yellow feathers of macaws and toucans from the lower skies; and hanging below waist level are the black feathers of the ground-dwelling curassow.[3] These three categories of birds overwhelmingly dominate Waiwai featherwork[4] (Fig. 5.8). Furthermore, the tripartite vertical schema is replicated within the details of each ornament. From the bark armlets hang streamers of black and white curassow feathers, while above them are shorter tassels of red toucan feathers; stuck into the top of the armlets is a fan of tall red macaw tail feathers, trimmed on the bottom with curassow and on the top with eagle feathers. The headdress shows the same layering of upper white eagle, middle red (and yellow) macaw, and lower black curassow feathers (Fig. 5.9). Again, the eagle down stuck to the oiled hair and sticky face paints complements the lower ornaments hanging from the nose, chin, and ears, composed mainly of red macaw and toucan feathers, which

Figure 5.9

Headdress showing the layers of eagle, macaw, and curassow feathers placed in the same order as the birds are found in nature (See Fig. 5.8).

Figure 5.10

Back view of Waiwai showing loincloth tassel of toucan feathers and hairtube with white eagle feathers and huge bulb of black curassow feathers hanging from his long ponytail British Guiana, 1954. Photograph by Jens Yde. (Material Culture of Waiwai, fig. 78, p. 211)

are then continued in the loincloth tassels, as if to frame the central torso. When the end of the loincloth is wrapped in back, the toucan feathers lie neatly between the white eagle feathers of the hairtube and the huge bulb of black curassow feathers hanging below (Fig. 5.10). Many other items of material culture reveal the same logic—for instance, the special arrows for ceremonial gift exchanges, which the hunters feather with curassow and toucan, then decorate with facial paints and cover with eagle down, because, they told me, "they should look as beautiful as the hunters who made them" (Fig. 5.11).

In sum, the way Kiwinik assembled his feather adornments exhibits a rigorous symbolic logic. Each of the parts (the individual ornaments) reveals the same three-tiered composition as the whole (the wearer's fully ornamented body); indeed, even subparts and subsets of the ornaments replicate the same order, creating a series of embedded part-and-whole relations. This is a remarkable instance of a venerable principle of poetics called "synecdoche" by Aristotle. More recently, Turner has explored how Kayapó and Bororo featherwork works with synecdoche when ritual dancers imitate the natural birds that supplied feathers for cultural performances; through such part/whole relations, he says, "orders or systems of relations (e.g., 'nature' and 'society'), which appear as separate totalities in everyday life, become suspended at the higher level created through ritual action. From [this] perspective . . . they appear as interdependent parts of a single totality" (Turner 1991:149).

Ultimately, the whole of which Kiwinik himself is a part is the cosmos at large. Traditional Waiwai cosmology features five vertical layers; of these, the central three—roughly parallel to the three categories of birds dominating the featherwork—are occupied by beings that play the most active roles in human life. The very lowest level is the dry underworld of the cicada people, seldom mentioned except as heralds of the dry season and as the mythological source of fermented drinks. Above it is the terrestrial level populated by humans, plants, animals, and wild *kworokyam* spirits; this level is further divided horizontally into center/periphery domains of village, gardens, and forest, and crosscut by land/river contrasts. The first heaven above us is the realm of the afterlife where the eye-souls of the dead go to dance unceasingly in their most beautiful and brightly colored finery. Above it is a heaven occupied by powerful *kakînaw* spirits, who represent the essence of each species of animals and plants, and whom shamans contact to obtain cures and names. Birds are especially active among the *kakînaw*, the harpy eagle in particular being a prominent mediator among all layers on behalf of shamans. At the very highest level, so distant that communication with it is rare, is the land of the powerful buzzard people (Fock 1963:22–23, 101–103).

In the logic of symbolism, each of the creatures incarnates certain characteristics and powers of the domain from which it comes; each can therefore serve as a representative of its domain in other contexts and bring along with it the powers from its place of origin. Birds are, in this sense, symbols or "fragments" of the heavens and of the forests from which they come. Because of their ability to fly and cross thresholds between cosmological layers, they are particularly apt delegates for communicating between them and linking them conceptually. Significantly, the Father of the Birds, a toucan *kakînaw* spirit in the form of a miniature man, is decorated at all times in a complete array of feather, bead, and festive wear (Fock 1963:31–32). In other words, his role as representative of the entire category of birds is visually displayed in his costume assembled from feathers and materials from all cosmological domains.

In sum, what we see in the full festive outfit worn by leaders such as Kiwinik is a microcosm of the cosmology charted out

FIGURE 5.11

Hunter bringing ceremonial gift arrows which, like himself, are adorned with painted designs and featherwork to make them both beautiful. Kaxmi village, Brazil. 1986. Photograph by the author.

on the body (Roe 1989a:2). Furthermore, we can see a converse operation at work: the semantic expansion of the person in space and time to macrocosmic proportions. The process of arranging the set of ornaments into a harmonious whole on the body thus dramatizes the articulation of the cosmos into an integrated whole. Man can indeed serve as a measure of all things.

Each spatial domain (and hence its occupants) also has its distinctive kind of time. The underworld works on the oscillation between the dry and rainy seasons, and between night and day. The terrestrial level is characterized by numerous rhythms, most notably the temporality of the human life cycle and its gradual processes of birth, growth, maturation, death, and decay. The first heaven above, home of the dancing eye-souls purified of their mortal bodies, is a realm drained of human temporality, in perpetual motion but without change or decay. The next layer, however, is a realm which can cause great transmutations, even reversals, in human states of being by *kakînaw* when they impinge on earthly affairs, e.g., through direct contacts, illnesses and cures, shamanic trances and dreams, and names. As the domain of archetypal essences, it is an ancient realm of spirits who existed long before the events of origin myths—perhaps even without beginning. By contrast, the uppermost realm of the buzzard people—carrion eaters who draw life from rotting carcasses—exists on the yonder side of death and putrefaction. In Waiwai modes of thinking, distance in space (vertical or horizontal) is correlated with depth in time. Both in turn are associated with varying degrees and kinds of natural, supernatural, and social powers.

Because birds move between these various zones, they are capable of articulating the various rhythms with each other.[5] Without some process of weaving them together, the universe would disintegrate into a disjointed muddle with its parts out of synchrony. For instance, a shaman may call on the Father of Birds above to ensure a good day's hunt out in the forest (Fock 1963:130)—thus coordinating different vertical rhythms with the oscillation of the hunter between forest and village. On the other hand, different temporalities must sometimes be kept separate to avoid disharmonies, as when a mourner, embroiled in the immediate terrestrial rhythms of the body and mortality, must refrain from wearing any feather ornaments, which would connect him to celestial rhythms of perpetuity.

In one of the upper heavens is located the sun, considered a manifestation of a certain *kakînaw* spirit who looks like a human being. Waiwai myths and rituals reveal many associations between the sun and the ceremonial diadem (*aroko*) made of orange cock-of-the-rock feathers with accents of red and black toucan feathers.[6] The brilliant feathers are bound to a circular bamboo splint, with longer tufts protruding at certain intervals, creating a crown that strikingly resembles the sun and its rays (Fig. 5.12). Long ago, the Waiwai say, the sun spirit was surrounded by rain clouds because he wore a black-feathered diadem, until some shamans braved his flames to replace it with a red one (Fock 1963:33). Shamans can still use these diadems to persuade the sun to shine. Their magic involves offering dry manioc bread to the sun and calling upon various *kakînaw* birds, neighbors of the sun; later,

> When the sun then shows itself a little, the *yaskomo* [shaman] lays out on the open-air cassava [manioc bread] drying shelf . . . his diadem of [toucan] feathers (*aroko*), his armlets with red macaw feathers . . . and various red feather tassels, saying: "Behold sun, here are your adornments so that you can shine."
>
> These adornments remain lying on the cassava shelf for three days . . . [so] the sun will have had sufficient time to have taken to itself the *ekatî* (soul, picture, strength) of the brilliant adornments

FIGURE 5.12

FIGURE 5.13

Diadem (SA 529b).
Traditional shamans
would offer these diadems
to the sun on rainy days to
persuade it to shine.
Karape River, Brazil.

Waiwai family in their hammocks, 1913–14. The woman sleeps in the hammock
nearest the ground, her husband in the hammock above, and the child on top.
*Photograph by William Farabee. (*The Central Caribs, *pl. VII)*

and then itself be as clear and radiant as a diadem. It is said of the sun that it wears the diadem of the *yaskomo*. (Fock 1963:34)

We can interpret the efficacy of this ritual by remarking that the shaman is offering to the sun what the Waiwai consider the quintessential humanizing food, manioc bread, and then "feeding" the sun with the feather ornaments' *ekatî*—their energy, vital essence, or double. Perhaps we would be closer to Waiwai attitudes by saying that the sun is made to resemble the diadem rather than the other way around.[7]

FIGURE 5.14

Three girls of a Parakuoto (southern Waiwai) village in Brazil, 1914. Rather than using the elaborate featherwork of men, women wear copious strands of highly valued glass beads. (The Central Caribs, *pl. XIII–b*)

FIGURE 5.15

A contemporary Waiwai girl with a pet macaw. In addition to the profuse bead strands, she also wears a bead pendant portraying a macaw. Kaxmi village, Brazil. 1985. Photograph by the author.

FEATHERWORK AND THE SEXUAL DIVISION OF LABOR

A question that people often ask is: why are Waiwai men more elaborately adorned in featherwork than women? To understand why, we have to look at Waiwai concepts about gender and power, hierarchy and complementarity.

Gender contrasts are strongly marked out in the Waiwai conceptualization of the cosmos, the upper realms being associated with male powers, and the lower with female. In garden work, for instance, men fell trees while women harvest manioc tubers from the soil. In preparation for village festivals, men repair the thatching on the roof of the feast house while women weed the plaza. "Men are the basket makers; they cut tall reeds," the Waiwai told me, "while the women are the potters; they dig clay from the ground." Men sit on stools, women on bark cloths on the ground; similarly, husbands hang their hammocks immediately above those of their wives (with children above both; Fig. 5.13). Menstruating women are said to be *roowo po*, "sitting on the ground," and are thought to be dangerous to shamans, whose souls travel to the upper heavens; in other words, women in their most intensely feminine and carnal state must be kept separate from men in their most powerful masculine and spiritual role as shamans.

Consequently, there is a distinct association of men with birds insofar as they are predominantly creatures of above. Furthermore, the fact that birds are obtained through hunting makes featherwork even more clearly a masculine prerogative. A suitor at an intervillage festival, for instance, will do his best to be especially well ornamented with featherwork to impress his potential in-laws with his skills as a hunter capable of providing them with ample supplies of meat after marriage. Ogilvie states:

> The ceremonial dress is an indication of the owner's status, his wealth and above all, his prowess as a huntsman. The youth just entering manhood has to shoot every feather he wears, and it takes him some years before he gets enough to make all the variety of ornaments necessary. He cannot devote his whole time to hunting. He has to cut, burn and plant a field, and assist the village in all communal work. He has his own arms and ornaments to make and countless other duties, so that it is generally not until a man is well over 20 years of age that he can become one of the dandies of his tribe. (n.d.:212)

Women have fewer associations with featherwork: they do not hunt birds, make feather artifacts, or wear as much feather ornamentation as men do. The most elaborate feather adornment that women wear is the festival corselet worn over the small of the back, consisting of rows of beads hung between two wooden slats and draped with thick layers of toucan feather streamers that bounce seductively when the woman dances (see dancer in Fig. 5.4). Although they wear some feather ornaments, they lack the profuse, towering, and augmented kinds of feather dress that make men look so commanding. On the other hand, women are the gender most strongly associated with beadwork, highly esteemed as a complementary "wealth" item (Fig. 5.14). Beads, in Waiwai thought, are related to seeds, stones, and fish eggs, items that consistently contrast with birds and feathers (Howard 1988). When the Waiwai make some special link between birds and women, it tends to be with ground-dwelling species, or with the stage of cooking their husbands' game into a meal, or with domesticated pets (such as the parrots trained to talk, see Fig. 5.1). These feminine connections are congruent with women's symbolic link to the earth and their roles in food processing and child care in the Waiwai division of labor. Sometimes all three of these aspects are condensed into one, as in the belief that pregnant women get cravings for curassow meat.

In other words, men and women transform birds in different ways: men convert them into featherwork, women convert them into food or humanized pets. Correlatively, full-grown wild birds fetched by men from the "wild" forest can yield both feathers for adornments and meat for food; but tamed birds raised by women in the "socialized" village are never eaten (nor are any domesticated animals), and their feathers are seldom used for ornaments (Fig. 5.15).

In the Waiwai division of labor, hunting is the male pursuit par excellence; agriculture is most strongly associated with women, and fishing is linked to both sexes. Spatially, this means that women are linked to the nearby gardens and men to the outlying forests, and both to the rivers that connect them. Thus, there is not only a vertical gender division, but also a horizontal one, mapped out in a series of concentric domains moving outward from the village. Men traverse greater distances than women, both outward and upward, signaling the mastery of powers that are more difficult to control, more dangerous, and more potent because more foreign (logically and spatially) than humankind. Because birds come from the skies and from the forest, they are superbly able to represent both vertical and horizontal distance in the cosmos. I would suggest that the capturing of birds and the transforming of their feathers into ornaments are means of symbolizing the male mastery of both dimensions of external powers. Not only do men tend to use more feather ornaments than women, but they use the most "expansive" kinds radiating above and beyond the body; these are visual means of representing men's greater control over cosmological space and time. This in turn symbolizes their greater power over other people and resources—their broader "extension" of influence in political arenas. In Waiwai society, men are the ones who exercise control in the public domain of village politics, while women are responsible for domestic affairs in the household. This aspect of male/female relations is conceptualized socially and spatially as a hierarchical differentiation.

However, the relationship between the sexes is not simply hierarchical, but also complementary; each gender has its distinctive powers indispensable to the social whole. When hunters return from the forest, they turn over the game to the women, who feed them with tapioca and bread (garden manioc products). Such a transaction is conceptualized by the Waiwai as an exchange of complementary foodstuffs necessary for a complete meal, which thereby models the social totality. In the material culture, women make items of dress out of glass beads—aprons and corselets for themselves, hairtubes and belts for men, necklaces and strands wound around the joints for both sexes—but they hand them over to their husbands to finish off by attaching feathers.[8] Conversely, men depend upon women to spin cotton thread for them to use for attaching feathers, making arrows, and weaving loincloths. This complementarity of beads, feathers, and cotton expresses the reciprocal interdependence of women and men—and complementarity is part of what makes things "beautiful" in Waiwai eyes. My informants told me, for instance, that there was no point in taping only the men or only the women singing, because it took both groups to make the songs *centaporem*, "pleasing to hear." Again, the various designs on combs are made by interweaving women's purple-dyed cotton with men's blond *buriti* palm fibers (Fig. 5.16). The "beauty" of the contrastive design is a tangible reflection of male/female cooperation. Furthermore, the complementarity of the dyed cotton and the fiber reflects other gender-linked contrasts as well: gardens/forest, bush/tree, ground/sky,

FIGURE 5.16

Two Waiwai combs. The contrasting design is produced by interweaving women's purple cotton thread and men's blond palm fibers—visually representing the "beauty" of cooperation between the sexes. Kaxmi village, Brazil. 1985. Photograph by the author.

cultivated/wild. Suitably, the comb is finished off with tufts of bright macaw feathers and used, of course, to beautify the hair. We can see in such items a reflection of a social system and a symbolic landscape.

BEAUTY AND SOCIAL INFLUENCE

Beauty is not a trivial pursuit for the Waiwai, but a profoundly political matter. It is not coincidental that Kiwinik was the most splendidly dressed of his compatriots as well as one of the most powerful leaders in the region. The influence that leaders of renown exercise ripples out beyond the household and village to affect neighboring villages and tribes as well. If the array of featherwork adornments visually represents control over powers from the natural environment, it also represents control over the social environment. The "expansion" of the person politically through influence and visually through featherwork marks two interconnected attributes. Along such lines, Munn (1977:49) states, "This 'enlargement' is the pivot of personal power and social relationship summed up in the idea of 'being attractive.'" To be influential and to be beautiful both entail the attraction of other people toward oneself through the exercise of persuasion—that is why beauty and power are so closely meshed in Waiwai society.

Young men and women seeking potential spouses at collective festivals are also elaborately adorned in their finest wear. A subtle but distinct element of competitiveness marks this display of "beauty" and attractiveness. In the first place, rivalry runs deep among suitors over potential spouses; the efforts put into beautification are one of several means of displaying one's suitability as a good candidate for marriage, a kind of visual persuasiveness that is directed as much to the opposite sex as to potential in-laws. In the second place, once a selection has been made, the new relationship between the parents-in-law of the couple engages powerful rivalries. Control over dependent in-laws is a key feature of political power in Waiwai society. The enormous debt that a son-in-law owes his parents-in-law for their gift of a daughter is usually met by his coming to live with the wife's parents, where he is at their beck and call for labor on gardens, houses, hunting, and basketry. It is therefore noteworthy that macaw feathers are used to decorate the basketry items a man makes for his wife and in-laws, such as covered baskets, sieves, fans, trays, and other items (Fig. 5.17).[9]

Residence with the wife and her family after marriage is not, however, a rigid rule; the most powerful leaders in fact will attempt to retain both their married sons and sons-in-law, building up a retinue of followers. Since often the fathers of both the young husband and wife are jockeying for advantage, an acute (though understated, in typical Waiwai fashion) competition ensues. Affines (the range of in-law relations) are necessary for biological reproduction and social continuity over time, but the competition between the two sides for where the couple will live represents a struggle of persuasion, influence, prestige, and political power. The greater the social distance to be overcome in drawing in a son-in-law, the greater the potential prestige to be acquired—just like the conquest of birds from great spatial distances. Since the older men of marriageable sons and daughters have reached the point in their life cycle when they compete for political power and leadership, it is not surprising that they are often the most splendidly ornamented. In this respect, not only are the accouterments of beauty physically attractive, but they also

FIGURE 5.17

Basketry container (half-opened) with bird designs. Macaw feathers decorate baskets like this one woman by a son-in-law for his father-in-law, a highly "social" relationship. Kaxmi village, Brazil. 1984. Photograph by the author.

FIGURE 5.18

Men returning from ceremonial hunt wearing game birds and animals attached to their belts and eagle down in their hair. Kaxmi village, Brazil. 1984. Photograph by the author.

FIGURE 5.19

Hunter dressed like his prey wearing bird wings, and monkey-fur beard and wig, loaded down with game, blowing trumpet over ornamented smoked bird. Kaxmi village, Brazil. 1986. Photograph by the author.

FIGURE 5.20

Carved wooden bird and animal targets that will be placed in rafters of feast house. Kaxmi village, Brazil. 1986. Photograph by the author.

serve as symbols of one's *control* over processes of attraction, i.e., persuasiveness: "In adornment, persuasion takes the form of visible qualities of the body . . . the beautified person persuades by exhibiting his or her persuasive potency as a visible property of the self" (Munn 1986:102). While we may not be accustomed to thinking of items of decoration as the stuff of *realpolitik*, for the Waiwai, the spectacular array of feather and bead adornments, body paints, and glistening oils is a "civilized," aesthetic form of "waging beauty." Indeed, the ceremonial clubs and weapons they display in rituals are decorated with featherwork, just like those who wield them.

Beauty is associated with influence not only at the level of individuals, but at the collective level as well. Featherwork is one of several means that the collectivity uses to represent its control and influence over nature. An example of how the Waiwai make various references to birds to symbolize the conquest of external "natural" powers by society is found in the ceremonial target shooting which I witnessed men perform when they returned from their week-long collective hunting expeditions to provide game for village festivals. The hunters and their prey metaphorically represented each other in many overlapping ways, almost like a play of mirrors. The men would emerge from the forest making "wild" noises by hooting, whistling, and tapping arrows against bowstrings. They would be wearing animals and birds attached to their belts and a thick covering of eagle down in their hair (Fig. 5.18). One year, they also wore wigs and beards made of fur; another year, "costumes" of meat draped over frameworks arching above their heads. As a counterpart to this "naturalization" of the hunters, some of the game were "humanized" with satirical versions of feather ornaments, while smoked game birds, "beautified" with down, were tied to the front of bark trumpets and coated with human breath transformed into eerie, otherworldly music (Fig. 5.19). The hunters would encircle the huge central building (*umana*) used for collective rituals, then file inside where the women were waiting to serve them manioc drink. Perched high up in the crossbeam rafters of the *umana* were wooden sculptures carved and painted to represent a wide variety of birds and other animals (Fig. 5.20). This part of the *umana* ceiling is conceptually linked to the heavens, the wider cosmos, and powerful spirits, as well as physically linked to them via a 50-foot-long central pole extending out the roof toward the skies. One by one, the hunters would take aim and shoot as everyone shouted challenges such as "Show the women how we shot the game in the forest!" "Shoot that macaw there on the left!," naming each species and even jokingly comparing them to humans.

I would suggest that, having spiraled in from the distant forest to the inside of the *umana* in the village center, the men not only reenact what happened on the hunt, but indeed funnel and compress the powers from distant realms into the center of the village. These powers are life-giving (for instance, the powers of nurture represented by the game as food) as well as dangerous (such as those represented by the threats of wild animals and spirits). The Waiwai confirm their skills, knowledge, and abilities to "capture" these powers and import them into the heart of society. The symbolic equations set up in the course of the ritual between hunters, prey, and targets are a way of transforming the *umana* into a model of the world. Over the many days of the ensuing festival, the *umana* becomes the arena within which symbolic operations, performed through human actors, reorder and renew the fundamental principles of the cosmos. For yet another season, Waiwai society thus guarantees the perpetuation of a world order within which it draws its sustenance.

W e can push our "reading" of the socio-geographic symbolism of adornments even further and consider certain myths that deal with ornaments and the birds that provide feathers for them. We have seen how the three main layers of featherwork arranged on the body draw on three principal categories of birds—curassow, toucan and macaw, and eagle—which occupy the lower, middle, and upper domains of the cosmos, respectively; we have also seen how these correlations take on social and political meanings. I will now turn to the myth about the origin of featherwork (epitomized in central toucan and macaw decor) and then to myths about the curassow and the harpy eagle. I will then compare the social relations that are portrayed in the three narratives—relations concerning the nuclear family, lovers, and in-laws—as a way of shedding some light on Waiwai values for the ideal society, celebrated in their rituals of "joyfulness" and "beauty."

The first myth, concerning the origin of feather and bead adornments, features the Anaconda People, masters of terrestrial waters. I mentioned above that rivers and fishing are associated with both men and women. To be more specific, they appear to be linked in Waiwai thought to women and foreign men. This contrast can be broken down into two related oppositions: in certain contexts, land and water are contrasted as male to female; in others, as "insiders" to "outsiders." Men from other villages and tribes can become linked to one's home village through trade and feast invitations, but above all through marriage to resident women. "Foreign" men are, in other words, a sort of prototypical brother-in-law. The myth of feather adornments, I will suggest, dramatizes the attempt to establish relations with foreign in-laws that can be repeated over time through reciprocal exchanges of women and valuables; it also illustrates the profound competitiveness of such in-law relations.

The Anaconda People appear in myths that deal with the origin of women, sexuality, and proto-alliance relations. These beings are first encountered in the principal origin myth which recounts how the Waiwai creator hero, Mawari, fished up from the Anaconda People's riverine domain the first women's goods (cotton and spindles, bead aprons, menstrual barkcloth mats, body paints, etc.) and finally a woman, daughter of the Anacondas, whom he took to wife. Some mishaps marked the first attempts at intercourse until Mawari fashioned correct sexual organs and got it right. Their offspring gave rise to the Waiwai people (Fock 1963:42, 46). In a later episode, the Anaconda People come seeking a Waiwai girl in compensation for the daughter stolen by Mawari. Frustrated in this attempt, they leave behind the first bead and feather ornaments for their Waiwai brothers-in-law.

This second episode opens with all the residents of a certain Waiwai village departing for a festival in another settlement, leaving behind an adolescent girl and her grandmother, who were then visited by the aquatic creatures in human form:

> When the Anaconda-people and their party arrived at the clearing they did not enter the house but danced outside . . . as though they awaited drinks, but in reality they only waited for the girl whom they wanted to take with them as wife. All were clad in ceremonial dress with feather and bead decorations which the Waiwai had never before seen, the tiger fish with long nose feathers, and all had tall arm feathers etc. . . .

. . . Finally the Anaconda-people became resigned to the fact that the girl was not there, and prepared to leave the village. As a last song they sang: "I wanted to lie in the embrace of the old woman's grandchild." They then removed all their feather and bead finery: upper arm and calf bands of beads, ceremonial hair tubes, chin, mouth corner and nose feathers, women's ear ornaments, bead criss-cross. All these things they put in the roof of the house and left there, saying: "Here is something for *poimo* [brother-in-law] to look at when he returns from the dance," and then they departed . . . (Fock 1963:48–49)

Collective dance, song, drink, ornaments—all are widespread Amazonian symbols of beauty, sexuality, and procreativity. It was entirely fitting that the Anaconda People should manifest "joyfulness" and "beauty" in their effort to attract, seduce, and persuade the Waiwai to yield a woman as a return for the one they had lost. Indeed, the Waiwai warn menstruating girls not to bathe in the river, lest they be kidnapped by the Anaconda People who are trying to this day to obtain compensation for their daughter captured by the Waiwai ancestor. This reciprocal kidnapping of each other's women prefigures the logic of proper Waiwai social relations, which should be based on the positive complementary exchange of women through marriage between families and across generations. Such multiple intermarriages solidify alliances by transforming random, isolated instances of sexual intercourse into organized collective relations that can be replicated over time. They transform raw, "natural" sexuality into "social" affinity. Furthermore, they "socialize" the "natural" family by giving it the means to establish connections with outsiders, thereby allowing it to spawn future generations.

Just as vivid, expansive featherwork enables the body to extend beyond itself perceptually, so too the group extends itself by seeking social relations through marriage. Hence the Anaconda People try to balance out the exchange of women and initiate a social structure, as it were; short of success, they leave gifts of beautiful feather- and beadwork adornments as its symbol and its substitute. The myth continues:

When the villagers came . . . they also found all the ornaments that had been left behind by the Anaconda-people . . . They were very enthusiastic about all the finery, but the fine beads proved to be fish eggs which soon became soft and rotten, and the beautiful necklace plate was a small, flat fish which could not keep, either. But the adornments of the Anaconda-people had been so lovely that the Waiwai never forgot them, but spoke of them from generation to generation, saying: "That is how the Anaconda-people looked, they really were beautiful . . . !"

The Waiwai learned from the Anaconda-people the use of feathers for decorative purposes as employed today. (Fock 1963:50)

I would suggest that these brightly colored feather and bead adornments represent the vivid, sexual, biologically and socially generative aspects of male/female and in-law relations. The adornments stand in the place of the potential marital and affinal relations proposed by the Anaconda People. Just as these first-attempt ornaments dissolved but gave the Waiwai the *idea* of beautiful decor, so the adornments left behind suggest the *concept* of affinity; both will be consummated in the future with more appropriate materials—real feathers and beads, and people, not anacondas, as in-laws. Both work on the model of appropriating natural energies and channeling them to social reproductive ends. Because of these associations, such ornaments can stand in the place of potential affines; furthermore, each is the means of acquiring the other. The myth aptly expresses the latent struggle between families related by marriage: the Waiwai do not want to lose their daughters to foreign men/monsters—but they will risk such contacts in order to bring in outsiders' women.[10]

The list of feather ornaments described in the myth are, interestingly enough, mostly those adornments that are made of red toucan and macaw feathers. Recall that the Waiwai say that the Father of Birds, a toucan man, wears the full array of feather ornaments. In other respects too the bright red feathers of the toucan and macaw epitomize the use of featherwork in general. Two other myths, dealing with the curassow and the harpy eagle, complement the myth of the origin of ornaments.[11] These are of course the birds associated with the lowest and uppermost portions of the tripartite arrangement of feather ornaments on the body, bracketing the medial ornaments of toucan/macaw.

The myth of the Curassow Man portrays the dangers of the nuclear family closing in upon itself and refusing to share with others. Summarized briefly, it tells of someone who overhunted the birds until reprimanded by a Curassow Man, who adopted him for a while and fed him well (an inverted image of the care of pet birds by humans). Later, the Curassow Man sent him home with a packet of food that, when opened, would grow abundantly. Showing no restraint, the man and his wife shut themselves up inside their house and greedily consumed the products of the miraculous food packet between themselves in secrecy, sharing with no one. But when he went to open a garden, the man disappeared and was never heard from again (Roe 1990:6–8).

The myth of the Harpy Eagle Man presents a terrifying vision of predation and cannibalism between in-laws. A man who had married into a certain village turned into a harpy eagle one day by donning its "clothes" and then went hunting, using his talons and beak as weapons. His in-laws found out and told his wife, who then quarreled with him. Angered, he left the village, taking his son with him. Both put on eagle "clothes" and became dangerous birds of prey. The Eagle Man returned to capture the villagers, his affines, as food. They baited him by tying a grandmother to a long rope like prey, but no one was able to vanquish him, until finally his brother-in-law succeeded in shooting both the Eagle Man and his son. The villagers tore out their wings and down, which turned into eagles and hawks (Fock 1963:79–82; cf. Roe 1990:8–10).

As I see it, each of these two myths dramatizes tensions in everyday social relations that, if unchecked, threaten to develop to extremes: either movement toward an extreme "interior" or movement toward an extreme "exterior." Both narratives follow out the consequences of antisocial behavior by the main character and end with their disappearance or death. The man in the Curassow myth who shares food with no one but his wife, and the Harpy Eagle Man who treats everyone but his son as food, represent two polar extremes that undermine society. The myth of the Anaconda People represents an attempt to balance these conflicting forces through the gift of feather and bead ornaments. Let us examine these points more closely.

The Curassow myth is about nuclear family relations and physical nurture within the home, as well as the necessity for the family to open its boundaries to participate in a wider network of exchange relations with other households. While nurturant relations within the family are portrayed in the myth as something positive, the family must generalize such relations by exercising self-restraint and generosity towards the rest of the village. Consumption and its more radical form, greediness—one of the most highly censured behaviors in Waiwai society—are ways of undermining or even reversing the ability of the family to reach out and develop constructive social relations with other households. As a unit based on relatively more "natural" relations (sexuality, child rearing, food, etc.), the nuclear family is "socialized" by extending its connections outside itself and being incorporated into the community (Turner 1979). This same impetus to expand relations with a broader network of others should also operate at the intervillage level. In his role as sponsor of these festivals, the village chief (*kayaritomo*) is called "the owner of the drink" (*wooku yosom*), precisely because of the copious amounts of manioc drinks and foods (prepared by his wife) he offers to the guests. He is, in other words, acting as the greedy man of the Curassow myth should have, sharing plentiful foods with as broad a spectrum of people as possible.

At the other extreme is the Harpy Eagle myth. Whereas the the myth of the Curassow Man portrayed the negative outcome of confining "nurture" to an extreme "inside" within the nuclear family, here the Harpy Eagle myth narrates the devastating results of failing to control in-married foreigners, who alienate themselves so drastically that they put themselves beyond the limits of society as a whole and turn into powerful enemy birds. While the Anaconda myth portrayed the competition between affines in the sublimated form of seduction and beautiful ornaments, the Harpy Eagle myth depicts the dissolution of all semblance of civility as the potential threat lurking in affinal ties reels out of control. The in-law relationship, which should be the most "social" of all, is here ejected into nature: the brother-in-law turns into a wild creature and hunts down his affines, using his claws and beak instead of the mediated weapons of bows and arrows. Eagles are never eaten by the Waiwai, nor are almost any carnivores. But in this tale, in-laws become outsiders to an extreme and prey upon the Waiwai in a horrifying cannibalistic inversion. Indeed, the motif of affinity as cannibalism is not uncommon in lowland South America.

When the Eagle Man is finally conquered by his human brother-in-law, the last vestiges of any threat are destroyed when the villagers dismember the birds and tear out their feathers, which then reproduce into the species of eagles and hawks hunted by the Waiwai of today. When contemporary Waiwai make "civilized" arrows with eagle feathers, coat their hair with down, and fabricate "beautiful" ornaments with feathers from these birds, they are in essence reenacting the victory of that archetypal hunter, attaching to their weapons or their bodies symbols of mastery over the powerful external forces embodied in the Eagle Man (Fig. 5.21). Indeed, in covering themselves with eagle feather ornaments, the Waiwai in a certain respect "become" eagles themselves. In many of their rituals, wearing the "clothes" of birds and wild animals is a type of impersonation in which humans avoid becoming the prey of dangerous creatures by wresting their place. Moreover, as Turner (1991:150) says of featherwork and ritual imitation, to "become a [bird] is to become fully human, in the sense of a social being capable of transcending and recreating the structure and meaning of social life."

In summary, these three myths correspond to the three vertical levels of feathers used in ceremonial wear: the myth of the Curassow Man and his copious vegetable foods; that of the Anaconda People and their bead and feather finery, epitomized in the toucan; and that of the Eagle Man and his predation upon his affines. We can imagine a logic, almost a narrative, to this sequence of "reading" the fully adorned male from bottom to top. In each of these myths, the principal characters try to manage relationships that will help them meet basic challenges to social life: how to guarantee sustenance for the nuclear family without sealing its boundaries as a consumption unit and becoming isolated "below" the level of society; how to establish sexual liaisons "between" social groups that can be replicated through marital exchanges that endure over time; and, once having consolidated bonds with affines, how to maintain the relationship without losing control and ejecting it into nature "beyond" the limits of society. The sequence from one myth to the next is correlated with the move from narrower to broader social relationships (nuclear family, lovers, affinal groups), which replicates the

FIGURE 5.21

Drummer wearing eagle down stuck on his face paintings and oiled hair, recalling the mythical hero who conquered the dangerous Eagle Man and tore out his feathers for adornment. Kaxmi village, Brazil. 1985. Photograph by the author.

order of feather ornaments worn on the body from bottom to top (curassow, toucan/macaw, eagle). It is as if the hierarchy of relations comprising the "social body" were visually mapped out in the hierarchy of feather ornaments arranged on the individual's body.

Although the myths narrate the failure of these attempted relationships, they portray society in the making and call attention to what went wrong. It is left to current-day Waiwai to work out viable solutions. The success of that project is symbolically represented by the fully ornamented adult male leader who demonstrates on behalf of society how to master diverse natural powers and harmonize them into an integrated social totality which can endure beyond the lifetime of its individual members.

CONCLUSION

This excursion through the Waiwai world of featherwork has taken us along many paths. To understand the whys of feathers, we had to explore the whys of adornment and beauty in the broader social and cultural context. We looked at the arrangement of feather ornaments upon the body, how this reflected patterns found in nature, and how these in turn symbolized the spatial and temporal organization of the cosmos. This led us to consider how birds and featherwork are correlated with social distinctions between men and women, leaders and followers, visitors and hosts, dominant and subordinate in-laws. By tracing the "cultural biography" of the transformation of "natural" feathers into "social" ornaments, we discovered that the person who wears them is likewise "socialized" and transformed.

This transformation of actor and artifact alike is an example of actions that increase a person's social "extension": "the capacity to develop . . . relations that go beyond the self, or that expand dimensions of the . . . control of an actor" (Munn 1986:11). We saw how the process of beautification involves adorning the body with symbolically potent items constructed from raw materials drawn from certain spatial and temporal domains of the cosmos—and thereby "extending" the actor's reach to such domains, both horizontally and vertically. Thus beautified with visible symbols of cosmological control, the actor—especially a leader like Kiwinik—is able to display himself as a persuasive person who can extend his influence over others in social and political matters. Influence in questions of marriage, residence, resources, labor, and so on is ultimately a matter of influence over the capacity of society to rejuvenate and perpetuate itself.

Featherwork therefore illustrates a theme we have seen running throughout Waiwai culture: that natural potencies from external sources are essential for the vitality of the society, but they must be mastered, incorporated, and reconstituted in order to be usable by society. Waiwai society gives order to such natural, anarchic energies, containing their dangers and thereby rendering them "pacified" (*tawake*); society in turn is rescued from arid sterility by being reinvigorated with generative, reproductive powers (Fig. 5.22). As a result of these complementary transformations, Waiwai society realigns itself in the "center" of the world, radiating its control over the "periphery."

Let us return to our initial problem: understanding the Waiwai concept of "beauty." We have seen many

FIGURE 5.22

*Naturalized dancers who
socialize nature by
dancing with birds
attached to their backs.
Kaxmi village, Brazil.
1985. Photograph by the
author.*

principles involved in it: hierarchy, complementarity, concentricity; spatial and temporal distinctions; competition and cooperation; and so on. These principles are expressed in everyday life in various combinations, but rarely all together; sometimes they may even work at odds with each other or spin off on their own and become exaggerated, as in the myths reviewed above. This is where the periodic rituals of "joyfulness" (*tahwore*) come in, by engaging the entire village and its neighbors in a project of activating and staging *all* of these principles in such a way that they become coordinated and synthesized into a larger totality that embraces them all. The "beauty" of the featherwork worn by the actors is both a *part* of this ritual whole, and a visual model of it—a heightened synecdoche of society itself.

The way the Waiwai use featherwork to express fundamental cultural values is by no means an exceptional or exotic example; indeed, they can teach us something about adornment, beauty, and bodily enhancement in general. As Turner put it,

Decorating, covering, uncovering or otherwise altering the human form in accordance with social notions of everyday propriety or sacred dress, beauty or solemnity, status or changes in status, or on occasion of the violation and inversion of such notions, seems to have been a concern of every human society of which we have knowledge . . . The surface of the body, as the common frontier of society, the social self, and the psycho-biological individual, becomes the symbolic stage upon which the drama of socialisation is enacted, and bodily adornment (in all its culturally multifarious forms, from body-painting to clothing and from feather head-dresses to cosmetics) becomes the language through which it is expressed. (1980:112)

Acknowledgment

Fieldwork data for this paper are drawn from information collected during my doctoral research project on Waiwai exchange systems and ethnic identity, conducted through the Department of Anthropology at the University of Chicago and sponsored by the Department of Anthropology at the Museu Nacional, Universidade Federal do Rio de Janeiro. Financial support for institutional research and fieldwork in Brazil (1982–86) was provided by IIE Fulbright-Hays, the National Science Foundation, and the Organization of American States.

FEATHERS ARE

by Patricia J. Lyon

VIII. Bororo arrows (L–24–10).

"FROM THE POINT OF VIEW OF THE SOCIETIES WHICH PRACTICE THEM, ALL TECHNOLOGIES A

FOR FLYING

FIGURE 6.1

*M*ap showing the approximate locations of ethnic groups in South America (except for Peru, see Figure 6.9) that are discussed in this chapter.

IN THE CONTEXT OF THE SOUTH AMERICAN TROPICAL forest, feathers immediately call to mind elaborate headdresses and other elegant and colorful adornments, especially materials used in ritual. In our own culture, although we spend considerable portions of our excess wealth on ornamentation, we tend to think of it as nonutilitarian. Thus we would consider these feather creations and the use of feathers on them to be nonutilitarian. There is one item, however, virtually a hallmark of Native South American culture, that we can all agree is extremely utilitarian and that depends for its utility on feathers: the arrow. Bows and arrows are the traditional weapon most commonly used in both hunting and warfare throughout lowland South America. Thus, the supremely utilitarian contribution of feathers to both protection and subsistence may be balanced against all their supposedly less useful functions.

In view of their importance to survival, it is startling how little is known about the manufacture and function of South American bows and arrows. Doubtless one reason for the lack of reliable information is that most research on archery, especially experimental work, has been carried out on the English long bow and the Turkish composite, recurved bow. South American bows and arrows, while exceptional for their great length, are neither the most powerful nor the most accurate known and hence of little interest to sport archers.

To illustrate the extent of our ignorance in this area let us consider a few questions regarding the use of feathers on arrows. For example, how necessary are feathers to the functioning of an arrow? Of course the answer depends to a certain extent on how the arrow is to be used. Arrows used for shooting fish seldom bear feathers since they generally need not fly and therefore do not need the steadying effect of feathers. Moreover, wetting would damage feathers. It seems intuitively obvious, however, that arrows expected to fly should have feathers. Nonetheless, a number of peoples, especially in northeastern South America, do not feather any of their arrows. Among these peoples are the Makú of the upper Rio Negro and the Barí of the Colombia-Venezuela border, both of whom are competent hunters and depend heavily on hunting for food (Fig. 6.1). There are also other areas of the world, for example New Guinea, where feathers are not used on arrows. Thus it would appear that feathers are not entirely necessary to the proper functioning of an arrow.

The Cashinahua, however, showed Kenneth Kensinger the difference between the flight of a fletched arrow and that of an unfletched one, and it was obvious to him that for accuracy over any considerable distance, say from the forest floor into a tall tree, feathers are indispensable (Kensinger, personal communication). That some groups do not seem to find such accuracy necessary may suggest a difference in hunting techniques or perhaps in preferred prey. Heath and Chiara, in their discussion of Brazilian hunting techniques (1977:99–105), emphasize the desire of the hunter to approach his prey closely and discuss several means used to achieve this end. But it is hard to get very close to a troop of monkeys or a flock of birds high in the forest canopy.

DEQUATE AS LONG AS THEY PROVIDE FOR THE SOCIETY'S MATERIAL NEEDS." – *RALPH LINTON*

FIGURE 6.2

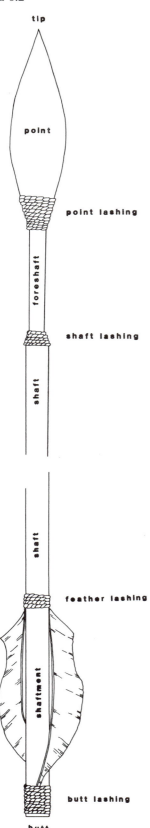

tip

point

point lashing

foreshaft

shaft lashing

shaft

shaft

feather lashing

shaftment

butt lashing

butt

Schematic drawing of a Peruvian arrow as a key to terminology. Note how the feathers are fastened in a spiral. Drawing by the author.

Some experimental data would be useful in settling the question of how necessary feathers are, but little is to be found. The reports I have seen have been preoccupied with distance rather than accuracy so that bows, not arrows, were being tested, clearly a reflection of the experimenters' own preoccupation with archery per se rather than subsistence.

Since we cannot answer the preceding question, and since we are concerned with arrows that do use feathers, let us now consider how many feathers are used. Here we are on somewhat firmer ground. In contrast to the practice in North America, where three feathers are generally used, most South American arrows are fletched with two, relatively large, wing or tail feathers; the specific types of feathers used will be considered shortly. There are, however, reports of three or even four feathers being used in certain, though unspecified, circumstances (Métraux 1949:241), and Heath and Chiara (1977:57) seem to suggest that the use of three feathers was general among Uaupés River groups for certain types of arrows. So we know that two feathers were used except when three or possibly four were. No one, however, suggests why there should be more than two.

One of the more frequently mentioned features of some South American arrows is the attachment of the feathers to the shaft so that they form a spiral, thus causing the arrow to spin in flight (Fig. 6.2). Characteristically, the feathers of Peruvian arrows, for example, are given a 90° spiral by fastening one end of the feather a quarter turn around the shaft from the other end. The use of the spiral is independent of the means used to attach the feather.

Archery specialists often liken the use of spiraled feathers to rifling in a gun, so we find such statements as the following: "It seems not a little remarkable that rifling, which is supposed to be a modern invention, should be discovered and practiced by savages; but it is undoubtedly true" (Hough 1891:63). Apparently no one has ever asked those who do so just why they spiral their feathers, and Heath and Chiara suggest that the spiral is not deliberate, but rather a result of the natural curvature of the large feathers that are used on these arrows (1977:63). This explanation sounds logical except for the fact that the same-sized feathers are also attached without a spiral.

The confusion continues. There are two definite statements that spiraling cannot be used on arrows with three feathers because the spin of the arrow would cause the feathers to be jostled by the string, thus spoiling the aim (Hough 1891:63), or to be injured in loosing (Flint 1891:65). Flint, who experimented with spiraling three feathers on "modern" arrows, further notes that the spiral motion slowed the flight and gave no greater precision (1891:65). Unfortunately for these gentlemen, we have statements from two excellent observers to the effect that the three feathers on the arrows of the Uaupés region were spiraled (Heath and Chiara 1977:57). It does not seem to have occurred to anyone except Mr. Flint to experiment to find out how the use of spiraled feathers affects distance and accuracy.

If we do not know much about the effect of feathers and their arrangement on arrows from the South American tropical forest, there are still a number of things that we do know. Using what we do know we can find out other things.

The bows and arrows used in the South American tropical forest are generally much longer than those of North America. Bows range in length from about one to three meters, arrows about the same. Since those dwellers in the mountains and plains of South America who used bows and arrows used short ones similar to those of North America, it is tempting to explain the differences on the basis of environmental factors. Such explanations are not always convincing, however. There is no obvious advantage, for example, to using a short

FIGURE 6.3

Feathering of some
Peruvian arrow styles (left
to right, three Culina
arrows, two Amahuaca,
two Amarakaeri, and
three Cashinahua). There
are variations in feather
trim, mode of attachment,
butt lashing, and kind of
feather. The Amahuaca
and Amarakaeri have
cemented feathering.

FIGURE 6.4

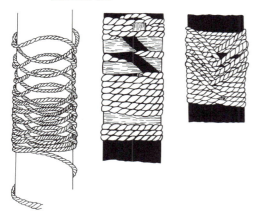

Details of butt lashing of Guarayo, Alto Purús, and Conibo arrows (left to right).

FIGURE 6.5

Front and back (reflected in a mirror) of an Amarakaeri arrow with composite feathers created by combining segments of feathers from two kinds of macaw.

bow in open areas, while maneuvering a long bow and a fistful of equally long arrows through dense tropical growth is not especially easy.

The length of the bow appears to be the limiting factor in any case, since it is impossible to shoot a short arrow with a very long bow of the strength and material generally used in the South American tropical forests, although long arrows could be shot with short bows. Given the distribution of the long bows in South America, it may well be that the crucial factor is the distribution of the palms used by all the dwellers in these areas to make their bows. These palms split into long straight pieces most suitable to shaping and smoothing into bows, and their wood is both strong and flexible.

Arrows are generally, but not always, somewhat longer than the bows with which they are used. The length of the feathers used depends to a certain extent on the way they are fastened to the shaft. Heath and Chiara (1977:51) give an average length of about 15 cm for the fletching of Brazilian arrows, but I found the cemented feathering of some Peruvian arrows to be some 5–7 cm longer (Fig. 6.3). The need for large feathers limits the number of birds suitable as feather sources. The most commonly used feathers seem to be from the wing and tail of the curassow. Wing, and occasionally tail, feathers of the macaws are also used, as are wing feathers of the guan and feathers from various (usually unspecified) hawks and eagles. Much less commonly mentioned are vultures (both black and turkey), perhaps because they are seldom killed. I found two mentions of duck and one of jabiru stork. This listing differs from that of Heath and Chiara, who list curassow, macaw, white heron, wild duck, hawks, "etc." (1977:51); but is in agreement with Steinen (1894:230). Given the nature of the sample, such disagreement is probably insignificant.

Within any community of arrow makers, the feathers of only one or two kinds of birds are usually employed. The Sirionó of eastern Bolivia, for example, insisted that they used only curassow and harpy eagle, the latter only on bamboo-pointed arrows for hunting larger game (Holmberg 1969:32); nevertheless, Holmberg also saw a few guan feathers in use. Ryden, in contrast, lists only the guan as being used by the Sirionó (1941:59). Guppy (1958:262) reports that the Waiwai used harpy eagle, macaw, and curassow, while Yde allowed them only curassow or guan and harpy eagle (1965:108, 128, 131–32). Boglár (1965) reports that the Nambiquara use curassow, parrot, or eagle feathers. The Palikur (Nimuendajú 1926:35) use mostly duck and hawk, while the Cashinahua use curassow and macaw most commonly (Rabineau 1975:222–24), but will use harpy eagle and vulture when such feathers are available (Kensinger, personal communication). The Yanomamö and their relatives seem to use only curassow feathers (Biocca 1966:158; Wilbert 1972:28). Henry reports that the Kaingáng fletch two of their three types of arrow with feathers of the black-fronted piping-guan, while hawk feathers are used for the third, iron-pointed type because, he was told, the hawk feathers "come from such a powerful bird" (1964:167). Lane (1959), reporting on a collection of Kaingáng arrows in the Museu Paulista, provides the following identifications: macaw tail feathers (fletching 36.5 cm long), ornate hawk-eagle, bare-faced curassow, red-throated caracara, king vulture, Muscovy duck, turkey vulture, and a dark hawk identified as *Hypomophus urubitinga*. The two iron-tipped arrows in the collection bear feathers of the ornate hawk-eagle.

We all recall Western movies in which the hero glances at the arrow still quivering in front of his nose, and utters knowingly, "Aha! Apaches." While such knowledge is not easily won, a detailed study of many arrows reveals numerous small differences that may be used to distinguish among the groups that made them. Indeed, there are repeated statements that individual arrow owners can be identified, certainly a useful feature in the case of a communal hunt, for example.

FIGURE 6.6

Amarakaeri arrow with composite feathers. The shaftment is covered with small red macaw feathers.

FIGURE 6.7

Stylistic differences in the attachment of feathers to Peruvian arrows. On the top, the feather rib was lashed flat against the shaft; the rib of the bottom example was partly fastened, then doubled over, and finally lashed in place.

Identification may be based not only on such gross differences as the shape of the points used and the material from which the shaft is made, but also on less obvious elements. For example, cotton thread is generally used to secure the wooden point and the extremes of the feathers to the shaft, as well as to cap the end of the shaft in the absence of a carved or inserted nock. The way in which this thread is wrapped, sometimes combined with other materials such as grass or feather tufts, helps define a given style of arrow manufacture (Fig. 6.4). The Sharanahua of eastern Peru use two-ply cotton thread to secure the points and feathers to their arrows, as do many other groups. The Sharanahua, however, use two plies of contrasting colors, so that parallel diagonal bands of color run down any section of lashing (Lyon 1987). There are several ways in which feathers may be attached to the shaft and many in which they may be trimmed before attachment, or they may not be modified at all. None of these variables seems to alter the efficiency of the projectile in any way.

Pragmatism is the order of the day when it comes to bringing home dinner, and any elaboration found to interfere with the proper functioning of the weapon would surely soon be abandoned. Arrows, to be effective, need not be beautiful or finely finished but only straight, rigid, and as sharp as necessary. Nevertheless, throughout South America we find much more care and elaboration expended on them than are needed to provide a reliable weapon. The considerable time and effort spent on such elaborations suggests that they may have functions not immediately obvious to outsiders.

In a study of the arrows of eastern Peru, I found that individual cultures are readily distinguishable by arrow style, but also fall together into larger stylistic units that share a number of features serving to distinguish them from adjacent units. In general, there is not a single characteristic, but several that serve to assign a given arrow to its proper group, although some features are limited to a single group or stylistic unit. Such a feature is the Sharanahua use of contrastingly colored cotton plies.

The Amarakaeri, uniquely to my knowledge, sometimes create composite feathers by alternating segments of two different kinds of macaw wing feathers, one that is blue on one side and red on the reverse and the other blue with a yellow back (Fig. 6.5). The result, after trimming, appears to be a single feather that is solid blue on one side and striped red-and-yellow on the other. This technique is possible only to an arrow maker using cemented feathering, in which the feather is split down the rib, leaving only a paper-thin sliver holding the feather barbs, and then the rib segment is fastened to the arrow shaft with beeswax. After both quills have been glued down, they are carefully lashed through the barbs with very fine plant fiber, sometimes palm, which is finally covered with a coating of beeswax or resin. The Amarakaeri sometimes elaborate still further by covering this area between the feathers (the shaftment) with tiny red macaw feathers, a treatment they share with the Bororo (Fig. 6.6).

The Bororo expend great effort in the adornment of their arrows. *The Enciclopédia Bororo* devotes to arrows more than 20 pages, many spent in listing specific decorations that belong to particular subclans (Albisetti and Venturelli 1962:932–53). Such decorations are located in the shaftment area and generally include one or more kinds of feather often combined with other elements such as porcupine quills, paint, or thread patterns. The feathers may be tied, as tufts or rings, to cane shafts or glued in a mosaic onto palm shafts. One decoration, for example, consists of little tufts of red and white feathers together with tiny motifs of porcupine quill braided with black cotton thread. "Slight differences in the disposition of the feathers or of the braids mark the subclan that owns it" (ibid.:947). Another subclan's

FIGURE 6.8

Points and foreshafts of three Peruvian arrows (left to right, Amarakaeri, Amahuaca, and Cashinahua). Point shapes differ as do the lashing patterns, and the length and thickness of the foreshaft. Painted patterns on the Cashinahua lashings are the same as those used on other artifacts and in body painting.

arrows are marked with small rings of black, red, and yellow feathers, and so forth.

Among the Peruvian arrows, I found significant differences in the way the butt end of the arrow was treated, in each of the feather lashings, in the way the feather was attached and trimmed as well as the kinds of feathers used, in treatment of the shaftment, the shaft, foreshaft, and point, and in the materials that were used (Lyon 1987) (Fig. 6.7, 6.8). It may be that, as among the Bororo, some of these differences are the property of certain social groups to which the owner belongs, as is apparently the case of the geometric designs used by the Cashinahua, for example, to decorate some kinds of points as well as the thread wrapping on some arrows (Dawson 1975:147–48). Without further field investigation, however, there is no way to tell what other features in the Peruvian arrows are thought by their makers to be significant or what they mean.

Even without knowing their precise meaning we can use the stylistic groupings to say something about Native South American culture. For example, a number of anthropologists and archaeologists believe that there is a connection between language and culture such that art styles follow linguistic groupings. In eastern Peru this belief has been reinforced by the existence of a large number of groups belonging to the same language family most of whom share similar pottery styles. My research was designed to find out whether the relationship was peculiar to pottery in this area, or whether all material objects would follow language distributions.

I was able to establish four stylistic units, each named for its general location (Lyon 1987). The Ucayali Style includes three groups (Cashibo, Isconahua, Conibo-Shipibo), all of whom speak Panoan languages. The Urubamba-Apurímac Style includes three groups (Machiguenga, Piro, Campa), all of whom are Arawak-speakers. The Alto Purús Style includes four groups, three of whom (Cashinahua, Sharanahua, Amahuaca) speak Panoan, while the fourth member (Culina) speaks an Arawak language. The Madre de Dios Style includes three Harakmbut-speaking groups (Wachipaeri, Amarakaeri, Mashco) and the Tacana-speaking Guarayo (Fig. 6.9). The factor connecting the styles in all cases appears to be geographic rather than linguistic communication.

While this finding may seem esoteric and far from the cares of our daily world, it can be important in how we interpret the past as revealed by archaeology. While, as in the Panoan case cited above, modern distributions may show a tendency for style and language to coincide, they also often show, as in my study, some lack of coincidence. A study of Guatemalan pottery, for example, shows historical factors to have operated in such anomalous cases (Reina and Hill 1978:205–206). The archaeologist, however, seldom has access to historical information regarding the materials he or she is excavating. Therefore, in any given case, there is no way to be sure whether two groups with the same pottery or arrow style actually spoke the same language or not.

It is likely that the growing interest in and emphasis on ecology will lead to more and better studies of South American bows and arrows. The well-established and intricate connection between Native South Americans and their environment must certainly extend to the weapons they use to acquire their food. The rapid replacement of bows and arrows by firearms, combined with the encroachment of outsiders on traditional hunting territories, has already resulted in changes in traditional practices. The fact that both guns and ammunition must be purchased not only establishes a relationship of dependence on the dominant culture but also requires the acquisition of money, not infrequently by the sale of pelts of endangered species. Some groups, or at least individuals, however, still prefer the bow and arrow since it is a silent weapon and permits killing more than one animal in a group without frightening the rest away. Some also say that the noise of gunshots results in the general movement of game out of areas where shooting occurs. Nonetheless, given the prestige of meat in South American cultures (Kensinger 1989; Siskind 1973:84–85) and the general

FIGURE 6.9

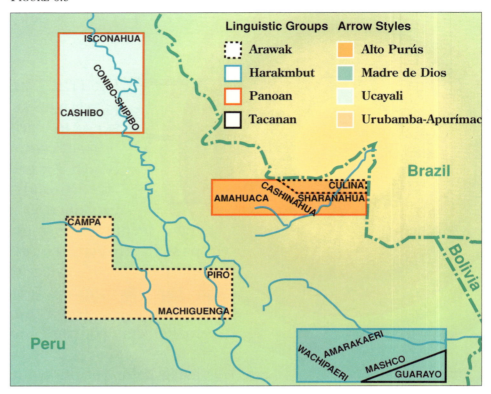

Map showing the location of arrow styles, and their component linguistic and ethnic groups in central and southeastern Peru.

advantage of guns over bows and arrows in securing it, the ultimate fate of the latter would appear sealed. Such replacement will surely result in increased cultural distortion, reducing still more our chance of understanding how these people have managed to live in the tropical forest for so many thousands of years without destroying it as we are doing today.

Acknowledgments

Research on Peruvian arrows was funded by a Museum Research Fellowship from the Wenner-Gren Foundation for Anthropological Research. It was carried out in 1970–71 at the Lowie Museum of Anthropology, University of California at Berkeley; the American Museum of Natural History, New York; the Peabody Museum, Harvard University; and the Laboratory of Anthropology, University of Illinois, Urbana, all of which were wonderfully helpful. All the specimens illustrated here are courtesy of the Lowie Museum of Anthropology, University of California at Berkeley. The black-and-white photographs were taken by William M. Lake, the color ones by Lee Brumbaugh.

I especially wish to express my gratitude to Kenneth M. Kensinger not only for contributions to the original research but also for his aid and encouragement in the writing of this paper.

FIGURE 7.1

*R*ikbaktsa headdress *(89–1–5) collected in 1983 from the Juruene River, Brazil. This is a traditional chief's headgear. The woven headband of this headdress is covered with feathers from the Scarlet Macaw, Blue-and-yellow Macaw, and toucan together with human hair. Body feathers are also tied to cords which hang vertically, giving the illusion of a rope of feathers.*

FOR THE INDIANS OF SOUTH AMERICA, ORAL narratives such as myths, stories, and legends serve to clarify the otherwise unexplainable. The brilliant coloration characteristic of many species of South American avifauna is believed by some "traditional" South Amerindian peoples to be explained in mythological events. Their ancestors have accounted for such radiant colors in various legends passed along through generations, and it is to these communicative devices that we must turn in order to find their "traditional" understanding. Such legends reflect not only their point of view, but the importance the birds, and their magnificent plumage, hold for the Indians.

Oral narratives frequently explain that avian color results from the birds having been "painted" by certain agents, such as blood, fluids from internal organs, and fire. The incidence of such stunning colors (reds, yellows, oranges, blues, whites, blacks, and greens) on the feathers of birds may have required justification, and it is within the confines of mythology that the rationale for the origins of this process can be found. Among nonliterate societies, such as those in South America, myth presents an elaborate stage, on which actors portray certain events. These depictions often revolve around some supernatural event which explains a puzzling incident or phenomenon. In the myths presented in this essay, birds are the actors in a drama that explains the creation of the present-day colors in their feathers.

It must be remembered that although some of these stories do not appear to be wholly rational, and deviate from accepted scientific knowledge, such myths need not conform to modern understanding; the information they convey is not to be taken literally by us, but as an account passed down over many generations, and part of the "traditional" learning of children. Contemporary ornithology states that many species of tropical birds have developed colorful plumage because camouflage is not necessary. This runaway evolution occurs as a result of the minimal threat of

"IN CEREMONY AND IN MYTHOLOGY THE EXPRESSIVE SIDE OF LIFE APPEARS I

OF AVIAN COLORATION
BLOOD & FIRE

by *Jon F. Pressman*

IX. *Rikbaktsa headdress (89–1–5).*

ORMS PLAINLY RELATED TO THE PERSISTENCE OF SOCIETY." – *ROBERT REDFIELD*

predation, and bright feathers do not place the bird at a disadvantage (Ayensu 1980:82). Some South Amerindians are perhaps aware of this explanation, yet still retain "traditional" lore because it is an integral part of their cultural heritage.

As is commonly the case with myth, not all the members of a given society have knowledge of the complete story, and opinions regarding content do vary among individuals; what is interesting is that although the versions may be different, there is a central theme among them that remains the same. The overall relevance of these myths regarding the coloration of the birds is that they describe a cause and effect, a "curiosity" shared by linguistically and geographically diverse groups among the South American population.

Among the mythological conceptions concerning the colors of birds, an extensive pattern exists in the mythological narratives from many South American groups. There are two general means that they use to account for the birds' color: (1) birds bathing primarily in the blood, and less frequently in the fluids from internal organs, of a mythical character, often an animal, and (2) birds burned by fire, or other hot items. The similarities in the narratives among the 15 societies that have a "blood" myth, and the six societies that have a "fire" myth, are quite pronounced.

Most of the narratives that follow have been collected and translated from the original Indian languages by ethnographers and linguists who spent time observing and participating in the life of a group. Some of the legends may have been actively sought by the anthropologists, or freely given by one or more informants. The content could have been affected by the translation, or by the presence of a stranger, but the core concepts constitute a basic portrait of the Amerindians' world-view. These concepts of the "traditional" Indian groups warrant our attention because they attempt to explain how the birds came to be what they are today.

The two agents of coloration (blood and fire) will be presented separately, and a selection of myths will document the findings. All narratives, from as many various groups as possible, have been selected to underline the basic processes responsible, from the Indians' viewpoint, for avian coloration. Yet not all the groups in South America are represented in our sample, due to the unavailability of narratives. One of the best sources from which to draw information on some of the groups (Toba, Chamacoco, Warao, Mataco, Chorote, Bororo, Guajira, Nivakle, and Mocovi) is the compilations of myths edited by Johannes Wilbert and Karin Simoneau (see References). This series contains independently published myths, and myths collected by individuals that have not been previously published. Only those myths related to our subject (birds) were selected from this and other sources, and this sample constitutes only a fraction of thousands of myths explaining or describing many other natural and supernatural phenomena besides avian coloration.

FIGURE 7.2

Map indicating those groups which have a "blood" myth.

BLOOD ON THE FEATHERS

Blood is highly regarded by many "traditional" groups of people (Fig. 7.2). Describing the Shuar Indians of Ecuador, Victor Von Hagen observes the power and value ascribed to blood by this group:

> I noticed the great place that blood plays in the ceremonies of the Indian. The native does not consider blood in its material aspects as we do. We regard it as a liquid that circulates in accordance with the impulses given to it by the contraction of the heart. Its coagulation on leaving the body we recognize as a chemical action and a property common to all blood. But to the primitives, the coagulation is most important. For them, far from being a mere liquid without which life would not function, it is endowed with a great supernatural power. It is a vital principle of immeasurable potency. It has magic virtue, and helps as a charm against witchcraft. (1937:160–61)

Not intended to represent the opinions of all the groups discussed, this statement gives some insights as to why blood is such an important fluid.

A common process of avian coloration involves the birds bathing in the blood of some mythical character. This individual is often a foe attempting to do the birds harm, and when defeated, this figure colors the birds with blood. One learns through myth that the blood, due to subsequent coagulation, putrefaction, or unexplained change, can be responsible for several colors besides the typical deep red. The colored fluids of internal organs, such as the liver and spleen, also figure in the myths, as well as the color of fatty tissue. In this manner, the myths account not only for the reds of plumage, but the blues, yellows, and greens.

The "blood" myths have been ordered according to a preliminary classification of stylistic region, used for the distribution of feather objects (see Fig. 9.4); this arrangement shows distinctive regional similarities in the myths. Comments will follow each group, mentioning points of interest when comparative analysis is possible. Similarities in narratives provide a certain marker to each region, and supply a basis for cultural distinctions to be made among different regions.

Northern Montaña Region

Wayú (Guajiro) People

Maleiwa [culture hero] was shut up inside the stone. Then he called all the ants and they began to dig. "There! We've made a little path!" said the ant. Maleiwa squeezed through, but in the process he scraped against the stones, and he bled copiously. Then he called the birds. "Go and fetch me a cup!" he ordered. Filling the cup with blood he called the parrot, the cardinal, and many other birds, which remained red since that time. "Bathe in this blood!" he said to them. (Perrin in Wilbert and Simoneau 1986:75)

This single narrative for the Guajiro of the Northern Montaña region is an example which may contain elements that have a wider distribution. The blood that colors the birds is that of a culture hero, Maleiwa, who orders the birds to bathe. It should be noted

FIGURE 7.3

Asháninka string of birds (SA 635a) collected in 1913. Birds: Paradise Tanager, Blue Dacnis, Green Honeycreeper, Black-necked Aracari, Turquoise Tanager, Green-and-gold Tanager, and a species of toucan.

that only those birds like the parrot and cardinal have a red color because they obeyed and bathed in the blood. In this case, at least, the mythological blood coincides with the color of natural blood, and no other coloring agents are mentioned.

Southern Montaña Region

Asháninka (Campa) People

His [serpent] blood forms a lake, and at his bidding birds came to bathe therein. Some of the birds, including all the sacred birds, bathe only once in the blood and emerge with beautiful plumage. But others, including the demonic birds, are greedy, not satisfied with their good looks after bathing once, and bathe again, emerging with ugly plumage. (Weiss 1975:328)

Shipibo People

Evil Inca falls into a trap, a hole in the ground. He is killed with arrows and his body is dragged out of the pit, blood spurting from his many wounds. Then various birds, allies of men, bathe in his blood, those who are the first getting their brilliant red colors, those last receiving their dusty orange colors. Finally, the tardiest bird swallows his liver and is tainted a dark green by the bile. (Roe 1982:184)

Cashinahua People

One day the animals all decided to kill Yawashikonawa [a selfish mythical monster]. They decided to make a tunnel to near his home, and then shoot him with arrows. After several attempts, a tunnel was made, and the bow-men took up positions. They were "paucares" of the Isko family. They are birds [oropendolas] that live in bands, make great nests in the shape of bags, sometimes thirty in a single tree. Boi Isko shot first. He missed [instead] hitting the roasted manioc Yawashikonawa was eating. In an eyeblink, Koman Isko shot and killed Yawashikonawa. In memory of this, Boi Isko has a white beak, like the manioc, and Koman Isko has a small red spot on the point of his beak: the blood of Yawashikonawa. Some animals, curious to see Yawashikonawa's gall bladder, cut him up. It was enormous and they began to play with it. The ancestor of Ishana, the bird they call "azulejo" [blue jay], punctured it. The contents wet his body and he turned blue. Other birds also took a bit of the bile of Yawashikonawa and they have brilliant tones in their feathers, blue or green. (d'Ans 1975:82)

In the myths from the three groups of the Southern Montaña region, we can see several corresponding points. In each story, a definite sequence seems to emerge regarding the order in which the birds gain their respective colors. The Shipibo narrative demonstrates this well when three distinct episodes of coloration are described, and the birds who have participated in each sequence all emerge with a different color. According to the Shipibo, birds that are red have taken part in the first "bath," birds that are second to arrive receive a dusty orange color (presumably from the dwindling supply of blood), and finally, the last birds to appear gain a dark green color, not from the blood (perhaps the quantity of blood was not enough to color the last bird), but from the green fluid of the liver.

The Cashinahua legend describes something similar, but with four different coloring periods. The first bird gains a white beak from the burned manioc, the second acquires a red spot on his beak from the actual blood, and the third bird, having punctured the gall bladder, is stained by the gall fluid, which is blue. The fourth bird gains a blue-green color from being stained by the monster's bile. No single color seems to be more important than any other in the myths, but according to the Campa, those "greedy" birds pay for their avarice by having ugly plumage.

Guianas Region

Waiwai People

When Petali [anaconda] had been cut in half the riverbanks swam with blood . . . the bird people bathed in this with the result that they were transformed into proper birds. After a bath in the serpent's blood a heavy shower took place . . . so the Kworo-yenna [red-and-green macaw people] hastily began constructing a house in which to shelter. Some bird people, however, did not build houses and therefore lost the red colour they had acquired . . . the woodpecker people hurriedly placed some leaves over their heads, and consequently these birds now have red heads. The Shafi-yenna [blue-and-yellow macaw people] arrived [too late for a bath in the blood]. However, some gall was left and they bathed in that instead. For this reason they became yellow, but where the rain fell on them they turned blue. As the rain also dripped through the roof blue patches likewise appeared on the wings of the kworo. (Fock 1963:63–65)

Warao People

The woodpecker had just carved her [daughter of the anaconda] sex to make her a suitable bride for the sun, master of all birds, when out poured suddenly a flood of blood. With it the head of the red-headed woodpecker was stained . . . The macaw arrived and stained his breast. But her blood [daughter of the anaconda] had the peculiarity of changing its color; luckily those birds with the brightest colors were stained first. Later the blood turned white like milk, and the herons came and were stained white . . . even later when the blood had coagulated and putrefied the zamuro [vulture] arrived and rolled around in it and was left, since then, painted black. (Barral in Roe 1982:184)

In the two Guianas myths, various stages of coloration are described, and each is associated with a different hue. The Waiwai legend describes how certain birds (red macaws and woodpeckers) bathed in the blood, and then took action to retain their red color by protecting themselves from the rain, while other birds neglected to do so and lost their redness. Other birds (blue-and-yellow macaws) arrived later, too late for a bath in the blood (akin to the "tardy" bird in the Shipibo myth), and therefore had to resort to the yellow coloration afforded by the gall fluid, not blue as formerly seen in the Cashinahua myth. For the Waiwai, the bird is blue because it has been stained by rain.

The Warao myth presents the unique property of the blood to change, and the changes in the color of the blood result in different colors for the various bathing periods. The blood is first red, then white, and then black, changes that coincide with the stages of coagulation and putrefaction. Each bird reflects in its color the timing and order in which it received its coloration. Although in myth anything can happen, in this region the phenomena presented in the myths appear to be very close to the natural processes of blood. Blood left out in the open does coagulate and finally putrefy.

Mato Grosso Region

Mundurucú People

The eagle called upon the other birds to help him devour the terrapin; but first they had to open his shell. The toucan pounded at the hard shell with the side of his beak (which accounts for its present shape), but to no avail. Then the carpinteiro, a kind of penicapau [woodpecker], pecked at the shell until it broke. The birds all ate and decorated themselves with the red blood, the blue fluid from the gall bladder, and the yellow fat. The toucan put the blue fluid around his eyes and placed yellow fat on the trunk of his tail and in a band across his breast. He also placed blood on his tail. The penicapau put blood on his head, and the pipira [tanager] covered himself completely with blue gall. The mutum [curassow] put blood on his legs and beak and then called out to the galsa [unidentified bird], who had just arrived, "Let us smear some white clay upon ourselves. You go first." He did this to keep the galsa from using any of the terrapin dyes. The galsa covered himself with the white clay and then said, "Now you." The mutum, who did not intend to paint himself white, flew away, but the galsa reached out to grab him. He caught only the tail of the mutum, which to this day is white. (Murphy 1958:128–29)

Rikbaktsa People

. . . the ancestors [the birds] were out one day in the forest and found their ancestor, the sloth, up in a tree eating fruit. They [birds] asked him to throw some down, but he refused, saying that the fruit was not ripe. They threatened him, saying that they would rip out his tail. He continued to refuse, and so they ripped out his tail. Various birds poured the sloth's blood onto parts of their bodies: the two species of red macaw. The red crown parakeet sulked, and his red feathers thus darkened; he cried as he cries today. The yellow macaw . . . had none, and covered himself with corn meal. (Hahn 1976:60)

Mehinaku People

The redness [of hawk's feathers] is men's blood from ancient times. (Gregor 1985:136).

Different colorants are found in the myths of the Mato Grosso region, ranging from blood (red) and gall fluid (blue) to fat or cornmeal (yellow) and clay (white). It is important to note that in both the Mundurucú and the Rikbaktsa myths (as in the Cashinahua and Warao myths), specific birds are the creators of the blood flow, making it available to the other birds. This is done by shooting arrows (Cashinahua), carving (Warao), pecking (Mundurucú), and ripping (Rikbaktsa) at the involuntary donors.

FIGURE 7.4

Chamacoco anklet (SA 955a). Fiber netting, comprised of numerous interwoven and knotted fiber strings, to which are tied body feathers, forming a dense mat. Bird: parrot.

Chamacoco People

When he [eagle] played his whistle [to acknowledge that he had severed the leg of a boy] she [woman] arranged the containers below. Soon afterward the blood came flowing from above where the leg [of a boy] was. Whenever a container was full she would move it aside and put another in its place. All kinds of colors resulted: yellow, black, blue, green, white, red; all the colors that exist. They filled the containers. Then he [eagle] told her that he wanted to bathe in the blood, that he wanted to be painted. The woman asked: "What colors do you want?" "Only black and white; that's all." She painted the eagle's body completely black and painted white stripes on his tail feathers. She left his beak white, like the beak of the hawk. When she finished he went away. Then she said: "Now I can paint the other birds any color they wish!" She called all the birds and asked each one: "What color do you want?" The heron wanted to be white, and she painted him white and sent him away. Another bird wanted to be red, and she painted him red. Another wanted to be red and blue, and she painted him those colors. One wanted to be white, another wanted yellow legs, and yet another wanted black legs. She gave them all what they wanted. (Cordeu in Wilbert and Simoneau 1987a:268)

Chorote People

A heavy stream of blood came out of Sakiti [man-eating celestial eagle]! His blood was of different colors. The strongest people went into the stream, stayed there, and were colored. Each one selected the colors he now has; they all came from Sakiti's blood. That was how all the people who are now birds got their colors, for earlier they had none; they were white. Wosiet, the cardinal, immersed himself in the blood and painted himself red; Petohoi, the great kiskadee, painted himself yellow; Ele, the parrot, painted himself green; Som, the blue magpie, painted himself yellow and blue. But they pulled Eskinini, the piculet, away from the blood, and that is why he does not have enough color. (Siffredi in Wilbert and Simoneau 1985:194)

Mataco People

Takjuaj [mythical man] was very swollen, and the birds, who were people, talked among themselves, saying: "Who is missing?" "Who is missing?" "Who can save this man?" Then they saw that a little bird was missing, the very small woodpecker, and as the rest of the birds couldn't do anything, they called upon him. The woodpecker gave one peck in the wax that stopped up the mouth and pulled it out. The blood of Takjuaj splattered over the birds. The dirty blood farthest in flowed over the raven; that is why it is black. All the birds that have red feathers were spotted by the blood of Takjuaj. (Palavecino in Wilbert and Simoneau 1982a:198)

Toba People

The family returned and found Fox sleeping. They gathered mud and stopped up his anus, his limbs, his mouth, his eyes, and his ears [because he had killed their child]. They stopped him up completely. Fox swelled up. Nobody was there to remove the mud. All the birds with strong beaks tried to cut the mud with their beaks. The yulo [unidentified bird] came and struck him near the ear. Blood spurted and stained him. That is why yulo birds have a red throat. (Métraux in Wilbert and Simoneau 1982b:249)

The woodpecker had to make the fox lie down, for while he was standing up nothing could be seen. Then the bird started to stab the fox as though to pierce him completely. He was stabbing and stabbing. As he pierced the fox, water and blood spurted out. They say that the cap of the woodpecker was white, but it turned red from the spurt of the fox's blood. The cardinal was standing a bit further back, and he got some of the blood on his crest too. Since then cardinals have had red crests. The ovenbird was further back and he only got a little bit on him. Ever since then the ovenbird's feathers have been a dark brownish color, because he got spattered just a little bit. (Teran in Wilbert and Simoneau 1982b:250 and Wilbert and Simoneau 1989:293)

Mocovi People

Woodpecker told Fox that he would begin pecking at his anus [which was clogged]. A whole bevy of birds came to see Woodpecker cure Fox. Finally Woodpecker pecked through the clay and opened up Fox's anus. Blood and fecal material splashed out. It splattered Woodpecker's head and ever since then he has had a red cap. The cardinal was there, too. He got some of it on his head and he, too, since then has had a red head. All the birds who have some red feathers in their plumage have them because they were there on that occasion. (Teran in Wilbert and Simoneau 1988:84)

Nivakle People

The woodpecker went over and got under the buzzard's wing. After he got under the buzzard's wing, he began to peck. He pecked little by little, then he would rest and listen. The he went back to pecking. When he saw that the blood was about to gush out he pecked even harder. The others [birds] were very frightened when the buzzard's blood began to flow and to gush out. They all jumped on the woodpecker and threw him aside, about a hundred meters away. Then they all began to bathe in the buzzard's blood, but it harmed them and itched. When they felt their bodies itch, they bathed again and cleaned themselves with ashes and coal. There were birds who cleaned themselves with the ashes in order to clean off the blood which caused them to itch, and these all became white again. Those who bathed in coal became black. Only their eyes remained red, because they could not paint them or rub out the blood. The flamingo and the spoonbill were the only ones who could stand the itching caused by King Buzzard's blood. That is why they have remained red until now. (Tomasini in Wilbert and Simoneau 1987b:240)

Of all the regions, the Gran Chaco gives us the largest number of myths dealing with this process by which birds become colored by blood, and several distinct regional observations can be made. In the myths of this region, the Nivakle, Mocovi, Toba, and Mataco all say that the woodpecker was responsible for creating the initial flow of blood by pecking at various individuals. In the Toba and Mocovi narratives, that individual is the fox; in the Nivakle and Mataco it is the buzzard and a mythical being. Unlike the other societies, which account for only the red of feathers (with the exception of the Mataco, who believe the black color results from "dirty blood"), the Chorote and the Chamacoco both depict the blood's transformation into all the other colors, or suggest that it contained all the necessary colors for "painting" from the start. Also in

FIGURE 7.5

Map indicating those groups which have a "fire" myth.

only the Chamacoco and Chorote narratives, the birds possessed free will regarding their coloration: they got to choose the colors they presently have. It is important to note that although these people have myths to explain brilliant avian color, they do not use these feathers in their ornaments. This absence of brightly colored feathers is without explanation, yet is a distinct regional "marker."

Conclusion

In this discussion of "blood" myths, we note that several common mythological elements are present in most of the narratives. Blood is invariably associated with the color red. Various societies present several agents for the colors blue, yellow, green, black, orange, and white, but only one agent, blood, for the color red. Another pattern that runs through many of the stories is the notion of sequential coloration, that is, birds who appear at different times acquire different colors. One final theme is that the blood and fluids did not simply appear, but were "donated" by another individual. The stories are quite specific in that they not only account for the origin of avian color, but also tell who and what the source of the colors was.

FIRE ON THE PLUMES

Many groups in South America have myths which tell of birds having gained their coloration through exposure to fire, or hot items such as coal, ashes, and smoke. Further, in some instances, brightly colored birds are the products of humans' being consumed by flames, and subsequently emerging from the fire, transformed into various avian species. This theme not only accounts for the birds pigments derived from the colors of the flames, ashes, coal, and smoke, but also explains the metamorphosis into bird from nonbird, specifically, a person. Fire colors the already existing birds, and transforms humans into birds, establishing in these myths a close kinship between humans and birds. These myths from different groups are presented and analyzed for similarities and differences.

Southern Montaña Region

Cashinahua People

One day Chere, the parrot, tired of not having fire and eating raw corn, decided to steal it from Yawashikonawa [by making disturbing noises]. Furious, Yawashikonawa's wife picked up a fistful of embers and threw it. Crying more quietly, the parrot waited until they were not paying attention, then he picked up the ember in his beak and flew away. At that time, Chere had a big beak like a toucan. The other birds made a pyramid of their bodies around the embers, to protect it from the rain [sent by Yawashikonawa]. Closest was Shawan, the red macaw, who got his color from the live fire. Above him was Kain, the big-headed macaw, a little less red. Then the rest of the birds, ending

FIGURE 7.6

Kayapó headdress (89–1–12a,b) from the Mato Grosso, Brazil, collected in 1980. The colorful yellow and red feathers are tied to a cotton band and suspended in a bent fiber bow frame. Birds: Oropendola and Scarlet Macaw.

with Oka, the locrero [black cacique]; his body is black because only smoke reached his feathers. (d'Ans 1975:77)

Although the myth only briefly mentions that the parrot used to have a large beak, it can be inferred that fire affected the physical appearance (size) of the bird's beak: the parrot's beak was shortened because it was burned away. In the myth, the intensity of the red coloration is due to the proximity of the bird to the fire. Those birds with the most vibrant reds were closest to the flames, while those farther away had only the smoke touch their feathers.

Guianas Region

Taruma People

Two or three days after this Duid [culture hero] was looking after the fire when a maroudi [unidentified bird] picked it up and flew away with it. When Ajijeko [another hero] came home Duid told him of the loss of the fire again. The maroudi was called back; she returned the fire undamaged, but her neck was so burned that it has always remained red. (Farabee 1918:146)

It is clear that the bird acquired its red neck because it had come into contact with the flames. The maroudi is an unidentified species.

Mato Grosso Region

Bororo People

All the Bororo that threw themselves in [the midst of the flames] emerged immediately, transformed into birds of magnificent plumage, painted the prettiest colors or decorated with pleasing designs. Magure turned into a splendid macaw with red plumage, but Okoge Erugo who had barely reached the periphery of the fire emerged transformed into a macaw with yellow feathers, as the heat had not been sufficient to turn them red. The Bororo say that in the old days all the birds already existed, but that only after this event did they have different, many-colored feathers. (Albisetti and Venturelli in Wilbert and Simoneau 1983:134)

Kayapó People

. . . the jacu and the jaho (two small game birds), ran along swallowing all the sparks that fell from the [stolen fire] log, thus acquiring their red throats and thereby "eating" fire. (Turner in Roe 1982:211)

In the Bororo myth, even when undergoing transformation, the birds obtain their respective colors in relation to their distance from the fire. The notion of heat in this case is essential to coloration, as if this myth follows a simple rule: the hotter the bird, the brighter or redder its color. The macaw with red plumage was colored in the hottest part of the fire, and subsequently became red, a primary color in the flames. The other macaw obtained only yellow feathers because he had reached only the periphery of the flames. The Kayapó myth is straightforward; where the fire touched, the color red appears.

Mocovi People

Before the fire both the male and the female brasita de fuego [red-crested finch] had the same brownish feathers. However, after the fire the female's feathers turned another color; she was now red [because only she had been burned]. Ever since then the female brasita de fuego has red feathers and the male brownish ones. (Teran in Wilbert and Simoneau 1988:71)

Nivakle People

"Let's make a big fire and jump into it," said the chief to his people. They built an enormous fire. One of them jumped headlong into it. "I want to be a stork," he cried as he jumped. That is why the stork today has a red neck, because he was slightly singed by the fire. (Chase-Sardi in Wilbert and Simoneau 1987b:218)

Toba People

When he [parrot] opened his mouth they [women] put a burning coal inside. They put the hot coal in his mouth, burning it, and he was not able to speak anymore. This is why parrots have a black tongue. (Wright in Wilbert and Simoneau 1989:140)

The three myths from the Gran Chaco region are similar to the other "fire" myths in that birds acquire their colors according to the distance they are from the fire. The transformation from person into bird is seen in the Nivakle myth as well, further enhancing the human-avian bond in this region.

Conclusion

One common pattern is revealed among the "fire" myths. The intensity of a bird's color as derived from its place in the fire (periphery vs. interior), whether involving a stipulation of heat or not, is a theme that appears in the stories of various regions.

VEGETABLE AGENTS OF COLORATION

We have become familiar with the two most frequently cited mythological explanations the Indians of South America used, and some of the most "traditional" people continue to use, to account for a variety of avian colors. It is clear that, according to the myths, some birds were once without color or had different pigmentation, and then, undergoing various processes, they emerged with the radiant colors each species has today. Specifically, blood and fire are the agents of color that have "painted" the birds. Pablo Wright, an Argentine ethnographer working among the Toba, observed that the Indians truly believe in these mythical stories, and continue to tell tales about the colorizing activities of mythical

FIGURE 7.7

Mythical Toba Fox Trickster. Drawn by Angel Achilai, a Toba shaman from Misión Tacaagle, Formosa Province, Argentina. Collected by Pablo Wright, 1983.

figures, such as the Trickster Fox-man depicted in Figure 7.7 (Wright, personal communication).

The Cashinahua, Nivakle, and Mocovi are the groups in our present sample which use both blood and fire to explain avian coloration. However, the bird species mentioned in the blood myth is never the same as the species mentioned in the fire myth. Both myths are evidently considered necessary to explain the various colors of each species. The Toba might be included in this group because they have both kinds of myths, but their fire myth, unlike the narratives from the other groups, is concerned with the color on the tongue of the parrot (as opposed to the feathers). The Cashinahua blood myth makes mention of the oropendola and the blue jay, while the fire myth of the same society deals with the color of the parrot, red macaw, big-headed macaw, and black cacique. In the Mocovi legends, the blood myth talks about the woodpecker and the cardinal, while the fire myth refers specifically to the red-crested finch. The Nivakle blood myth talks of the flamingo and the spoonbill, while the fire myth talks only of the stork. The coloration processes of blood and fire each apply to different avian species, and although it may appear to the Western mind that the red color from fire is akin to the red color from blood, this is not the case for the Indians. The reason behind the need for two completely separate coloring agents (blood and fire) has not been found in the narratives or in ethnographic materials. Nevertheless, the pattern exists, and it may be of interest to pursue this line of research with additional fieldwork.

Throughout this survey, blood and fire have been cited as colorants for the birds, and they have a widespread distribution. These are the two most common agents, but there are additional procedures within the realm of mythology to explain the origins of color on the birds' feathers. Such explanations are often not as explicitly stated, and often birds' coloration by these agents can only be inferred; it is necessary occasionally to "read into" the narrative to find pertinent insights—as illustrated in the following accounts.

Mato Grosso Region

Bororo People

The parrot that says "Kra, kra, kra" was in past times a very gluttonous boy who had the habit of gulping down his food without chewing it. Once when his mother, who had found some fruit of the mangabeira vine, roasted it over some coals, the boy ate the fruit without letting it cool. It is a sticky fruit which stays hot for a long time, so the boy's throat was burned. He began to say "Kra, kra, kra," forcing himself to vomit up the fruit. He grew wings and feathers and turned into a parrot which today still says "Kra, kra, kra." (Colbacchini and Albisetti in Wilbert and Simoneau 1983:151)

Gran Chaco Region

Mocovi People

So finally Woodpecker agreed to go. There were many birds watching him work. He began to peck at the Fox's anus which was a piece of clay. He began pecking slowly and then finally hard. Then water came out, tinted red from all the mistol [edible fruit]. Woodpecker bent down, and so did his helper, the cardinal. They both ducked. Woodpecker's cap was colored red, and so was the cardinal's crest. The little red-chested sparrow got really splattered (which is why he got his red chest). Then the ovenbird approached. He came toward the end, and by now the liquid was half-red, half-brownish. The ovenbird got splattered too. Other birds who have the same color were also there when all this happened. (Teran in Wilbert and Simoneau 1988:86)

Chorote People

Then Ele, since he is a parrot—he is roguish to this day—took a leaf from the tree where he was sitting and threw it down. It landed right on the leg of one of the girls. The girls then took a dry black cactus fruit and threw it at him, hitting him in the mouth. That is why Ele has a black beak. (Siffredi in Wilbert and Simoneau 1985:34)

A man wanted to turn into a rhea. He thought: "What can I do to become like a rhea? I think I shall get some ashes from the hearth." He started swallowing ashes, and soon he had turned into a rhea. (Verna in Wilbert and Simoneau 1985:253)

Fruit and other vegetable products frequently figure in legends, and are used to account for the creation of some avian colors. Among the Bororo, the fruit is used in conjunction with fire to transform a boy into a parrot. This myth can be seen as a narrative about coloration in that parrots are red, and so too are the fruit and the fire. The narrative never specifically refers to color, however, and all that is told is that the boy grows feathers and makes the appropriate sounds of the bird. The Mocovi myth is similar in drama to the "blood" narrative, only in this case the blood has been replaced by the fruit. The first Chorote myth does not account for the color of plumage, but of the bird's beak. The second Chorote myth requires the greatest amount of imagination, but traces of a coloration can be seen when it is realized that the rhea is a bird that has the color of ashes in its feathers.

The brilliant colors in many birds once motivated the creation of myths, for such a spectacular display requires explanation. It must be remembered that myths incorporate stories of the origins and characteristics of many different animals besides birds, and that birds are no more important to the Indians than any other type of animal; this exhibit is concerned primarily with birds, as are the articles in this catalogue. Knowledgeable leaders and shamans are still recounting these myths to their people, and to outsiders interested in their culture, when queried about how the birds came to be so stunning. It is in their myths that the "facts" have been recorded. Kenneth Kensinger, who spent many years among the Cashinahua, observed the recitation of myths and legends during the initiation ritual of the children, and the importance of teaching such stories to the next generation of adults (Kensinger, personal communication).

The myths of the birds speak of origins, referring us back to a time when the birds were first bathing in blood, burning in the flames of a fire, and being "painted" with fruits. The feathers became radiant and distinctive, and have been used in objects which are transformed, from the Indians' point of view, into "beautiful" adornments. The "harvesting" (collection) of these feathers has become extremely significant. They are necessary for ritualistic and ceremonial occasions, and through the art of featherworking, these objects, like the myths, reflect the Indians' cultural heritage and "traditional" knowledge.

Acknowledgment

The information for this essay was gathered during my term as a research assistant to the University Museum Featherwork Project, in the summers of 1989 and 1990, under the direction of Dr. Ruben E. Reina. The essay was written during the fall of 1990 and guided by Dr. Reina, who was instrumental in the production of the final text. I would also like to thank Ms. Kay Candler, who made many insightful comments; Professor Kenneth Kensinger for ethnographic details and editorial suggestions; and Mr. Pablo Wright, who graciously contributed the drawing of the Toba Trickster. Additional appreciation goes to Mr. John Hastings, whose assistance with computer instruction and programming was crucial to achieving the present results.

CROWNS
BIRD AND FEATHER SYMBOLISM

by Peter T. Furst

x. Kayapó headdress (89–1–15).

"... LEARNING THE LANGUAGE OF ANIMALS, ESPECIALLY OF BIRDS,

FIGURE 8.1

*K*ayapó headdress
(89–1–14). Birds:
*Amazona species, Scarlet
Macaw, and parrot. Collected
from the Juruena River, Brazil,
in 1986.*

O F ALL THE PLACES WHERE PEOPLE USE feathers to adorn themselves, beautify their world, and display wealth and social position, only the New Guinea highlands rival Amazonia in the size, splendor, and variety of headdresses and other body ornaments fashioned from the brilliant plumage of tropical birds. But in Indian South America the feather diadem and feather symbolism are not just meant to improve on nature or proclaim rank and affluence. Birds are sacred beings, transformations of the divine Sun and other deified phenomena of nature, as well as allies of the shaman, whom they assist in his role as mediator between the human and nonhuman realms. Thus, in South America birds and the use of their plumage are inextricably bound up in the ideology and techniques of shamanism.

In the beginning, so goes the creation myth of the Desana, the only two beings in the world were the Sun Father and his brother, the Moon. Not all South American Indians conceive of the Sun and Moon as male, or as older and younger brother; often it is the Sun who is male and the Moon female, the latter standing in a direct relationship to women, menses, and female fertility and fecundity. But among the Desana, the Moon is younger brother to the Sun, libidinous and untrustworthy.

At the dawn of the world Sun and Moon wore brilliant crowns made of the feathers of tropical birds that lit up the sky with their beautiful light. Elder Brother Sun, the Sun Father, was a great shaman—*payé* in the Tukano language—and even then he had all the magical paraphernalia shamans use today. The Sun Father also established the special knowledge shamans possess of disease and curing, their magical songs and invocations of the spirit world, and the use of tobacco and sacred ritual hallucinogens. For the Desana, these are especially the potent snuff called *vihó*, made from the inner bark of the *Virola* tree, and *yajé*, a brew made from a vine belonging to the genus *Banisteriopsis*, reinforced with extracts of other psychoactive plants.

For a long time Sun and Moon lived all alone. But then the Sun had a daughter, and she lived with him as his wife. Moon did not have a wife and, being jealous of his older brother, tried to make love to her. This angered the Sun, and he vowed to punish his younger sibling. A dance was held in the sky, and when the Moon came to join in the festivities, the Sun took away his beautiful feather headdress, leaving in its place only a small feather crown whose light was much paler, and a pair of earrings made of dull copper instead of brightly shining gold. The Sun also banished his errant brother from his sight to a distant part of the sky. That is where he has remained ever since, far distant from the Sun, wandering about in the night and sometimes descending to earth to seduce women in their sleep.

In the origin mythology the Desana ancestors were great shamans who could transform themselves into jaguars. This they did by fasting and taking *vihó* snuff, which originally belonged to a great supernatural jaguar who went about devouring his enemies. They also had a macaw, whose brilliant feathers decorate the crowns used by shamans as well as ordinary men. Like the primordial shamans, the macaw also fasted and inhaled *vihó*. He did this to transform himself into a jaguar. When a jaguar-man fails, so goes the myth, the macaw replaces him in jaguar form, going about with other jaguars devouring human enemies (Reichel-Dolmatoff 1975:110).

In Desana thought, the macaw is preeminently the bird of the Sun Father, its brilliant plumage flashing like the Sun's rays through the dark forest canopy. But myths and rituals that establish the connection between the spectacular macaw-feather diadems and the Sun abound throughout Amazonia. So, for example, in the cosmology of the Sipo, the first dawn at the beginning of the world broke when the Sun, appearing in the east as a man of black skin color, donned a great crown of flaming scarlet macaw feathers. Night fell when the Sun was killed by a man who dropped a heavy bundle of tree fruit on his head, making him sink down into the earth. The killer made off with the Sun's headdress of fiery feathers, but not for long. The Sun had five sons, and they pursued the killer and took the headdress away from him. The first four brothers tried the headdress on themselves, but each in turn found its heat too terrible to bear. Finally the fifth and youngest, who was black of skin like his father, put on the red-hot feather crown, and when the others saw that he alone could withstand its heat long enough to light up the world, he fell heir to his dead father's office and instituted the cycle of day and night.

Because of their connection with the Sun the red feathers of the scarlet macaw are often described as so "hot" that only shamans can handle them safely. That, too, goes back to the beginning of the universe: in many Indian traditions it is from primordial shamans that the Sun got its fiery headdress in the first place, and with it the power to light up the world. Their supernatural heat, then, more than just practical considerations, may help explain why the feathers are often attached not to a simple band but to a circular frame that keeps them from direct contact with the head—at least this is how Indians who use these frames account for it. It is also why an ordinary man often prefers to ask the shaman to handle the headdress and ritually place it on the head of its owner instead of doing it for himself.

Frames are by no means universal in Amazonia or outside it; for example, according to Curt Nimuendajú (1914), the shamans of the Apapovuca-Guaraní wore soft headbands of woven cotton set with feathers, rather than the more rigid feathered frames of other tribes. In this case the preferred feathers were the scarlet crest plumes of the crested woodpecker, and the tail feathers of the thezoura (*Colonia colunus*), because these were considered to have special power. For the Guaraní generally the feathers a shaman (*pazé*) wears on his head are the souls of the birds that serve as his personal assistants, i.e., the spirit helpers the shaman recruits at the conclusion of his initiatory training and his first ascent into the Upperworld. That is probably why the shaman is sometimes required to obtain his feathers—particularly those attached to the top of his rattle—not from dead but from living parrots. According to an Arawakan shaman, the rattle feathers had to come from a live parrot of the species *Psittacus oestivus* (Roth 1915).

Harvesting feathers is apt to be a dangerous enterprise, because it may require the shaman to put life and limb on the line in trapping the birds, plucking, them and releasing them, otherwise unharmed, at the top of trees a hundred feet or more up in the air. He may also have to travel far from his home to collect the various components that go into the making of his rattle.

FIGURE 8.2

Warao gourd rattle (87–34–29). Collected in Venezuela in 1987. Birds: Scarlet Macaw and Blue-and-yellow Macaw.

THE "RATTLE OF THE RUFFLED FEATHERS"

This applies particularly to the *hebumataro*, the sacred rattle (Fig. 8.2) of the Warao *wishiratu* shaman, the "Master of Pain" (Wilbert 1974:90–93, and personal communication). Among other things the sacred calabash rattle is for the Warao the model of the earth, with the center shaft as axis mundi. The whooshing sound the small quartzite stones inside the hollowed-out gourd make when the shaman shakes and whirls this powerful instrument are his principal means of communication with the higher powers. These sacred stones—250–300 in number for an experienced shaman, far fewer for the novice—are his spirit-helper "family." But no such stones exist in the Warao environment (the Orinoco Delta), and so the shaman has to obtain them from the island of Trinidad or from Guyana. Wilbert, who has been studying Warao religion and shamanism for more than 35 years, accompanied a shaman on his quest for the different materials, and watched him ascend a 120-foot manaca palm (Euterpe spp.) for the parrot feathers that are the rattle's all-important "hair."

As Professor Wilbert explains it, harvesting these feathers from live birds is tied to the growth cycle of the palm, because the birds come only when the palm fruits on which they feed are ripe. Further, really tall palms—great height is a requirement—are rare in the lower delta, requiring the shaman of a group living there to travel across several village boundaries to find the right fruit-bearing specimen in the upper and intermediate delta. The *manaca* is itself the "shaman of all the trees," and so has special powers. But to be "right" for the feather quest the palm selected must not only be very tall and have ripe fruit, but be one from which the shaman, in his initiatory tobacco trance, and also subsequently, obtained the stipules from which he makes the wrappers for the two- and three-foot cigars whose smoke Warao shamans swallow in enormous gulps to pass into ecstatic trance (Wilbert 1987). The stipules are harvested when they fall naturally and are caught by lower vegetation, for to be used by a shaman as wrappings for his sacred cigars they must not have touched the ground.

Wilbert's account of the shaman's quest continues: the chosen tree was marked with the shaman's machete, to signal to the supernaturals that he was still smoking, i.e., still shamanizing and feeding the gods with the tobacco they crave. Once he had located the right tree, the shaman ascended the 120 feet into the swaying crown, where he made a blind by bending over some of the fronds. Holding on for dear life, he laid out a little sling around the fruits and waited patiently for the parrots to come and roost for the night. Several birds had to be trapped, plucked, and released again to get a sufficient number of the coveted feathers without depriving the birds of their ability to take wing. This compelled him to remain precariously balanced at the top of the palm tree for some considerable time. The wood for the center shaft is also unavailable in the shaman's own environment, and so he has to visit several neighboring groups to ask permission from the local chief to collect the ingredients for his sacred instrument. These travels and intervillage contacts by the shaman, in turn, establish rapport between local Warao groups and help identify marriageable partners across subtribal boundaries.

FIGURE 8.3

Rucuyen shaman, wearing bird wings and feather crown, treats patient with a powerful blast of tobacco smoke. Illustration from Jules N. Crevaux's Voyage dans l'Amerique du Sud *(1883). Courtesy of Johannes Wilbert.*

THE POWER IN THE RATTLE AND THE DIADEM

As a musical instrument the gourd rattle as such is no more exclusive to the shaman than the feather crown. But there are rattles and rattles, and there is a considerable qualitative difference between a gourd rattle owned by an ordinary man and used by him in the dances, and the feathered rattle that houses the shaman's spirit helpers and that he treats accordingly with enormous respect and reverence. There is a corresponding qualitative difference between the diadems worn by ordinary participants in the great ceremonies and dances and those of the shamans, even if to the uninitiated eye there is no difference in their appearance.

That is because everything connected with the shaman is "non-ordinary," imbued with special powers that he acquires in the course of initiatory training and that emanate from his or her spirit allies. Because of its symbolic functions as a replica of the cosmos, the feathered shaman's rattle serves not just to produce rhythmic sound for the dances but to communicate with gods and spirits and activate magical power. In the same way the shaman's feather crown and other feather ornaments are charged with supernatural power that does not adhere to those of ordinary men, at least not in the same intensity. The shaman can even use his diadem to cure, for by touching the feathers to the patient's body he transmits therapeutic qualities from himself and his helping spirits to the patient. This attribution of healing powers to the shaman's headdress is not limited to South America but has been reported also from such areas as the Northwest Coast of North America. Conversely, he can employ it as an instrument of magical death, even across long distances.

Finally, the feathers of his diadem confer on the shaman a special kind of x-ray vision. Thus, the Tama or Tamao, another of the western Tukanoan groups, say that it is the shaman's feather crown that helps him to see into other worlds (Preuss 1921). This concept is shared by many other peoples.

The concept of heat and power of such intensity that it puts the ordinary man, but not the shaman, at risk is very much the case with the feather crown called *ankungitana* in the language of the Tapirapé. Wagley (1959) and Zerries (1977) describe how the Tapirapé deal with its awesome qualities: Any adult man may wear the feather crown, but its power is so great that in practice the *ankungitana* is mainly the attribute of the shaman. This is because he alone can endure, or is willing to risk, not only the great heat emanating from the red macaw feathers, but other supernatural powers that adhere to the *ankungitana* headdress or that it attracts in the manner of a magnet. He can even use it as a magical weapon. Shamans often challenge and fight each other, or, to put it another way, they send their spirits to enter into combat. When a shaman sees the soul of an adversary in his trance, he can fling his feather crown to immobilize and take it prisoner. Thus deprived of his soul the hostile shaman falls ill and, barring last-minute recovery of his abducted spirit, dies. In the same way a shaman can also bring magical death to an ordinary person, for his own reasons or at the behest of a client.

FIGURE 8.4

Kofan shaman and expert in making of curare arrow poison, with his feather crown, feathered nose and ear ornaments, and jaguar tooth necklace. Photograph by Richard Evans Schultes, 1945.

FEATHER POWER AND THE SEASONS

The ambivalent power inherent in the *ankungitana* crown comes into play especially at the beginning of the rainy season, a dangerous time because among the spirits the headdress attracts to itself is the great Thunder Spirit Kanuána. Kanuána, taking the form of a lightning bolt, can strike a man wearing the headdress and render him senseless. To lessen or prevent this danger, the shamans conduct a Thunder Ceremony in which the whole village participates. All the adult men have their feather crowns, but do not wear them until the shaman has cooled down their supernatural heat and assuaged the spirits by wafting the feathers slowly back and forth while chanting magical formulas and blowing tobacco smoke on them before placing them on their owners' heads.

To protect the village at this perilous time, the shamans, wearing their own diadems, inhale enormous quantities of tobacco smoke until they fall into a deep ecstatic trance. In the form of birds their souls travel to the House of Thunder in the distant sky. With Thunder live the souls of many dead shamans, called *ankunga iunwara*, as well as Thunder's spirit helpers, the thunderers called *topus*, who also own many red macaw feathers, which they wear in their crowns. To keep the *topus* from harming the people with violent thunderstorms, the shamans have to deprive them of their power, which resides in their feather diadems. The *topus* put up fierce resistance, but for the most part the shamans emerge victorious.

These cosmic battles of the shamans against the thunderers must be fought over and over again at the beginning of every rainy season, for the thunder spirits, and also the souls of dead shamans, seem to have an inexhaustible supply of red feathers. No matter how often the thunderers lose their crowns to the shamans, there are always more.

To learn why, a shaman went traveling in his dream through the forest. On and on he went until he came to a hill near the confluence of the Tapirapé and Araguaia rivers. Inside the hill lived a giant red macaw. This was the bird from which the thunderers got their feathers. The macaw was very big indeed, and he had many fiery red feathers, so many that there were always as many after as before someone came to pluck them out. So the shaman saw that no matter how many times he and his fellow shamans won over the thunderers and year after year deprived them of their headdresses, the thunderers could always come back the following year and pluck more to fashion into *ankungitana* crowns (Wagley 1959:405–23).

The oral poetry of tropical forest peoples often credits the way things are with the sun and birds and the alternation of day and night to the manipulation of feather crowns by ancestor shamans. The Waiwai tell of a time long ago when the sky was always dark with heavy rain clouds. Two shamans went into the medicine hut to divine why this was happening. They sang themselves into a trance and traveled up to the sky, where they encountered a bird spirit, who was the father of the Sun. When they told him they wanted the Sun to shine and make the world bright, he replied, "Visit the Sun yourselves!"

He led them to the Sun's house, where they nearly perished from the heat. Peering out, the Sun told them that the reason it was always dark on the earth, even in daytime, was that he was wearing a diadem made of the black feathers of the *kuyukoimo* bird. The Sun instructed the shamans to travel further into the forest, and when they found black feathers, they should take them away. They came upon a patch of burning brush that was like a piece of the forest that had been cleared for planting. The burning brush was surrounded by black

FIGURE 8.5

*Detail of a Hixkaryana
diadem (SA 529b)
collected from the Karape
River, 1913–1916. Birds:
Channel-billed Toucan
and Crimson Fruitcrow.
See Fig. 5.12.*

feathers. The shamans circled the clearing, removing all the black feathers and replacing them with the red feathers of the scarlet macaw and the toucan. The two shamans returned to their medicine hut on earth and regained their ordinary consciousness. The following day the Sun shone brilliantly from a cloudless sky.

In another Waiwai tradition a great shaman put an end to a long rain when he addressed a special song to the Sun and offered up his own diadem of red toucan feathers, his armbands of red macaw feathers, and several red feather bundles. He placed these on a slab of cassava bread and held them high up into the sky on a long pole so that Sun might absorb the *ekatî*, or soul, of the fiery ornaments (Zerries 1977).

FEATHER CROWNS AND THE SHAMAN'S STATUS

Considering the close relationship of the magnificent multicolor feather diadems to celestial deities—especially the Sun—in these and other instances, one would have expected there to be a one-to-one relationship between the relative size and splendor of the feather crown and social status, or personal wealth, and, for shamans, degrees of esoteric knowledge and supernatural power and corresponding prestige. But such is not the rule at all. Of course, prestige attaches to these splendid adornments, and sometimes they also denote personal wealth. They are so highly valued that among some groups shamans who charge for such personal services as curing may be paid in feathers and feather crowns.

Nevertheless, more often than not, the feather diadem functions mainly as a marker of developmental stages from adolescence to the grave, or of the wearer's domains of action. For the shaman it may denote not so much his prestige as first, his connection generally with the feathered kingdom and bird spirits; and second, a relationship to specific birds, as initiators, personal tutelaries, and power sources, or as rulers of the cardinal points, and weather phenomena associated with the directions, to whom he relates in his capacity as a weather prophet.

Whatever else may be conveyed or implied by the size and colors or other characteristics of a feather crown, for shamans or ordinary people, it is only initiation into manhood that entitles a youth to wear the great diadems that are the marker of adult status. And that applies as much to adolescent boys learning to be shamans under a master shaman as it does to the rest of the male members of the society (women, it should be noted, wear feathers, often in striking combinations, as ear and body ornaments, but except in certain relatively rare situations, feather crowns are the prerogative of men).

Before initiation into adult status a boy wears a crown at the ceremonies that is generally made of feathers of small birds—parakeets instead of parrots and macaws, for example. Yet feather crowns of relatively modest appearance, at least to the outside observer, are also worn by adult individuals to whom a special spirit power is ascribed and who enjoy considerable prestige. Among the Colombian Desana these are the shaman-priests called *kumú*, a highly respected class of specialists whose functions differ from those of the regular shaman in that, among other things, a *kumú* does not cure common organic ills. Nor does he engage in magical manipulations and

FIGURE 8.6

*Rikbaktsa headdress
(89–18–3). Collected in
the Juruena River region,
Brazil, in 1986. Birds:
Yellow-rumped Cacique,
Scarlet Macaw, Blue-and-
yellow Macaw, and hawk.*

negotiations for game with the supernatural Master of the Animals, called Vai-mahsë, who is conceived as a red, phallic dwarf whose outsized penis is engorged with the seeds of the useful plants.

In Desana belief, Vai-mahsë releases game animals needed by the people to the shaman in return for the souls of dead persons who have transgressed the rules of life, for example by committing incest. This reciprocal exchange derives from the Desana conception of the natural environment as a kind of closed circle of energy, in which everything taken out for sustenance diminishes the whole. To prevent ultimate depletion, and with it the collapse of the whole energy system, what is removed must be replaced by something of equal value. In this case it is the soul, or spirit power, of a human for that of the slain game animal. Vai-mahsë has his home near a prominent cliff in the forest, to which the shaman, having placed himself in an ecstatic trance by inhaling hallucinogenic snuff, travels with his wish-list and from which he returns after having bargained the souls of human transgressors for game animals (Reichel-Dolmatoff 1967:107–13).

The *kumú* is above such everyday concerns for the physical welfare of his social group, his principal domain being the moral order. Another thing that sets him apart is that he does only good, whereas the ordinary shaman can harm as well as cure—for example, send illness and even death to enemies by means of magical sickness projectiles. Needless to say, such capabilities expose the shaman to criticism, fear, or envy, whereas the *kumú* is without enemies.

Kumús, whose office is hereditary, being passed on from father to son, traditionally belong to the sib Umusí-porá, the Sons of the Oropendola (family *Icteridae*), a tropical bird whose yellow tail feathers associate it with the fertilizing powers of the Sun. At the same time, its pendant nests, which are suspended like long purses in grapelike clusters from the branches of trees, have a double association: on the one hand, they carry a uterine meaning as "bags that contain the brood"; on the other they are likened to testicles (Reichel-Dolmatoff 1971:196–97). According to Reichel-Dolmatoff, the office of *kumú* was "created by the Sun Father who determined that these men should be called upon to perpetuate moral teachings in the highest ethical sense." These teachings emphasize, among other things, the interpretation of hallucinatory visions and the development of wisdom and serenity in the settling of social conflict. Ever since, the *kumú* has been the repository and guardian of sacred traditions, who sees to it that they are transmitted correctly through the generations. On a much higher level than the ordinary shaman, he "is a luminous personage who has an interior light, a brilliant flame that shines and unveils the intimate thoughts of all the people who speak to him. His power and his mission are always compared to an intense light that is invisible but perceptible through its effects" (ibid.:137).

Given all this, and in the absence of familiarity with its symbolic value, the outsider might be surprised to see that the *kumú*'s feather crown, called *abé berö*, "Sun-circle," is relatively modest in appearance, lacking the long, radiant blue macaw tail feathers that make the splendid ceremonial headdress worn by the men during religious and social get-togethers such a feast for the eye. Instead, the *abé berö* consists only of red and yellow feathers, colors that manifest the essential complementarity of "male and female phallic fertilization and uterine productiveness [which] form a pattern of recurrent motifs in most cosmogonic and cosmological ideas and pervade, through ritual, practically all aspects of existence" (Reichel-Dolmatoff 1975). This is clearly one case where clothes decidedly do *not* make the man.

FIGURE 8.7

Textile border (SA 3523)
from the south coast of
Peru (see also Fig. 1.8).
The condor head and
wings attached to these
flying figures may indicate
that they are supernatural
beings or shamanic "alter
egos."

THE SHAMAN AS BIRD

The case of the kumú is especially interesting because this class of shaman-priests belongs to a descent group whose members not only are related to one another by blood, but consider themselves to have blood ties to a species of bird whose appearance, ecology, and social behavior carry complex sexual and social connotations for Desana society as a whole. But this is only one aspect, specific to one group, of the general relationship between shamans and the world of birds that is visually expressed in the ornithological costume that distinguishes the shamans of so many Amazonian peoples.

Indeed, the *kumú* does not content himself with the relatively modest red and yellow feather crown he customarily wears at the great dances, nor is this his only use of feather symbolism. He occupies a central and highly honored place at the kin-group gatherings held in the *maloca*, the large circular communal dwelling that is common to many tropical forest peoples. On these occasions he wears a red, skirtlike barkcloth garment covered with short feathers. His head is circled by a ring of small white feathers, and on his arms he wears several wide bands woven of very fine fibers and adorned with feathers and interwoven diamond motifs. Suspended from his left elbow is a large hollow black palm seed in which he keeps some little red and white feathers and a red vegetal pigment used for face painting. Finally, around his neck he wears a short cylinder of quartz crystal similar to those worn by other shamans in northwestern Amazonia. This translucent amulet symbolizes lightning and also the Sun Father's fertilizing semen, but quartz and rock crystals are important in the shamanic arts virtually everywhere, often as the visible manifestation of ancestors and helping spirits.

For the *kumú* to dress himself in the manner of a bird is very much part of shamanic mythology and symbolism. Feather crowns, feather capes and skirts and aprons, feathered body ornaments, effigies of birds, even the bird-bone nose pipes widely employed to ingest hallucinogenic snuff, all associate the shaman with birds, as supernatural patrons of the ecstatic trance and winged spirit helpers who guide and protect him, or, on the relatively rare occasions where the shaman is female, her[1], on the flight to the Upperworld, where shamans seek guidance from the ruling powers of the sky. Conversely, diving birds and shore birds serve as guides on travels to the watery Underworld, and so the shaman's magical paraphernalia and adornments may include feathers also from these species. Beyond this there is the shaman's ability to "become" bird himself, by way of complete or partial ornithological adornment.

The ornithological costume of the shaman greatly impressed the first Europeans who ventured into the Amazon in the 16th century, even if its deeper meaning eluded them. Several full-length feather capes covered with scarlet feathers were acquired in the mid-16th century and survive today in European museums, one of the most spectacular, its colors as brilliant as when it was collected four and a half centuries ago, being in the National Museum in Copenhagen, Denmark. The dramatic account by the German merchant-soldier Hans Staden of his adventures and observations among the Tupinambá, first published in 1557, was widely circulated and reprinted, accompanied by woodcuts that were later redrawn with more attention to detail by the Belgian Theodore de Bry (1528–98). One of the latter, dating to 1592, depicts three Tupinambá shamans, dressed in feather crowns, feathered waistbands, and long feather capes, dancing with large feathered rattles inside a circle of other men who are also adorned with feathers (Fig. 8.8).

Two of the shamans are blowing tobacco smoke from large tubular cigars at the dancers circling around them; they and the shamans directing the ceremony also have feathers glued to their legs or torsos. The dancers' buttocks are covered with the large circular shields of rhea tail plumes that Tupinambá men wore for ceremonial occasions and for war and that could measure several feet across.

Staden visited Brazil twice, the first time in 1548 and again a few years later, when, after being shipwrecked, he was taken prisoner by the Tupinambá. His captors mistook him for one of the detested Portuguese slave raiders, fit for nothing but fattening up, cooking, and eating. Staden was held captive for nine months, ample time to make observations of Indian life and customs, including the complex set of rituals that attended the execution and subsequent ceremonial consumption of enemy prisoners. Staden, who spoke the Tupian language, eventually gained his freedom, boarding a French ship and reaching Antwerp in 1555. Two years later he published his story in Marburg, in the dukedom of Hesse. Given the prejudices of his time, his observations on the Tupinambá have turned out to be remarkably accurate.

The birdlike dance of the shamans depicted by Staden's illustrator and elaborated later by de Bry had to do with the investment of the feathered rattles with magical power and the voice of the spirits. Staden writes that there were among the Tupinambá certain men called *paygi* (*piai*). These men were greatly respected as soothsayers (i.e., shamans). Women, he noted, could also become *paygi*. Once a year these men traveled about to visit all the houses and inform the people that a spirit had come from afar who gave them the power to invest their rattles with the magical gift of speech and to grant whatever they asked for. Those who wished their rattles to be granted this power prepared a great feast with dancing, drinking, divining, and other "strange ceremonies."

On a day appointed by the shamans a dwelling was ritually prepared and cleared of women and children. The shamans commanded the men to paint their rattles red, decorate them with feathers, and appear before them to have their rattles—each of which had a slit cut into it resembling a mouth—invested with the power of speech. When all had assembled and the shamans as well as the rattles had been honored with gifts of feathers, arrows, ear ornaments, etc., the visiting shaman took up each rattle and, after fumigating it with tobacco smoke, held it close to his mouth, shook it to give it voice, and addressed it as follows: "*Nee kora*, speak now, let yourself be heard, you who are within." Then, reports Staden,

> . . . in a low voice, he makes an utterance that is hard to hear. Whether it is the rattle that is doing it, or he, the others believe that it is the rattle. But it is the soothsayer himself who does it, and so he proceeds with all the rattles, one after the other. And each one is now convinced that his rattle has great power. Then the soothsayers tell them to go to war, to capture enemies, because the spirits residing in rattle desire to eat intelligent flesh, and thereupon they go to war.
>
> And now that the soothsayer *Paygi* has turned all the rattles into gods, each man takes his rattle, addresses it as 'dear son,' and builds its own little house for it, and when it [is] stood inside places food before it, and just as we ask of the true God, requests of it all that of which he has need, and these then are their gods. (Zerries 1962)

A contemporary of Staden, the French friar André Thevet, who visited Brazil the year Staden's story appeared in Europe, identified the rattle deity as Toupan (Tupa), the spirit of thunder who after the coming of the missionaries was promoted from secondary status among Tupinambá supernaturals to the rank of the Christian God

FIGURE 8.8

In 1555, the German merchant-soldier Hans Staden observed these feather-clad shamans of the Brazilian Tupinambá purifying the feathered rattles of fellow tribesmen with tobacco smoke and investing them with the supernatural power of speech. Engraving by Theodore de Bry, 1592. After an earlier illustration published by Staden in 1557.

FIGURE 8.9

Engraving of a man-bird transformation on a shell cup (National Museum of the American Indian). This drawing is taken from on of the numerous shell objects recovered from the great Precolumbian mortuary-temple complex centered on Spiro Mound in eastern Oklahoma, A.D. 1200–1400. This and related representations fit perfectly into the widespread North and South American concept of the shaman as bird ascending into the sky.

(Métraux 1945:128). Like the Thunder Spirit of the Warao, Tupa appears to have been conceived as a bird.

TRANSFORMATION, NOT DISGUISE

All the evidence suggests that appearing as birds in the dances is not limited to shamans. Still, there is a difference. The ordinary tribesman might put on the dress of a bird in the reenactment of a myth and thus take on the identity of that spirit for the duration of the drama. The shaman's feathers, on the other hand, define his relationship at all times with the celestial powers and with avian tutelaries and spirit helpers to which only he has access.

The point is that in no case, shaman or ordinary person, is the bird costume meant to disguise. Rather, it manifests a shift in shape from human to bird, or, in the case of an animal skin or mask, to mammal or some other creature. In the traditional religions and world-view of Native American peoples all life forms, in particular animals and humans, are qualitatively equivalent, the outer garment—be it feathers, fur, or the bare human skin—being the "form soul," that which lends every being its distinctive outer shape. "Lends" is quite the appropriate term here, for in the belief systems of many peoples, human beings may change into one another, or some other life form of their choice, simply by putting on or taking off the outer garment. There are countless stories about this sort of transformation, from the Arctic to Tierra del Fuego, in the oral poetry and literary traditions of Native North and South American peoples.

These ideas are deeply rooted in shamanism—indeed, they are basic to the shamanistic world-view that some scholars are certain underlies all Native American religions, whatever the formal differences between them. To effect transformation it is not even necessary for a shaman to change the whole outfit. He might "become" jaguar just by putting a jaguar fang or claw around his neck, wearing a belt of jaguar skin around his waist, or imitating a jaguar's growl (Furst 1968).

FIGURE 8.10

Waiwai jaguar skin belt (SA 351) collected from the Brazil-Guyana border region in 1913. Birds: Red-and-green Macaw, Scarlet Macaw.

INTERSPECIES COMMUNICATION AND METAMORPHOSIS

The importance of this aural aspect of the shaman's identification with animals and birds cannot be overemphasized. Many writers have commented on the remarkable ability of Indian peoples to imitate predators and game, including birds, with such uncanny accuracy that even members of the same species are fooled. But generally these skills, which children practice from an early age, are mentioned mainly in relation to the food quest, rather than as a shamanic technique of interspecies communication and transformation.

If a shaman can turn into a jaguar with a mere growl, or, as among the Tacana, by diving or leaping or turning somersaults (Hissink and Hahn 1961:397–99), with the same deceptively simple techniques he can feel himself transformed into a bird. A brief passage of birdsong or a whistle may be enough. A Karina Carib shaman (*pudai*) needs, with certain ritual preparations, only to imitate the voice of a bird spirit, one of the *iakurai*, to turn himself into one of the Bird People. He constructs a little hut into which he retreats to communicate in lonely vigil with the spirit world. After a while he begins to sing in the voice of the *iakurai*, the bird spirits whom he recruited in his initiatory training as his supernatural helpers, or who selected him, and who are always ready to heed his call. He has become one of the *iakurai* himself, and when his spirit helpers hear him sing they come at once to his assistance, for that is their function. Moreover, once the Karina shaman himself has transformed into an *iakurai*, he no longer has to do a thing, because his bird spirit helpers will do it in his place.

The shamans of some groups need only to sound their bird-bone flutes to transform themselves into birds—that is, to send their spirits winging their way as birds to the other world to do battle with disease spirits. Not so the Akawaio shaman, who has to use birdsong and a special kind of feather ornament, both called *malik*, in conjunction to effect transformation and take flight in the shape of a bird.

The art of transformation by imitating the voices of the helping spirits extends from the Karina shaman to the bird spirits themselves, for it is one of the main criteria for a shaman's choice of a helping spirit that the latter can also transform by imitating the songs and voices of other birds, animals, and humans. Not surprisingly, the list of bird spirits capable of making the right sort of "magical racket" is headed by the parrot family, birds that are not only notoriously noisy but also gifted mimics, so much so that a parrot imitating human speech can give one a real start.

As part of his initiatory training, the Karina shaman also has to familiarize himself with the feeding habits of all the different spirit-helper birds, as well as any other animal he might call upon for assistance. In Karina belief what the spirits eat they destroy, and because sickness is thought to be caused by animals, it is essential that the shaman pick as his spirit helpers birds and other creatures whose natural prey are animals his diagnosis has pinpointed as the source of his patient's malady (Zerries 1977).

FIGURE 8.11

Cashinahua headdress (65–10–15). Kensinger (Ch. 4) suggests that Cashinahua headdresses are designed to replicate the visual effects of a hallucinogenic beverage. Birds: Trumpeter, Scarlet Macaw, and Harpy Eagle. Rio Curanja, Peru.

BIRDS OF THE SHAMAN

Many species of birds and their feathers figure in Amazonian shamanism, but two major classes of birds predominate. First place is held by the parrots, led by the scarlet macaws. Their well-known gift of mimicry surely contributed to the roles they play in shamanic mythology and practice, but this the macaw shares with other members of the parrot clan. Perhaps it has something to do with the hallucinatory experience, with its characteristic bursts of colors of great intensity, a whole houseful of whirling red feathers being one of the dominant sensations reported by Indians after taking the potent drink made from the *Banisteriopsis* vine. But apart from its spectacular plumage, there must be other things about its behavior and ecology that led to the macaw's prominence in South American shamanism, its identification with the jaguar in such origin mythologies as those of the Colombian Tukano, and the therapeutic (or harmful) magic ascribed to its feathers.

The second group consists of the raptors, a category that includes vultures, buzzards, hawks, falcons, and eagles. All figure in the myths and in Precolumbian art, as assistants, companions, and aerial guardians of gods, and spirit helpers and tutelaries of the great shamans of mythic times and the shamans of the present.

The vulture, which almost everywhere has a special affinity to the shaman, often appears to him in human form by removing its feather cloak. Conversely, it empowers the shaman to do the same in reverse. As carrion eaters vultures have a natural connection to death and the Underworld, the land of the dead being one of the other worlds shamans visit in their out-of-body travels. But that seems not to be the principal reason why vultures—in the Andes especially the condor, the largest vulture of them all—play such a prominent role in South American shamanism. What people seem to focus on, rather, is that the vulture can soar so high and so swiftly that it soon becomes a mere pinpoint in the sky or is altogether lost to the human eye, as though it had passed through the celestial vault; and yet, like the eagle, it is gifted with such extraordinary sight that from this great height it can drop down with lightning speed and uncanny accuracy on the smallest carcass or live prey. The vulture is itself a shaman, because like the shaman it can travel through the different planes of the multilayered cosmos and is gifted with that special sight by which the human shaman looks into other worlds. No wonder, then, that shamans often recruit the vulture as an especially effective spirit helper and guide to the celestial region, or why, conversely, the vulture often selects the novice shaman as its protégé.

In the mythology of the Taurepan or Taulipáng, a subgroup of the Venezuelan Pemón, his spirit-vulture wife hands the great shaman Maitxaule a feather cloak. The moment he puts it on he transforms into a vulture and wings his way with his vulture wife and her two brothers high up into the sky. There the vultures remove their feather cloaks and transform themselves into people. Maitxaule successfully undergoes a series of difficult trials and for the return journey puts on the dress of a nightingale, who accompanies him back to earth. Today, when a Taurepan shaman wants to summon the mythological Maitxaule to his assistance in doctoring a patient, he sings a chant that recapitulates his mythic predecessor's journey to the sky in the form of a vulture and his return to earth as a nightingale (Koch-Grünberg 1916). As Zerries (1977) notes, similar traditions exist among other Indian peoples of the Guianas, not just speakers of Carib languages like the Pemón, but also Arawakan peoples in Suriname and Guyana, as well as the Warao of the Orinoco

FIGURE 8.12

Bird warrior and winged messenger in Moche art. Illustration courtesy of Christopher B. Donnan.

Delta. It should be noted, however, that vulture transformation does not necessarily translate into widespread ceremonial or magical use of vulture feathers.

Finally there is the vulture as one of the more prominent bird patrons of ecstatic intoxication and the visionary trance. Of this the Cubeo provide a graphic example. The potent drink made from the *Banisteriopsis* vine, called *yajé* by the Desana and *ayahuasca* by speakers of Quechua, the Cubeo know as *mihi*. *Mihi* is consumed individually in the context of shamanic curing, and communally on major ritual occasions, such as the *oyne* mourning ceremony, and also during the great drinking parties which the member sibs of larger related social units throw for one another and at which hosts and guests consume prodigious quantities of beer made from the manioc tuber. "*Mihi* has magical power which the bearers portray dramatically" (Goldman 1963:248). "They pretend to stagger under its weight because *mihi* has power to fell a man." The bearers of *mihi* prance, birdlike, with torso bent forward and knees kicked up high, whispering *he he he* and whistling. "These are the sounds of the spirits and they are the same as the sounds made by the guests when they circle the ceremonial remains during this dance." An effigy of a vulture as *mihi* bird, the supernatural patron of the ecstatic intoxicant, is suspended from a roof beam at the exact center of the house, "where it overlooks equally the male half and the female half... The bird hangs like a mobile. It is said to be 'drunk' on *mihi*, and it presides over the *oyne* to give the proper spirit of intoxication" (ibid.). Despite its obvious connection with death as a carrion eater, the vulture is here thought of not so much in that connection but "for its quality of soaring."

The vulture also plays a role as a tobacco spirit. As early as 1943, for example, de Goeje wrote that the Tukayana or tobacco spirit of Guianan Indians "often appears to the medicine man in human shape but sometimes adopts his gigantic vulture-shape or that of four large king-vultures."

In fact, tobacco spirits generally are birds, either vultures or some other raptor. Probably the most dramatic elaboration on this theme is that of the Warao. In their cosmology, the swallow-tailed kite (*Elanoides forficatus*), a remarkably agile hunter of the sky who turns up with some regularity in the shamanic mythology and cosmology of peoples from the Peruvian Montaña to the Guianas, is the creator bird and epiphany of the sun at zenith. He is also the originator of *bahana* ("white") shamanism, whose mythology and practice focus specifically on human reproduction, with its attendant physiological, psychological and social concerns (Wilbert 1985:145–82).

FIGURE 8.13

Elderly female shaman of the Tikuna on the Rio Acacayuca in the Columbian Amazon. Her arms and shoulders are festooned with the feathers of eagles and other birds, in the manner of wings, symbolizing her intimate identification with bird spirits and the power of flight to Otherworlds. She was a specialist in, among other magical knowledge, the properties of poisonous and intoxicating plants. 1954. Photograph by Richard Evans Schultes.

THE HARPY EAGLE AS THE SHAMAN'S ALTER EGO

There is, finally, the very special place the harpy eagle, *Harpia harpyja*, occupies in South American shamanism. This great bird, the largest of all American eagles, is the shaman's alter ego in the sky, matching, and often overlapping with, his qualitative equivalence with the jaguar on the ground. To put it another way, as the most powerful winged predator, the harpy eagle is to the Upperworld what the jaguar is to the earth, and both in turn relate to the shaman.

All the members of the harpy eagle group are very large, powerful, and rapacious birds. Because of certain characteristics, the bare tarsus, for example, they are assigned to the buzzard family. But whatever their anatomical relationship to buzzards, no one could ever think of them as such. And that applies especially to that real giant of the family, the strikingly colored harpy eagle. "The Harpy and Guinea Crested Eagle are both magnificent crested species inhabiting tropical forests, with the short wings and long tails characteristic of forest raptors," writes Leslie Brown. "The Harpy is unquestionably the world's most formidable bird. A male is impressive enough, weighing 9–10lb. (4.4kg), a female huge, weighing 15–20lb. (6.7–9kg) with a tarsus as thick as a child's wrist; she is about as big as a bird of prey can be while still able to fly easily" (1976:33).

Harpies kill monkeys with ease, flying among the tall forest canopy with incredible agility at speeds ranging up to 50 miles per hour. And while the harpy has yet to be studied in detail by ornithologists, it has obviously long been of special interest to the Native peoples of the New World tropics, especially the shamans, by definition the intellectual leaders and the most observant and learned students of the natural environment, for harpy eagle symbolism is found all through the New World tropics, from Amazonia to southern Mexico.

The Desana provide a graphic example of the close association of the harpy eagle with the jaguar and of both with the shaman (Reichel-Dolmatoff 1975:80–81, 128).

One of the first requirements for the novice *payé* is the acquisition, from the celestial sphere, of certain power objects he will use later in his magical practice. The essence of these objects is to be found in the House of Thunder, which the young shaman will visit in his initiatory trance. Thunder himself is related to the spirit jaguar and often appears in jaguar form. In the sky his companions and messengers are the harpy eagles and the jaguars. On his visit to Thunder's House the initiate will see only the essence of his power objects, which include different kinds of curing stones; white and translucent quartzite; sharp thorns or splinters that can be shot as sickness projectiles at an enemy, or, conversely, can aid the shaman in sucking out disease as a kind of counter-poison; and a special kind of hallucinogenic snuff that comes in the form of a hard, reddish resin.

Very important in shamanic initiation are the fluffy white down feathers of the harpy eagle and the fine white hairs from the underbelly of the jaguar. Stuffed into the new shaman's ears, these in combination will give him magical hearing and enable him to perceive and understand the spirit voices that speak to him when he has placed himself in an ecstatic trance with *Virola* snuff and *yajé*. There are also many other things the future shaman must acquire before he can practice, not least of them his feather crowns, his bird-bone snuffing pipes, his rattle, a forked cigar holder, and a special shaman's bench.

The Tukano say that if one meets a jaguar in the forest who wears harpy eagle down, one knows at once that this is not an ordinary animal but a sorcerer who has entered the body of a jaguar and made it aggressive and dangerous. Shamans have magical spells to ward off these dangers and tame the jaguar. "His ears are his ornaments," goes one of these incantations:

His ears are his ornaments.
They are the white feathers of the harpy eagle.
When he is thus adorned, he is fierce;
Then he is armed with his bow;
Thus he is adorned. (Reichel-Dolmatoff 1975:128)

The spell goes on to describe how the jaguar is made tame by depriving him of these feather ornaments and magical weapons. Without his bow and his harpy eagle feathers he is no longer dangerous and peaceably returns to his own house.

This attribution of power to harpy eagle down and feathers is widespread among Amazonian peoples. Eagle down plays an important role, for example, in the initiation of young Yanomamö shamans, as head and body decoration and also glued to an initiation pole said to symbolize a magical rock that is the home of the *hekula* spirits. Some 40 of these spirits, many of which are birds, are magically "shot" into the young novice's chest and will henceforth serve as his spirit helpers.

Among the Cubeo, the actual source of the shaman's power is a group of six magical substances which he absorbs into different parts of his body during his novitiate. One of these, called *kwitobo*, consists of harpy eagle feathers that are stuffed into the nostrils to lodge in the head (Goldman 1963:264). And among the Waiwai, the harpy is considered the most important of the four celestial spirit helpers of the shaman.

There is also a certain ambivalence about the harpy eagle, in that the bird, like the jaguar, is sometimes seen as a transformed sorcerer intent on doing harm, or as a bearer of supernatural illness. So, for example, there is a tradition among some Yanomamö groups that to come close enough to do harm to his intended victim a shaman can transform himself into a harpy eagle by dressing himself in its feathers. There are endless stories of shamanic transformation into jaguars, but this idea of the shaman becoming harpy eagle by way of the feathers is also deeply embedded in the origin mythology. Thus, Zerries (1977) relates the following myth of the Tariana:

In the mythic First Times, when the rocks were still soft and all beings, animals and humans, had the same form, three youths wished to become shamans but lacked the necessary harpy eagle feathers. There was a grandmother who hated the harpy eagle people because one of her boys had been devoured by them. She told the three aspiring shamans where the harpy eagle people could be found. To trap and kill them and strip them of their feathers, they should fashion a net of the fibers from the *tuturu* plant, which grew in the sky in front of the House of Thunder. They did as they were instructed. Because the material was not of this world, the net they wove was very strong. When they came to the House of the Harpy Eagle People they found only an old woman there, preparing curare (blowgun dart poison). But they also noticed a trumpet belonging to the harpy eagles. The sound of the trumpet was like that of the harpy eagles. When the harpy eagles heard the trumpet, they came flying to devour the boys. But instead they were trapped in the net and killed. The boys took the dead harpy eagles back to their house,

Figure 8.14

Novice shamans, their heads and feather crowns covered with eagle down, await their initiation during a yajé *ceremony in the Columbian Amazon. 1954. Photograph by Richard Evans Schultes.*

*Seven-tier frontlet
(65–10–1c). This train is
worn tied around the neck
and hangs down in front of
the body. The frame is
formed by seven wooden
bars fastened to each other
with split quills and black
cotton thread. Bird: Harpy
Eagle. (See Fig. 4.5D)*

stripped them of their feathers, and used them to make their shamans' costumes.

EAGLES AND CHIEFTAINS

The well-documented relationship between harpy eagle and shaman notwithstanding, the same majestic bird can also function as soul mate and as validation of high status and leadership for the village chief or headman. Some tropical forest villagers, especially on the upper Xingu river, raise harpy eagles as a living source of feathers, and in this unnatural, captive state the harpy is demonstrably less exclusively identified with the shaman than it is in the wild.

Still, the specifically shamanic connection occurs across a sufficiently wide spectrum of native societies throughout tropical South America, and can be recognized often enough in the art of Precolumbian cultures, to be taken as one of the dominant animal motifs in South American shamanism. The jaguar certainly comes first as the shaman's animal equivalent, spirit power source, and ally, but the harpy eagle is at least a close second.

There is also this: even if the conceptual links between the harpy eagle and the shaman are sometimes rivaled, or even eclipsed, by this magnificent raptor's ideological tie to secular power, it is equally true that there is, generally speaking, no sharp dividing line between the office of chief and that of shaman. Moreover, shamans usually enjoy great prestige, often rising, as Métraux (1945:130) reported of the Tupinambá, to considerable political power. Sometimes, indeed, shamans, those masters of ecstasy and celestial flight, come to exercise "unchallenged authority in their communities or even in large districts," being addressed with great respect even by chiefs (ibid.).

The Desana, whose myth of the rivalry of Sun and Moon over who was entitled to wear the shinier feather headdress opened this essay, are not the only group in whose origin mythology these two heavenly givers of light are also the first men on the earth as well as competitors for the original crown of power. It is safe to say that there probably is no Amazonian people that does not have at least one such story—for how else can one account for the sun's light being so brilliant while the moon's is so dim?

So the Eastern Timbira tell of a time when Put, the Sun, and Puduvri, the Moon, were so alone on the earth that they did not even know of each other's existence (Nimuendajú 1946:243–45). One day Moon saw human tracks. The next day he again saw tracks. The third time he followed the footprints. They led to a hut, inside of which Moon found Sun lying with eyes closed. Moon waited patiently, and when Sun opened his eyes, Moon asked, "Who are you?" "I am from here," Sun replied, "and who are you?" "I am also from here." They decided to keep each other company, with Sun suggesting two separate dwellings, but Moon insisting they build a hut in which each would occupy his own half.

One day while Moon was sleeping and Sun was wandering about on the steppe outside, he heard the pecking of woodpeckers. He looked and saw that one of these birds had just finished making a headdress of red feathers that shone like fire. Sun asked if he could have it. The woodpecker agreed, but warned Sun not to let it drop to the ground. Then he threw it down from the tree. The brilliant red feather headdress came flying down, twisting and turning and flickering like real fire. Sun caught it but it was so hot he had to throw it from one hand to the other until it was cool enough to wear. Then he went home. After storing his new feather crown in a safe place he went outside.

As soon as Sun was gone, Moon found this splendid new headdress of the Sun. When Sun returned Moon begged for a similar crown. At first Sun said no. But when Moon kept urging Sun finally took him to the woodpeckers. The birds agreed to give them another crown like the first and Sun positioned himself under the tree to catch it. Moon wanted to do it for himself, but Sun told him he didn't know how and there might be an accident. But Moon, thinking that Sun just wanted to keep this second feather crown for himself, insisted. The woodpeckers threw the headdress down and Moon caught it. But it was so fiery hot he dropped it. The headdress set the steppe on fire, forcing Sun and Moon to flee for their lives. Sun hid inside a wasp's nest that was resistant to the flames. Moon crawled into another one that was not fireproof, and soon the heat drove him out again. While searching for his companion, who had gone ahead without him, Moon came to a river. He swam across and finally caught up with Sun.

Sun went on to create the animals and foodstuffs that would feed the future human beings and otherwise arranged things on the earth. Moon, thinking he had equal powers, succeeded only in spoiling everything he tried. Then Sun made a young and handsome couple by jumping head over heels into a creek. Moon tried the same but succeeded only in making ugly and misshapen people. That is why there are good-looking and well-formed people and ugly ones with bodily defects.

When the world had all been put in order, each went his separate way. Sun, wearing his fiery crown of power, lit up the day, leaving night with its dim light to Moon. Moon demanded that he too have daylight, but Sun told him it was not his business to choose.

And that is how things have remained ever since.

FIGURE 9.1

Headdress (58–17–121). *The feathers are tied to a knotted, conical-shaped net. A twisted cord through the open end of the net allows the piece to be adjusted to fit the wearer's head. Collected from the Mato Grosso, Brazil in 1958.*

T HE ORIENTATION OF THE MODERN world, with its desire to collect and possess the beautiful and the unique, has accomplished yet another victory: the endangering of many species of South American avifauna. The birds are threatened not only by massive and unrelenting deforestation, but by the simple fact "that people want to own them" (Stern and Stern 1990:55). This has been practiced to the extent that the worldwide marketing and distribution of tropical birds may bring about the depletion of entire species. If exportation continues at the present rate, the once diverse ornithological species will rapidly diminish or disappear. The repopulation of some of the species has been attempted, but even when those endangered species born in captivity are reintroduced to their native environment, the birds are unable to survive on their own; they have become so accustomed to feeding times and metal bars that they no longer can defend themselves when set free in the forest. Their natural defenses and strategies to survive have disappeared, and they rapidly fall prey to other animals.

It was not always like this among South American Indians. Birds were, and in some cases still are, treated according to a different set of cultural values, and only a reasonable number of birds were hunted for food. Their feathers were not discarded, but used in the production of beautiful adornments for ritualistic occasions. Because the use of the feathers was guided by native cultural principles it had an impact on conservation; birds had an excellent chance to replenish themselves. The native peoples' approach is in part derived from the respect they have for this and many other resources of nature. The avifauna provided the Indians with plumes in colors not available in any other way, and enabled them to express themselves and create beauty in well-established cultural ways appropriate to their own group and recognizable by other native peoples. The question to be considered here is, how did South Amerindians traditionally secure birds and collect these feathers?

"... THE TEACHERS ARE NOT ALWAYS TO BE FOUND IN SCHOO

FEATHERS

by Ruben E. Reina and Jon F. Pressman

XI. Headdress (58–17–121).

OR IN GREAT LABORATORIES . . ." – *LOREN EISELEY*

111

DOMESTICATION

Figure 9.2

Map of distribution of the blowgun in South America.

Domestication is a practice used for the taming of birds such as parrots, macaws, curassows, guans, toucans, and rheas. To accomplish this process, the birds are caught young and trained to live in the company of humans in a village setting. Indians of the past and present generations have harvested their feathers as one would a special crop, paying special attention to assure the survival of the birds. Domesticated birds continue to exist in semi-natural surroundings within the village; they are easily approachable and seldom mistreated.

Westerners have seen domesticated parrots in many villages "strutting about or perched on top of the huts" (Blomberg 1961:83), enjoying themselves near their forest surroundings. In addition, some groups of South Amerindians practiced a method (*tapirage*) by which they could change the natural color of birds into more intense hues.

> The Tupinambá knew how to modify the natural color of the feathers of living birds; they defeathered a certain species of green parrots and coated their bodies with the blood of a toad. The new feathers which appeared had a red or yellow hue. This technology which the French Guiana creoles called "tapirage" was practiced not only by all the Indians of that colony, but also by those of British Guiana and Venezuela. This process, which seems to have been more common north of the Amazon, was nonetheless carried out to the south: Martius observed it among the Mundurucú and others. Roth and Nordenskiold [list] Macusi, Galibi, Wapisiana, Puinave, Achagua, Pomeroon, Uaupes, Mojo and Huanyam. [Métraux adds:] Paressi, Bororo, Mbaya, Guana, Cocama and Omagua. [Some groups—Puinave, Omagua and Cocama—change color of green parrots by making them eat fish fat.] (Métraux 1928:149)

Tapirage did not harm the bird, but was one more reason for domestication.

A Xingú village, visited by Vincenzo Petrullo in one of his expeditions for the Museum in the 1930s, had a harpy eagle in a cage, well fed by hunters and fishermen, and they would share their catch with the bird when they came back from their activities in the forest. The feathers of this powerful and highly admired bird were carefully gathered and stored in baskets in the men's house until the time of rituals, when feather ornaments were assembled. In this and many other cases, after removing the young birds from their parents for the purpose of domestication, Indians care for them and carefully gather their feathers. The domestication process brings strong human attachments to these birds; it has been reported that Indians nourished their domesticated birds very well, constantly feeding them from their own mouths, gently gorging them (Roquette-Pinto 1938:245).

Indians pluck the feathers of their companion birds, but according to ornithologists, this cannot be done too frequently. Overplucking kills birds, and Indians recognize this. While new feathers grow back, the villagers produce their elaborate adornments with available feathers, secured over a long period of time, to meet cultural requirements.

For some groups, feathers were and still are seen as having economic value; domesticated birds were considered by some groups a source of wealth. They were therefore valuable for trading between villages and were offered as gifts during ceremonial visits when marriages were arranged, or village alliances established.

FIGURE 9.3

Waorani Indian from the province of Pastaza in Ecuador, using a blowgun. Photographs by James A. Yost.

Amerindians were thus involved with the domestication of birds for two overall purposes: (1) as a source of feathers for ritual ornaments, and (2) as a means of exchange for specialized products from other ecological regions. As alternatives to capturing a young bird and domesticating it, hunting and trapping were methods widely used throughout South America.

HUNTING AND TRAPPING

There are several types of weapons used in the hunting of birds in South America. The blowgun is one such weapon (see Fig. 9.3). It operates on the piston principle; a puff of air delivers a sharpened or a blunted dart. Among some peoples, the darts are coated with poison made from the curare plant. It has been observed among the Jivaro (Shuara) of Ecuador that "the Indians are able to shoot as far as 30 or 40 meters, and in general they display remarkable dexterity with it" (Karsten 1935:158). Because the weapon is difficult to handle due to its weight and length, the hunter aims at a target by making a circular movement, finds the prey, and shoots quickly.[1] The Cayapa of Ecuador, the Panare and Pemón of Venezuela, and the Wapisiana and Macusi of Guiana all hunt birds with the blowgun. However, not all of these groups are able to produce blowguns; they may acquire them through trade with those people who are near bamboo sources and manufacture them. Blowguns are of different lengths, but in all cases the hunter has at his disposal the means—an almost effortless breath—to project a dart silently through the tube. This silent weapon is most useful for hunting birds and small mammals.

The Cashinahua of Peru, and their neighbors to the south and southeast, are strangers to the blowgun. Instead, they hunt with bows and arrows. Many of the traditional people continue to do so. Large bows are more characteristic of the forest groups, while the small bows are found in the open grassland. The Onas of Tierra del Fuego in Argentina, now extinct, had the shortest bow, which averaged four to five feet in contrast to the long bow of up to 12 feet. Some arrows consist of a thin palm-wood barbed point on a bamboo shaft, and always have feathers on them; another type was made with a trident point. Some groups use the blunted arrows so as not to damage and soil the feathers with blood from the wounded bird. In order to increase the surface area of impact in hunting small birds, the Onas attached a cross-stick to their arrows. The Nambicuara and Karajá of Brazil use two types of arrows according to their objective: the pointed arrows to kill, blunted ones to stun and capture alive.

In addition to blowguns and bows and arrows, many groups employ traps baited with seeds placed on tree branches, and are quite adept at using bird calls to attract the birds. The Karajá are not alone in this deceptive practice, for the Jivaro (Shuara), the Wapisiana, and the Cashinahua are ingenious not only with traps, but with their imitative sounds and mimicry. Among the other methods of capturing birds in South America are nets, decoys, and torches; here ingenuity and skill seem to be especially important. Netting is a form of trapping birds and it has been reported to have been efficiently used among many groups, specifically the Aymara of Bolivia: they drive the prey toward the net. Some groups of the Chaco, the Chiriguana for instance, catch wild pigeons by climbing trees where the birds roost and tying a live bird to a

FIGURE 9.4

	Southern Montaña (1)	Mato Grosso (2)	Guianas (3)	Gran Chaco (4)	Andean (5)	Northern Montaña (6)
Parrot	•	•	•	•	•	•
Toucan	•	•	•		•	•
Macaw	•	•	•		•	
Cotinga	•	•	•		•	
Egret	•	•	•		•	
Heron	•	•	•		•	
Tanager	•	•	•			•
Curassow	•	•	•			
Hawk	•	•	•			
Eagle	•	•	•			
Guan	•	•	•			
Oropendola	•	•	•			
Trumpeter	•	•				
Cacique	•	•				
Potoo	•	•				
Goose		•		•		
Rhea		•		•		
Aracari	•					•
Cock-of-the-Rock	•					
Dacnis	•					
Honeycreeper	•					
Motmot	•					
Hawk-Eagle		•				
Spoonbill		•				
Fruitcrow				•		
Ibis				•		
Vulture				•		
Chachalaca					•	
Jay					•	
Trogon					•	
Fruiteater						•
Totals	20	17	16	7	6	5

Key:

(1) Ameusha, Campa, Cashinahua, Conibo, Shipibo

(2) Bororo, Kayapó, Karaja, Mundurucú, Paressi, Rikbaktsa, Tapirapé

(3) Apalaii, Atorai, Cumiana, Diau, Kataw, Macoa, Mapidian/Mawayana, Parukoto, Tukano, Urukuena, Waiwai, Wapisiana, Warao

(4) Chamacoco, Guaná

(5) Coastal (archaeological), Aymara

(6) Guajiro, Shuara

Regional Significance of Bird Distribution

branch. Then, the hunter sits and waits for other birds to visit, and when they do, they are easy prey. The Terena of Brazil use loop-snares, and when these fail, men or boys swim under the desired water birds (ducks and geese) and come up underneath them, or surprise and kill them with sticks or stones.

Hunters disguise themselves with grass or palm leaves in order to conceal themselves and surprise the birds. This is a frequent practice among the Tobas of Chaco, while the nearby Choroti cover themselves to look like trees. The people of the Gran Chaco, the Tobas in particular, use a combination of self-concealment and skill to swim under wild ducks, pulling them down under the water to drown them; this group, like others to the south, also employ the slingshot and the bolas of the pampas in Argentina, particularly for capturing the rhea. Similarly, the Ona men use a sling to direct walnut-sized stones at the heads of the birds (Gusinde 1923:243). The Yanomamö of Venezuela hunt from elevated platforms, and construct blinds from leaves and vines to shield themselves from view.

Torches to blind the birds were used among the Onas; when birds were sufficiently confused and startled, a group of people descended upon them and clubbed them down, returning in the light of day to collect their prey. The Yaghan of Chile, also extinct, captured birds "with single or multiple noose snares, with the pole snare, and by torchlight" (Cooper 1946:110).

Once the gathering of birds (live or dead) is accomplished, the Indians are careful not to waste all that the bird can offer: meat for food if the bird is considered edible, and bones and feathers for decoration. Through various techniques of hunting, the Indians of different geographic regions were and still are able to provide themselves with the food and feathers needed by the members of the village. The Indians avoid killing for the sake of killing, and have traditionally taken from nature only that which is necessary for their own survival.

The feathers used to produce the objects seen in the exhibit were all "harvested" by the various methods described. They have all been examined by an ornithologist whose specialty is the avifauna of South America (see Robbins, Ch. 10). Robbins was able to identify the birds chosen by Indians from many thousands of available species for the creation of adornments. Figure 9.4 presents his findings based on the exhibit collection.[2] In this table, the birds represented in the elaborate featherwork have been found to have distribution in six distinct regions, and have been ordered in terms of regional significance. The choice of feathers (birds) and other technological features are characteristic of the groups of people who inhabit each region. There is a definite style when objects from the Waiwai (region 3), for instance, are compared with the objects of the Bororo (region 2), Cashinahua (region 1), Chamacoco (region 4), and other groups.

The parrot is the only bird represented in the objects of all groups from the six regions (Fig. 9.5). This observation indicates that the parrot is favored by groups throughout South America, although the specific placement of the feathers during the construction of adornments varies from group to group.

As one moves further down through the data in the table, the incidence of various birds becomes less widespread, steadily decreasing from the toucan—used in five regions—to all those birds (cock-of-the-rock, dacnis, honeycreeper, etc.) found in only a single region's objects. Due to their solitary presence in the feather artifacts, each of these birds is a unique marker for the overall style of the people in that region.

Figure 9.5

Rikbaktsa woman grinding manioc root. Pet macaw in background. Yalauapita Village, Brazil, 1990. Photograph by Michael Bernstein.

Figure 9.6

Rikbaktsa woman with child and pet green parrot. Yalauapita Village, Brazil, 1990. Photograph by Michael Bernstein.

Changes are inevitable and Indian groups have been responding to demands from the West for, among other things, the commercialization of birds. As the Indian cultures undergo changes through contact with outsiders, it must be very difficult for them to resist the offers and demands of traders. Indians too seek to benefit from the goods produced by modern society, such as shotguns, radios, watches, aluminum cooking utensils, and outboard motors. Trading their native products is a way to exchange with, and become incorporated into, the modern economic system.

Many groups realize that Westerners are seeking to obtain their feathered ornaments, and for some groups the production of touristic objects has increased. In these objects, Indians usually represent the overall style of their particular group, yet these adornments are not identical to those traditionally produced for themselves. Clear distinctions are made by the Indians between objects to be sold and traded, and objects to be used for their own ritualistic and ceremonial purposes. Nevertheless, these ornaments are attractive to outsiders and bring cash and other goods through trade. To satisfy the demand for more objects, some groups of Indians have intensified their search for feathers and placed greater stress on the birds from which those feathers are harvested.

Not only are ornaments traded, but many live birds are also exported from some regions by enterprising individuals of native groups who have made contact with outside middlemen. If this exploitation continues at the present rate, many species are in danger of extinction. The moderation of the past, once regulated by traditional ways, is rapidly disappearing. There are many reports confirming this process. For instance, Michael Harner states that among the Jivaro of Ecuador:

> The capturing and taming of . . . birds has increased because of the demand for these by Jivaro trading partners to the west, who trade them to the whites of the frontier (1973:206).

Disregarding the cultural practices of complex and well-established societies, systems just now becoming archaeologically apparent, is dangerous to the resources of nature, birds in particular. Birds are used for indigenous traditions and for those of foreigners. South Amerindians involved in this trade are now acting as if birds are an unlimited resource. Conservation practices, through either traditional culture or recommendations based on modern scientific methods, should be enforced so that future generations can appreciate the beauty and splendor of the birds, and continue to use the traditional feathered ornamentation. The negative influence of the West can be challenged only if the Indians are able to rekindle the cultural practices that they inherited from long ago.

THE SOURCES

by *Mark Robbins*

XII. Feather frontlet (65–10–1c).

"NATURE TEACHES, THOUGH WHAT IT TEACHES IS OFTEN HIDDEN AN

H arpy Eagle. No other bird in the New World signifies strength and power like the Harpy Eagle. It is the world's heaviest and most formidable bird of prey.

T HIS SURVEY PRESENTS AN OVERVIEW of the bird species used in the featherwork of the peoples of tropical and subtropical South America. A brief account of every bird species present in the "Gift of Birds" exhibit is given. Each account contains the bird's habitat requirements, behavior, diet, plumage characteristics, and voice (if known).

Selected birds play a prominent role in the lives of many groups, and this is reflected by the degree to which feathers appear in their artifacts. A common denominator among all of these groups, regardless of whether they lived within continuous rainforest, or along ribbons of it, was the use of the large and colorful parrots. It appears that color was a major criterion in deciding what birds were captured and used. One of the very few sources of vibrant reds, yellows, and blues is the macaws. Macaws are easily domesticated, and thus provide a constant source of these highly desired feathers (see Figs. 10.19–10.22).

Another important source of colorful feathers was the large *Ramphastos* toucans. Like the macaws, a single individual of these enormous billed birds could provide two or three colors. They too are frequently domesticated.

Only a very small percentage of the total number of avian species present were utilized. For example, in some of the richer Amazonian sites, where up to 500 species might be present over the course of a year, no more than 4% of the species were incorporated into these people's featherworks. All of the species that appeared in the feather artifacts are permanent residents.

Information about the natural history of the following species was gleaned from the sources listed in the References and from my field experience.

FAMILY RHEIDAE

FIGURE 10.1

Greater Rhea (*Rhea americana*). This large, ostrichlike species is native to southern South America. Hence, it was found only in the feather pieces of the Chamacoco. This flightless species lives on the pampas, where it feeds on insects and grasses. Rheas are gregarious, with an occasional group of up to 50 individuals seen. They lay their greenish yellow eggs on bare ground, frequently with several hens laying in the same nest. Rhea feathers are rough in texture, producing an almost hairlike appearance. The feathers are drab in color, mostly shades of gray and dull brown.

FAMILY ARDEIDAE

FIGURE 10.2

Great Egret (*Casmerodius albus*). Like the White-necked Heron, this large egret is distributed throughout South America (it is also widely found in North and Central America) and is found principally along watercourses. In addition, its feeding habits and diet are similar to those of the White-necked Heron. Like most other herons, this species breeds in tall trees in large colonies, known as rookeries. The entire body plumage is a single color, an immaculate white that gives this striking bird an elegant appearance. The Great Egret's large, pure white feathers are possessed by few other species in the interior of the continent, thus these unique feathers were an important source for the native peoples' featherworks.

White-necked Heron (*Ardea cocoi*). This large heron is very similar to North America's Great Blue Heron in habits and appearance. It is widespread throughout South America. It feeds on small to moderate-sized fish, frogs, and invertebrates that it encounters along rivers, lakes, and marshes. This heron is largely solitary, although relatively large concentrations occur at favorable feeding sites. Like the Greater Rhea, the White-necked Heron's plumage lacks brilliant colors. The feathers are mostly composed of grays, blacks, and whites.

FAMILY THRESKIORNITHIDAE

FIGURE 10.3

Roseate Spoonbill (*Ajaia ajaja*). The brilliant red and pink plumage, coupled with the unique spatulate tip of its bill, makes the Roseate Spoonbill one of the world's most striking birds. Although it is distributed from the southeastern United States through the Caribbean and Central America to southern South America, it is local throughout most of its range. One of the areas where it is locally abundant, at least seasonally, is in the vast marshes and riverways of the Chaco. Both the pink flight feathers and the brilliant red along the leading edge of the wing were used in the pieces.

FIGURE 10.4

White Ibis (*Eudocimus albus*). This beautiful wader is widespread, being distributed from the southeastern United States to the northern coast of South America. In South America, it is found primarily in mangroves and tidal areas along the Caribbean coast. Like all ibis, this species has a decurved bill that it uses to probe into shallow water for invertebrates. The breeding plumaged adults are immaculate white with black wing tips. The facial skin and bill are scarlet red. The legs are a less intense pink. The immatures are strikingly different from the adults, as they are largely brown with white underparts.

FAMILY ANATIDAE

FIGURE 10.5

Orinoco Goose (*Neochen jubata*). This relatively small, ornate goose is locally distributed along rivers and marshes in both savannah and forest areas east of the Andes. It is locally common in the Chaco, and

the glossy green feathers of the lower back and wings were used.

FAMILY CATHARTIDAE

FIGURE 10.6

King Vulture (*Sarcoramphus papa*). The multicolor, naked head, all-white body and wing coverts, and immense wingspan make this the most spectacular New World vulture. The King Vulture, like its cousins the condors, feeds primarily on carrion. Unlike the majority of the other vultures, this is a forest species. It is fairly common in the lowland rainforest. Featherwork of one group had body and wing covert feathers of both adult and immature vultures. Presumably, birds were captured with bow and arrow as they came in to feed on carrion—for example, deer, peccary—on the forest floor.

FAMILY ACCIPITRIDAE

FIGURE 10.7

White Hawk (*Leucopternis albicollis*). This raptor is one of the world's most stunning, as its plumage is primarily white, a very unusual color for a bird of prey. It is widespread, but local across most of northern and central South America, east of the Andes, where it inhabits mainly humid forest edge and deciduous forest. The White Hawk has a varied diet, as it is known to feed on snakes, lizards, insects, and small mammals. The distinct black and white banded tail feathers were found in one artifact.

FIGURE 10.8

Harpy Eagle (*Harpia harpyja*). No other bird in the New World signifies strength and power like the Harpy Eagle. It is the world's heaviest (reaching over ten pounds) and most formidable bird of prey. With its immense talons it snatches arboreal mammals, such as the sloth and kinkajou, from the forest canopy and subcanopy. Because it feeds on relatively large mammals, it needs large, continuous tracts of pristine rainforest to survive. As a result of deforestation, it has disappeared from a large part of its former range, southern Mexico south to southern South America. This eagle's bulky nest is typically located in an emergent tree that towers above the forest canopy. The nesting period is prolonged, lasting about seven months; this species breeds only every other year.

FIGURE 10.9

Ornate Hawk-Eagle (*Spizaetus ornatus*). This relatively large eagle is one of the most impressive raptors in the world. As its name implies, this is a spectacularly plumaged eagle. The adult's crown is highlighted with a long black crest that the bird erects when it is excited. The face is rufous and the underparts, including the feathering on the legs, are heavily vermiculated with black. The Ornate Hawk-Eagle is widely distributed from southern Mexico south through much of lowland South America (west of the Andes to southern Ecuador; east of the Andes to northern Argentina). Although it is found over a relatively large area, it is now much less common as a result of the clearing of large tracts of the lowland forest. Like most large birds of prey, it needs a huge area for hunting to meet its energy demands. A variety of prey items have been recorded, ranging in size from small rodents to small monkeys.

FAMILY CRACIDAE

FIGURE 10.10

Chaco Chachalaca (*Ortalis canicollis*). Chachalacas are gregarious, chickenlike birds that are generally drab in appearance. The

119

plumage is composed primarily of somber colors, mostly grays and browns. The word chachalaca is derived from the loud rollicking calls that all of the birds in this group make. The Chaco Chachalaca is restricted to extensive forests of southern South America. Groups of this species are commonly encountered foraging for insects and fruit on the ground or in low bushes within the forest. The long tail feathers were commonly used in the featherwork of the people in the Chaco.

FIGURE 10.11

Spix's Guan (*Penelope jacquacu*). Guans are also chickenlike birds, but are considerably larger than their smaller chachalaca relatives. Their plumage is largely blackish, with a greenish gloss. The tips of many of the breast and back feathers are edged with white. Guans are less gregarious than chachalacas, but also feed on fruit and insects. The Spix's Guan is fairly common throughout forested western Amazonia.

FIGURE 10.12

Marail Guan (*Penelope marail*). This species is very similar to the Spix's Guan in plumage and habits. The Marail Guan is restricted to the Guianas and northern Brazil north of the Amazon River. The long tail feathers were used in several feather objects by the people in this region.

FIGURE 10.13

Black Curassow (*Crax alector*). The curassows are the largest and most impressive cracids. They are confiding, and are typically encountered solitarily or in pairs in pristine forest. Like the guans, they commonly forage for fruit from ground level to the subcanopy. Unfortunately, these majestic birds' meat is delicious; as a result, they are commonly hunted and quickly disappear from an area where hunting pressure is at even a moderate level. Curassows, like the Harpy Eagle, are an excellent indicator of how pristine an area is. Both sexes of the Black Curassow have an erectable, short curly crest, a colorful cere (bare skin at the base of the beak), and glossy bluish black plumage. This species has a distribution similar to the Marail Guan's.

FIGURE 10.14

Bare-faced Curassow (*Crax fasciolata*). Unlike the Black Curassow, the plumages of the male and female Bare-faced are strikingly different. The male has a bulbous yellow knob, a relatively long black crest, and glossy bluish black plumage. In contrast, the female lacks the knob, the crest is largely white, the back is blackish, the upper breast and tail are broadly edged with white, and the lower breast and abdomen are a rich cinnamon-buff. This species is restricted to eastern South America (primarily in Brazil). Its habits are similar to those of the Black Curassow.

FIGURE 10.15

Razor-billed Curassow (*Mitu mitu*). The curassows are large turkey-sized birds. They have a well-deserved reputation for tasting good. As a result, this low-density bird frequently is the first species to disappear from an area once humans have arrived. The Razor-billed Curassow gets its name from the large, compressed red maxilla (upper jaw). Both sexes have a relatively large crest that is usually depressed, unless the birds are excited. The plumage is glossy bluish black, except for the chestnut belly and under-tail coverts. The tail is broadly tipped with white. The legs and bill are red. It is found throughout much of the lowland rainforest in western Amazonia, where it typically feeds on the forest floor.

FIGURE 10.16

Helmeted Curassow (*Pauxi pauxi*). The grayish, fig-shaped knob, referred to as a casque, on the maxilla of this curassow is unique. Unlike the preceding species the sexes differ considerably in plumage. The males are blackish with a green sheen, with a white belly and undertail coverts. The females are mainly buff-brown. Their backs, wings, and tails are vermiculated with black. The Helmeted Curassow has a much more limited distribution than the preceding species. It is found in the Upper Tropical and Subtropical zones in northwestern Venezuela and northern Colombia.

FAMILY PSOPHIIDAE

FIGURE 10.17

Gray-winged Trumpeter (*Psophia crepitans*). This unique group of birds were named for their loud resonating call. Trumpeters superficially appear like long-legged chickens; however, their plumage is primarily black, with a purple or green sheen. They are highly gregarious birds: often as many as a dozen may be encountered foraging for fruit and insects on the floor of pristine rainforest. They are readily domesticated. The Gray-winged Trumpeter is restricted to northern South America north of the Amazon River.

FIGURE 10.18

Pale-winged Trumpeter (*Psophia leucoptera*). This species is very similar to the previous species, but replaces it south of the Amazon River.

FAMILY PSITTACIDAE

FIGURE 10.19

Hyacinthine Macaw (*Anodorhynchus hyacinthinus*). The most ubiquitous feathers used in the featherwork of the people of lowland South America were those of the large and brilliantly colored macaws. Each macaw species' plumage is composed of one or more striking colors, with various combinations of vivid reds, yellows, blues, and greens. The very long (ca. 40 cm) tail feathers were particularly prized, as they appeared in a number of pieces. Macaws, the New World's largest parrots, are primarily found in the upper story of relatively pristine forest, where they feed almost exclusively on fruit. Their ear-piercing, raucous calls can be heard at a great distance. These spectacular birds use holes in trees for placing their one or two white eggs. Like most parrots they are highly gregarious and commonly kept as pets. The Hyacinthine Macaw, largest of all parrots, is found only in swampy forests of southern Brazil, where it typically feeds on palm fruit. This impressive macaw's plumage is almost entirely cobalt blue.

FIGURE 10.20

Blue-and-yellow Macaw (*Ara ararauna*). This splendid macaw is widely distributed across much of the northern two-thirds of the continent, where it is encountered principally along watercourses in primary forest. Dorsally, it is mainly rich blue, and ventrally it is a golden yellow.

FIGURE 10.21

Scarlet Macaw (*Ara macao*). The Scarlet Macaw is perhaps the most beautiful of all the macaws, as it is dressed in reds, yellows, blues, and greens. At least formerly it ranged from southeastern Mexico to northern Bolivia; however, as with many of the other macaws, it has been severely affected by deforestation. The long rectrices (tail feathers), wing coverts, and body feathers were commonly seen in a number of feather artifacts of the people in Amazonian South America.

FIGURE 10.22

Red-and-green Macaw (*Ara chloroptera*). This beautiful macaw is very similar to the Scarlet, except the red body feathers are deeper in color, and the wing coverts are green instead of yellow. The two species are frequently seen together at fruiting trees, or along riverbanks where they feed on salt deposits exposed by erosion. Feathers from this species were also commonly used, although not as frequently as those of the Scarlet, by the people of the eastern lowlands.

FIGURE 10.23

Blue-fronted Parrot (*Amazona aestiva*). The *Amazona* parrots are much smaller and less vividly colored than the macaws. They lack the trademark long tail feathers of the macaws. These parrots are gregarious and loquacious, and are most common in the upper story of primary forest, where they feed on fruit. The largely yellow-headed Blue-fronted Parrot is found in eastern South America.

FAMILY NYCTIBIIDAE

FIGURE 10.24

Common Potoo (*Nyctibius griseus*). The potoos are an unusual group of nocturnal birds; they have relatively large eyes and mouths which are special adaptations for capturing large night-flying insects, such as beetles and moths. During the day potoos typically perch upright at the end of dead snags, where their cryptic plumage makes them highly inconspicuous. If it were not for their disturbing, far-carrying vocalizations, they would go largely undetected. The Common Potoo's song is a descending mournful series of whistles.

FAMILY TROGONIDAE

FIGURE 10.25

Trogon or *Pharomachrus* species. The trogons and quetzals are well known for their brilliant, metallic-appearing plumage. In virtually all of the species, the back is an iridescent green, and ventrally the color is a vivid red or yellow, depending on the species. As many as five trogon species may be found in a single lowland rainforest site. If it were not for their oft-repeated calls, these solitary frugivores would often be overlooked, as they sit motionless for extended periods in the middle story of the forest. Trogons nest in tree cavities, where two white eggs are laid.

FAMILY MOMOTIDAE

FIGURE 10.26

Blue-crowned Motmot (*Momotus momota*). Motmots, like the trogons, are inconspicuous, as they often sit motionless for extended periods. Only their hootlike vocalizations reveal their presence. The plumage is mostly a subtle green, which closely matches the lower and mid-level forest vegetation where they typically perch. The most striking feature of their plumage is the racket tips on the central tail feathers. The long, distinctive tail is jerked from side to side as the bird calls from a horizontal limb. Like the trogons, they are primarily seen solitarily or in pairs. They eat virtually anything that they can swallow, ranging from insects and fruit to an occasional small rodent. In the lowland rainforest, motmots usually breed during the dry season, when the low water levels allow them to dig tunnels in the banks of streambeds. Three or four white eggs are laid at the end of a long winding burrow.

FAMILY RAMPHASTIDAE

FIGURE 10.27

Channel-billed Toucan (*Ramphastos vitellinus*) or *Ramphastos* species. Toucans are one of the most characteristic avian groups of the New World tropics. Their enormous beaks and plumage are typically adorned with a variety of colors. Their feather texture is unique, possessing an almost hairlike look and feel. Virtually all species are gregarious, often being encountered in groups consisting of from three to a dozen individuals. Although their diet consists primarily of fruit, they do feed on insects, lizards, small rodents, and even eggs and nestlings of other bird species. They use tree cavities for nesting. Toucan feathers played a major role in the feather-work of all groups, except in the Chaco region, where they were little used. Presumably this is a reflection of the rarity of these toucans in the area where the Chamacoco and Guana lived.

FIGURE 10.28

Aracari (*Pteroglossus* species). Aracaris are a group of small toucans that are most common at the edge of the forest. Like their larger cousins, they move through the forest in small bands, ranging from a couple of individuals to over a dozen. They typically feed on fruit, but they are opportunistic and will consume about any vegetable or animal matter that they can swallow. Virtually all of the species have dark greenish or blackish backs and wing feathers. Ventrally, however, they are much more colorful, with one or more bands of red or black on yellow breast feathers.

FAMILY COTINGIDAE

FIGURE 10.29

Spangled Cotinga (*Cotinga cayana*). This chunky frugivore is one of the most dazzlingly colored birds in the world. Males are entirely clad in a shining turquoise blue except for the throat and upper breast, which are reddish purple. Black bases to the turquoise blue-tipped feathers show through, giving the males a scaly appearance. The females, which alone attend the nest, are more cryptically colored, largely in light browns and grays. Cotingas are typically seen feeding at fruiting trees in the forest canopy; often several birds may be seen together at these feeding sites. Very little is known about their social organization. This species is widely distributed across the lowland rainforest in northern and western South America, east of the Andes.

FIGURE 10.30

Pompadour Cotinga (*Xipholena punicea*). Like other members of this family, the male's plumage is spectacular. Extensive white flight feathers contrast with the maroon red bodies of the males. The long stiff-pointed wing coverts of the males are apparently used for visual enhancement when courting females. The females also have white flight feathers, but are more somberly colored in gray, tinged with brown. This species inhabits the forest canopy, where it feeds on fruit. Very little is known about its natural history. It is found primarily in northern and central South America, east of the Andes.

White-tailed Cotinga (*Xipholena lamellipennis*). This lovely cotinga is closely related to the more widespread Pompadour Cotinga. It is restricted to north-central Brazil. The plumage of this species is quite similar to that of the Pompadour, except that the maroon is replaced by a deep purplish black in the male White-tailed. Although even less is known about this species than about the Pompadour, their diet and habitat preferences are quite similar.

FIGURE 10.31

Crimson Fruitcrow (*Haematoderus militaris*). This is the least known of the cotingas, as virtually nothing exists on its natural history. This fruitcrow's plumage is more spectacular than that of the Red-ruffed, as the male is clad in a brilliant crimson red. The female is similar, except her back is dark brown. One of the reasons it is so poorly known is its rather limited range, the Guianas and north-central Brazil.

FIGURE 10.32

Scaled Fruit-Eater (*Ampelioides tschudii*). This fairly common Andean cotingid is found from Venezuela south to northern Bolivia. It is found in humid, montane forest, primarily between 1000 and 2500 m in elevation, where it is most commonly encountered in the middle to upper story of the forest. As its name implies, fruit constitutes the bulk of its diet. As on most fruit-eaters, the body plumage is primarily yellowish green. The back and underparts are scalloped with black, producing a scaled appearance. The tip of the tail has a wide black band. The sexes are very similar in plumage; the males have a black cap that the females lack.

FAMILY RUPICOLIDAE

FIGURE 10.33

Andean Cock-of-the-Rock (*Rupicola peruviana*). The Cock-of-the-Rock is one of the most spectacular birds in the world. The males along the eastern slope of the Peruvian Andes are a brilliant orange (in Colombia and Ecuador they are red), highlighted with black wings and tail. The females are more cryptically colored, as they are clad mainly in dull olive green. This species has an unusual mating system wherein the males congregate at arenas, called leks. At these arenas they perform complex displays for attracting and mating with the females. The larger leks may have over 20 of the colorful males present. Typically the males clear all vegetation from the ground and branches within their display area. Most Cock-of-the-Rock leks are located near forest streams or in areas where there are rock outcrops. The female constructs her mud-based nest on the side of the rocks, where she lays two white eggs. This species, like its relatives the cotingas and manakins, is highly frugivorous. The Andean Cock-of-the-Rock is restricted to the South American Andes, usually at elevations between 1400 and 2500 m.

FAMILY CORVIDAE

FIGURE 10.34

Plush-crested Jay (*Cyanocorax chrysops*). Like most jays, the Plush-crested is very vocal and conspicuous. It is found in a variety of habitats, ranging from humid forest to more open agricultural environs. It is commonly encountered in small groups that forage on a wide variety of prey, ranging from small insects and fruit to lizards and small rodents. It is found from south-central Brazil south to northern Argentina.

FAMILY EMBERIZIDA

FIGURE 10.35

Green Honeycreeper (*Chlorophanes spiza*). Often the Green Honeycreeper, the Purple Honeycreeper, and the Blue Dacnis are seen foraging at the same fruiting trees. The male Green Honeycreeper is a beautiful turquoise green, with a black hood and red eyes. The female's plumage, a uniform green, makes her quite inconspicuous. This honeycreeper is widespread throughout most of lowland South America in humid forest. The song is a thin, high-pitched series of notes. A shallow cup nest, with two brown-spotted white eggs, is typically placed in the fork of a small tree or bush.

FIGURE 10.36

Blue Dacnis (*Dacnis cayana*). This small tanager is common and widespread throughout most of lowland South America. It inhabits forests ranging from dry deciduous to quite humid. Like most other tanagers it is commonly observed at fruiting trees in the canopy and at the forest's edge. Nonetheless, insects are an important component in its diet. The male is a deep blue, with a black throat, back, and wings. The female has a blue cap, but the remainder of its plumage is green. Both sexes have red irides and tarsi.

FIGURE 10.37

Black-faced Dacnis (*Dacnis lineata*). Like many of the other tanagers this dacnis is fairly gregarious. It is typically encountered in pairs or small groups in a wide range of forest habitats, from second-growth to primary forest. The Black-faced Dacnis is even smaller than the closely related Blue Dacnis. The yellow iris is conspicuous in both

sexes. The males are bright blue on the crown, rump, and underparts. The back and most of the wing are black. In contrast, the females are a dull olive green. Like other tanagers it feeds on insects and fruit. It is fairly widespread throughout much of western and northern Amazonia.

FIGURE 10.38

Swallow-Tanager (*Tersina viridis*). This unique tanager is common in clearings with scattered trees, and in forest edges and openings, particularly along riparian areas. Often several individuals are encountered together as they make aerial sallies to capture insects. Fruit also is a major component of this species' diet. Unlike virtually all other tanagers, *Tersina* lays three white eggs in holes in earthen banks and man-made structures. The male is a brilliant blue, with a black face, whereas the female is emerald green, with heavy green barring on yellow underparts. The Swallow-Tanager is widespread throughout much of the northern two-thirds of the continent.

FIGURE 10.39

Orange-eared Tanager (*Chlorochrysa calliparaea*). As a result of this species' largely green plumage it is often overlooked as it forages in the vegetation. The males are more brightly colored than the females; they have extensive blue on the

breast and belly that is absent in the females. The Orange-eared is found along the eastern slope of the Andes, between 900 and 2000 m, from southern Colombia to northern Bolivia. It feeds on insects and fruit.

FIGURE 10.40

Paradise Tanager (*Tangara chilensis*). In a group well known for being colorful, the Paradise Tanager could be referred to as the "rainbow" tanager, as it is adorned with vivid reds, yellows, blues, purples, and greens. The sexes are virtually identical; the young are less brilliantly colored. It is quite common in forest canopy and edge in northern and western Amazonia. Typically several individuals are encountered foraging at fruiting trees; however, insects are an important component of this tanager's diet. This tanager, like most, gives an uninspiring high, thin song.

FIGURE 10.41

Green-and-gold Tanager (*Tangara schrankii*). This tanager is largely green with bright yellow underparts. It is abundant in the lowland rainforest of western Amazonia, where it is commonly encountered in fruiting trees in the forest canopy and edge. At these fruiting sites, it is frequently seen in company with the Paradise and Turquoise tanagers.

FIGURE 10.42

Golden-naped Tanager (*Tangara ruficervix*). This pretty tanager, largely deep blue with a patch of buff-orange on the nape, is restricted to the Andes. Its elevational range is between 1000 and 2400 m. Its habits are similar to those of the other tanagers.

FIGURE 10.43

Masked Crimson Tanager (*Ramphoceleus nigrogularis*). In a group known for possessing extraordinary colors, the Masked Crimson Tanager stands out. The striking males (the females have the same pattern but are a little duller in color intensity) are clad in brilliant scarlet and black. This tanager is highly frugivorous and is typically found in woodland and forest bordering water. It is restricted to western Amazonia.

FIGURE 10.44

Opal-crowned Tanager (*Tangara callophrys*). This species is fairly common in the canopy and borders of forest in western Amazonia. It is usually seen in pairs or small groups as they forage on fruit and insects. The sexes are identical in plumage color. Dorsally they are mainly black, with an opalescent straw forecrown, stripe above the eye, and rump. The underparts are purplish blue.

FIGURE 10.45

Spotted Tanager (*Tangara punctata*). As its name indicates, this tanager's plumage is heavily spotted with black on a yellowish green background. As a result, this species is very difficult to see as it feeds on fruit and insects in the canopy and borders of forest. It has a disjunct distribution in South America. One population is found on the lower slopes of the Andes from Ecuador south to Bolivia, and the other is located in the lowland forest in the northeastern section of the continent (the Guianas and adjacent Brazil).

FAMILY ICTERIDAE

FIGURE 10.46

Yellow-rumped Cacique (*Celeus cela*) and oropendola species. The plumage of this relatively large blackbird is primarily solid black. However, the wings have a brilliant yellow patch and the rump and base of the tail are also clad in yellow. The ivory-appearing bill and bluish white eye stand out against the black plumage. This highly gregarious cacique is relatively common in a wide variety of semi-open habitats in the humid lowlands of northern and Amazonian South America (it is also found in Panama). Breeding colonies, ranging from just a few individuals to a few hundred, are often found at the edge of lagoons, where their loud and bizarre vocalizations give away their presence long before they are seen. The oblong nests are often in close proximity; at times they may almost touch each other. The eggs are bluish white with chestnut and brown spotting.

SOURCE OF FIGURES

10.1. *Greater Rhea (*Rhea americana*). Photograph by C. Munn. VIREO Project. Courtesy of the Academy of Natural Sciences, Philadelphia.*

10.2. *Great Egret (*Casmerodius albus*). Photograph by B. Volpe. VIREO Project. Courtesy of the Academy of Natural Sciences, Philadelphia.*

10.3. *Roseate Spoonbill (*Ajaia ajaja*). Photograph by H. Cruickshank. VIREO Project. Courtesy of the Academy of Natural Sciences, Philadelphia.*

10.4. *White Ibis (*Eudocimus albus*). Photograph by H. Cruickshank. VIREO Project. Courtesy of the Academy of Natural Sciences, Philadelphia.*

10.5. *Orinoco Goose (*Neochen jubata*). Photograph by J. Dunning. VIREO Project. Courtesy of the Academy of Natural Sciences, Philadelphia.*

10.6. *King Vulture (*Sarcoramphus papa*). Photograph by Steven Holt. VIREO Project. Courtesy of the Academy of Natural Sciences, Philadelphia.*

10.7. *White Hawk (*Leucopternis albicollis*). Photograph by W. S. Clark. VIREO Project. Courtesy of the Academy of Natural Sciences, Philadelphia.*

10.8. *Harpy Eagle (*Harpia harpyja*). Photograph by Steven Holt. VIREO Project. Courtesy of the Academy of Natural Sciences, Philadelphia.*

10.9. *Ornate Hawk-Eagle (*Spizaetus ornatus*). Photograph by R. and M. Hansen. VIREO Project. Courtesy of the Academy of Natural Sciences, Philadelphia.*

10.10. *Chaco Chachalaca (*Ortalis canicollis*). Photograph by J. Dunning. VIREO Project. Courtesy of the Academy of Natural Sciences, Philadelphia.*

10.11. *Spix's Guan (*Penelope jacquacu*). Photograph by J. Dunning. VIREO Project. Courtesy of the Academy of Natural Sciences, Philadelphia.*

10.12. *Marail Guan (*Penelope marail*). Plate from Delacour and Amadon 1973. Courtesy of the Department of Library Services, the American Museum of Natural History.*

10.13. *Black Curassow (*Crax alector*). Plate from Delacour and Amadon 1973. Courtesy of the Department of Library Services, the American Museum of Natural History.*

10.14. *Bare-faced Curassow (*Crax fasciolata*). Plate from Delacour and Amadon 1973. Courtesy of the Department of Library Services, the American Museum of Natural History.*

10.15. *Razor-billed Curassow (*Mitu mitu*). Photograph by J. Dunning. VIREO Project. Courtesy of the Academy of Natural Sciences, Philadelphia.*

10.16. *Helmeted Curassow (*Pauxi pauxi*). Photograph by Sid Lipschutz. VIREO Project. Courtesy of the Academy of Natural Sciences, Philadelphia.*

10.17. *Gray-winged Trumpeter* (*Psophia crepitans*). *Photograph by M. Robbins. VIREO Project. Courtesy of the Academy of Natural Sciences, Philadelphia.*

10.18. *Pale-winged Trumpeter (*Psophia leucoptera*). Photograph by J. Dunning. VIREO Project. Courtesy of the Academy of Natural Sciences, Philadelphia.*

10.19. *Hyacinthine Macaw (*Anodorhynchus hyacinthinus*). Photograph by J. Dunning. VIREO Project. Courtesy of the Academy of Natural Sciences, Philadelphia.*

10.20. *Blue-and-yellow Macaw (*Ara ararauna*). Photograph by C. Munn. VIREO Project. Courtesy of the Academy of Natural Sciences, Philadelphia.*

10.21. *Scarlet Macaw (*Ara macao*). Photograph by J. Dunning. VIREO Project. Courtesy of the Academy of Natural Sciences, Philadelphia.*

10.22. *Red-and-green Macaw (*Ara chloroptera*). Photograph by C. Munn. VIREO Project. Courtesy of the Academy of Natural Sciences, Philadelphia.*

10.23. *Blue-fronted Parrot (*Amazona aestiva*). Photograph by J. Dunning. VIREO Project. Courtesy of the Academy of Natural Sciences, Philadelphia.*

10.24. *Common Potoo (*Nyctibius griseus*). Photograph by J. Dunning. VIREO Project. Courtesy of the Academy of Natural Sciences, Philadelphia.*

10.25. *Collared Trogon (*Trogon collaris*). Photograph by C. H. Greenewalt. VIREO Project. Courtesy of the Academy of Natural Sciences, Philadelphia.*

10.26. *Blue-crowned Motmot (*Momotus momota*). Photograph by C. H. Greenewalt. VIREO Project. Courtesy of the Academy of Natural Sciences, Philadelphia.*

10.27. *Channel-billed Toucan (*Ramphastos vitellinus*). Photograph by C. H. Greenewalt. VIREO Project. Courtesy of the Academy of Natural Sciences, Philadelphia.*

10.28. *Aracari (*Pteroglossus flavirostris*). Photograph by Rob Cardillo. VIREO Project. Courtesy of the Academy of Natural Sciences, Philadelphia.*

10.29. *Spangled Cotinga (*Cotinga cayana*). Plate by Guy Tudor. From Hilty and Brown 1986.*

10.30. *Pompadour Cotinga (*Xipholena punicea*), upper two birds, and White-tailed Cotinga (*Xipholena lamellipennis*), lower bird. Reprinted from David W. Snow,* The Cotingas *in cooperation with the British Museum (Natural History) illustrated by Martin Woodcock (1982); by the Trustees of the British Museum (Natural History) used by permission of the publisher, Cornell University Press.*

10.31. *Crimson Fruitcrow (*Haematoderus militaris*). Reprinted from David W. Snow,* The Cotingas *in cooperation with the British Museum (Natural History) illustrated by Martin Woodcock (1982); by the Trustees of the British Museum (Natural History) used by permission of the publisher, Cornell University Press.*

10.32. *Scaled Fruit-Eater (*Ampelioides tschudii*). Photograph by Rob Cardillo. VIREO Project. Courtesy of the Academy of Natural Sciences, Philadelphia.*

10.33. *Andean Cock-of-the-Rock (*Rupicola peruviana*). Photograph by D. Wechsler. VIREO Project. Courtesy of the Academy of Natural Sciences, Philadelphia.*

10.34. *Plush-crested Jay (*Cyanocorax chrysops*). Photograph by G. Gerow. VIREO Project. Courtesy of the Academy of Natural Sciences, Philadelphia.*

10.35. *Green Honeycreeper (*Chlorophanes spiza*). Photograph by C. H. Greenewalt. VIREO Project. Courtesy of the Academy of Natural Sciences, Philadelphia.*

10.36. *Blue Dacnis (*Dacnis cayana*). Photograph by C. Munn. VIREO Project. Courtesy of the Academy of Natural Sciences, Philadelphia.*

10.37. *Black-faced Dacnis (*Dacnis lineata*). Photograph by J. Dunning. VIREO Project. Courtesy of the Academy of Natural Sciences, Philadelphia.*

10.38. *Swallow-Tanager (*Tersina viridis*). Photograph by C. Volpe. VIREO Project. Courtesy of the Academy of Natural Sciences, Philadelphia.*

10.39. *Orange-eared Tanager (*Chlorochrysa calliparaea*). Photograph by C. H. Greenewalt. VIREO Project. Courtesy of the Academy of Natural Sciences, Philadelphia.*

10.40. *Paradise Tanager (*Tangara chilensis*). Photograph by C. H. Greenewalt. VIREO Project. Courtesy of the Academy of Natural Sciences, Philadelphia.*

10.41. *Green-and-gold Tanager (*Tangara schrankii*). Photograph by C. H. Greenewalt. VIREO Project. Courtesy of the Academy of Natural Sciences, Philadelphia.*

10.42. *Golden-naped Tanager (*Tangara ruficervix*). Photograph by J. Dunning. VIREO Project. Courtesy of the Academy of Natural Sciences, Philadelphia.*

10.43. *Masked Crimson Tanager (*Ramphoceleus nigrogularis*). Photograph by C. H. Greenewalt. VIREO Project. Courtesy of the Academy of Natural Sciences, Philadelphia.*

10.44. *Opal-crowned Tanager (*Tangara callophrys*). Photograph by J. Dunning. VIREO Project. Courtesy of the Academy of Natural Sciences, Philadelphia.*

10.45. *Spotted Tanager (*Tangara punctata*). Photograph by C. H. Greenewalt. VIREO Project. Courtesy of the Academy of Natural Sciences, Philadelphia.*

10.46. *Yellow-rumped Cacique (*Celeus cela*). Photograph by J. Dunning. VIREO Project. Courtesy of the Academy of Natural Sciences, Philadelphia.*

EPILOGUE

FIGURE XIII

Detail of Karajá headdress (89–1–3a,b).

The destruction of the South American rainforest is under way and it will bring about a series of fatal consequences. The destruction of the trees will result in the eventual disappearance of the tropical bird population, diminishing the stock of feathers used by Indians for the artistic production of feather ornaments needed in rituals. Without feathers, the South American Indians will become strangers to many of their traditional values and beliefs. They will be cut off from their own environment, devoid of the emotional intimacy with the habitat that sustained them for so long.

As the trees are felled and the birds depart, the natives of this rainforest must confront a dearth in all spheres of life, a cultural want of significant proportions. The people may remain Indian but adopt a new lifestyle evolving in accordance with the economic principles of other world cultures.

However, if these South American Indians are given the opportunity to maintain their traditional philosophy as caretakers of this natural tropical habitat, they will reinforce their own identity. If the rainforest survives the present destruction, Indians may find strength and pride in keeping the fundamentals of their long-established culture and continue to build upon it without losing their rich heritage.

Ruben E. Reina

INTRODUCTION

1. After I had written this paragraph, I received from Peter G. Roe a copy of his paper "The Language of Plumes: 'Implicit Mythology' in Shipibo, Cashinahua and Waiwai Feather Adornments," in which he discusses the same four functions of feather art. Revision of this essay has profited greatly from my reading his paper.

CHAPTER 1

1. See Zuidema (1983) for a discussion of fox effigy headdresses in Inca times.

2. Although Salomon and Urioste (1991) have translated *caqui* as "toucan," Salomon comments that this identification is not completely secure. It is possible that *caqui* refers to one of the macaw species.

3. Zuidema (1990) provides an introduction to the complexities of Inca kinship and the role of women in Inca times.

4. Quilter (1985:293) found guano and "colorful bird down and feathers," probably from a parrot or other tropical forest species, in the same room with cotton, wool, and needles at the preceramic site of El Paraiso. This may have been a workshop for producing feathered textiles or ornaments, notable for the early date (probably around 1600 B.C.).

5. The first Incas, Manco Capac and his sister-wife Mama Oclla, are very clearly mythical. The last Incas, Atawallpa and Waskhar, were real men, living at the time of the Spanish conquest. It is very difficult, if not impossible, to tell which of the Incas in the succession of rulers between Manco Capac and Atawallpa were historical figures and which were mythical, or even how many there really were.

CHAPTER 2

1. Described in Rowe 1984:179–82.

2. The cord is Z-spun, 2S-plied, like the cotton yarns. A sample was taken from one end for identification. Unfortunately, the broken ends of the cord are both the only place where it can be sampled, and the most deteriorated areas. The fiber is neither cotton nor animal hair; an attempt at further identification will be made later.

3. Some of the sewing cords are four-ply (Z–2S–2Z).

4. The technique used to attach the crest feathers on one headdress, Rowe 1984: fig. 196, is known. This is the same headdress illustrated by Mead (1933:9, pl. III). The feather shaft was lengthened using a short length of reed or quill. A loop was made at one end, and the other end bound to the end of the feather shaft with fine cord, which also secured the loop. A cord was strung through the loops, and the feathers attached in pairs. This is slightly different from the technique used on the Caudivilla headdress, but the final effect is similar.

5. In accordance with Murphy's Law as applied to museum work, most of the Andean textiles were inaccessible for study at the time this article was written, as the collection was being moved into a new storeroom.

6. D'Harcourt (1962:132–33) illustrates three knotting systems, one of which (fig. 96A, knot b) occurs on the pieces I have examined.

Mead (1933:7) has one basic system of carrier and tying cords and two systems of sewing knots. His fig. 4 compares to Fig. 2.12. His fig. 5 uses a double sewing knot similar to Fig. 2.5B but the bent feather shafts are secured by individual binding as well as a tying cord; this technique has not yet turned up in the University Museum collection. I assume that the knots were observed on one or more of the three feather objects he illustrates (one headdress and two "ponchos"), but which system goes with which object is not clear.

Yacovleff (1933:145) shows feather strings made with a single carrier/tying cord, using a knot which occurs frequently in the University Museum collection. As he is clearly referring to Paracas material, perhaps the use of a single cord is a local variant. He also illustrates a method of keeping long feathers in alignment: a supplementary cord tied around each feather shaft at the midpoint. See Appendix, Nos. 5A,C and 7.

7. Rowe 1980:figs. 20B, 21. Compare Fig. 2.12C, and the sewing cord on Fig. 2.5A.

CHAPTER 3

1. Boe is the name by which the indigenous group from central Brazil identify themselves. Due to a misunderstanding by the first explorers, this group of people became known to Westerners as Bororo. They were also called Coroados, which means "the crowned ones," due to the magnificent feathered headdresses they wore.

2. This village was visited by Petrullo on an expedition of The University Museum in 1930 and the objects collected by his expedition are shown in the exhibition "The Gift of Birds." Both Petrullo's study (1931) and my study, and the research of many others throughout almost two centuries, confirm the existence of a strong cultural and artistic continuity in the Bororo society despite successive attempts by outsiders to dominate and change their culture.

3. Two clans of the Tugarege moiety, Aroroe and Paiwoe, were divided into small units due to conflicts between members of the subclans. The subclans were geographically relocated as shown in Figure 3.11.

4. The red pigment (*nonógo*) used for their body painting and for the coloring of raw materials for ornaments is extracted from *urucu* seeds, indigenously known as *nonógo á* The red pigment is extracted from the mature seed and mixed with animal fat for body painting or with latex for funeral ornamentation.

5. In contrast, there are only a few events outside the religious rituals when the owners of *aroe* are allowed to wear their own ritual pieces. The rights to use

of ritual pieces reflect another example of balance and reciprocity between the members of the moieties.

CHAPTER 4

1. In an earlier publication (Kensinger et al. 1975:69–83), I describe how the Cashinahua classify, manufacture, and use headdresses.

2. My teacher, Ward H. Goodenough, to whom I dedicate this paper, used to tell us, "If you want to know why people do what they do, ask them! You don't have to believe what they tell you but you'd better know what they mean by what they say if you don't believe their answer." This paper is an attempt to put that advice to work.

3. A man gets his name from his father's father and a woman gets her name from her mother's mother and/or her father's father's sister.

4. Every individual is a member of one of the two patri-moieties, which are subdivided by gender. A man is a member of his father's sub-moiety while a woman belongs to the sub-moiety of her father's sister and of her mother's mother, who normally is also her father's father's sister. The name of the male sub-moieties is often used to designate both gender sub-moieties. The patri-moieties are further sub-divided into two marriage sections or namesake groups. A man is a member of the same marriage section as his father's father and his son's son while a woman is a member of the same marriage section as her mother's mother and her daughter's daughter. At the same time a man's father and son are members of the other marriage section of his moiety and a woman's father's sister and brother's daughter are members of the other marriage section of her moiety. The moieties and marriage sections regulate marriage and ritual activity. A man marries a woman who is a member of the opposite moiety and of the same marriage section as his father's mother, and takes up residence with his wife and her parents, who ideally are his mother's brother and his father's sister.

5. There is an intentional pun involved in this phraseology. *Hina biden* also means "erect penis" as opposed to *hina pania*, "limp or dangling penis/tail." On those occasions when the women perform the fertility rituals, *kachanawa*, and wear headdresses with tail ornaments, men will frequently taunt their mothers-in-law by saying *Achin, min hina biden hayaki*, "Mother-in-law, you have an erect tail/penis." To which she is likely to respond, *Mina pania-ki*, "Yours is limp." Such an exchange between mother-in-law and son-in-law could happen only within a ritual context.

CHAPTER 5

1. The model of "fabrication" processes developed by Munn in studying Melanesian artifacts offers us a productive alternative to static Western ideas of meaning:

Fabrication taken in [the] broad sense has certain generic features: shifts of matrix or context are made (elements are separated from one context and entered into another), and shifts of organizational level ("new" objects or elements reformulate primary ones on another level). This view of fabrication sets the stage for a study of making processes not simply as, for instance, technological construction, but rather as developmental symbolic processes that transform both socially significant properties or operational capacities of objects, and significant aspects of the relations between persons and objects, between the human and the material worlds. Fabrication seen in this way does not end with technological construction, but consists of the total cycle of conversions effecting significant changes in an object. (1977:39)

2. To understand the cultural meanings behind the items displayed in the exhibit, the "ethnographic present" of this article focuses on roughly the period from the time of Farabee and Ogilvie's visit up through the expeditions of the Danish anthropologists Niels Fock and Jens Yde in the mid-1950s, before missionization and coloni-zation altered many of the Waiwai's practices, including featherwork usage. Although I see problems in the textual device used in anthropology of combining information from different points in time, I will draw on data from my own fieldwork (in 1984–86) or that of Peter Roe et al. (in 1985) when they are consistent with or illuminating of values and meanings that surrounded the use of feather items in the first half of this century. The interactive video in "The Gift of Birds" exhibit explores both past and contemporary Waiwai usage of featherwork.

3. Waiwai and Latin names for the birds these represent are:
harpy eagle: Waiwai *yaymo* (*Harpia harpyja*)
toucans (three species):
    yakwe (*Pteroglossus aracari roraimae*)
    kuyuru (*Rhamphastos vitellinus vitellinus*)
    kwicikwici (*Rhamphastos aurantiirostris*)
macaws (two species):
    red-and-green macaw: *kworo* (*Ara chloroptera*)
    blue-and-yellow macaw: *xaapi* (*Ara ararauna*)
black-crested curassow (also called powis): *pawxi* (*Crax alector Lin.*).
(Information adapted from Yde 1965:128–31)

4. Other birds that supply feathers used more rarely include a few species of brilliantly colored cotingas; the orange cock-of-the-rock; several kinds of green parrots (kept mostly as pets taught to speak); a few species of guans; hawks, buzzards, and chickens (sources of down); and a few other unidentified small birds (Yde 1965:127–33).

5. There are other means of integrating spatial and temporal domains, such as dance, song, tobacco, and exchange, which are not, however, explored in this paper.

6. Alternate sources of the feathers in the diadem can be used. Fock and Yde said toucan feathers were used, but a diadem I obtained used feathers identified as cock-of-the-rock (*Rupicola rupicola*) by Dr. David Willard, ornithologist of the Field Museum of Natural

History. The University Museum identified the feathers in the diadem Farabee collected as channel-billed toucan and crimson fruitcrow.

7. Further evidence for the human connotations of feather headdresses comes from historical reports that these diadems were treated as symbolic substitutes for persons. Coudreau, who explored the Waiwai region in 1884, reported that they rendered diadems to hostile tribes to prevent attacks (cited in Fock 1963:6)—in essence, giving feathers instead of their lives. Cary-Elwes, a missionary who visited the Waiwai in the 1920s, said that feather crowns were among the most important objects they traded with northern groups—suggesting they were a sort of emblem of tribal identity (Colson & Morton 1982:232).

8. I found it revealing when a middle-aged unmarried woman (a rare phenomenon in Waiwai society) complained to me that she could not make any seed necklaces to trade with me because she had no husband to provide feathers to complete their decoration. Full adult status requires a spouse; the capacity to produce items for exchange presumes such a status; economic and social "procreativity" are thus mutually dependent and reciprocally referential.

9. Practically the only exceptions are burden baskets, which are used in the gardens and forest, where featherwork is *not* used (being linked, as we have seen, to the village and socialized beauty); and *tipitis* (woven tubes used to squeeze the juice out of manioc mash), which I presume lack featherwork because the constant drenching makes it impossible to keep them attached.

10. This myth lies behind the other major type of intervillage ritual that the Waiwai traditionally held, the two-month-long Yamo dances, which the Waiwai said they learned from the Anaconda People. Men disguised as anacondas would dance around seated women who would sing, "Come, yamo, come, yamo, you are my *wayamnu* [lover]." (Fock 1963:170–71). Lovers would be taken from the category of persons from which spouses could be selected (classificatory cross-cousins). This ritual drew on themes from the ancient events recounted in the myth of the origin of feather ornaments. In periodically reenacting the myth in ceremonial settings, Waiwai society would touch base with its roots and thereby regenerate itself. This social regeneration was correlated on the individual level with the licensed sexuality encouraged between *wayamnu.*

11. Peter Roe (1990) recounts these two myths at greater length and analyzes them from his own theoretical model of "Solar" vs. "Lunar" birds. His narration of the myth of the Curassow Man is the only version extant in the Waiwai ethnographic literature, and he generously made available to me an earlier manuscript of this and other myths he collected, useful as I was writing up this present paper. Independently analyzing Waiwai featherwork, we have developed different though complementary interpretations. He remains responsible for the crucial insight about the cosmological layering of featherwork on the body.

CHAPTER 8

1. In tropical South America shamans are most often male. There are also female shamans, however, and in some societies—the Warao of the Orinoco Delta, for example—the wife of a *bahana* or "white" shaman is considered a shaman in her own right, with healing powers that are uniquely hers (Wilbert 1987:161–62). Ritual tobacco use in connection with the shaman's practice is also for the most part male, but there are exceptions. Female shamans among the Cuna use tobacco, and Jivaro women undergo a special ritual at puberty, marriage, and repeatedly in the course of later life, "in the course of which they drink quantities of tobacco juice to obtain dream visions" of abundance in food plants and animals; on these occasions, the women "take on a shaman's mediating functions" between the spirit world and human beings (ibid.:154–55).

CHAPTER 9

1. In the Museum's collections, blowguns from the upper Amazon range from six to eight feet in length and from two to five pounds in weight.

2. The findings presented in this table represent only this museum's collections and any conclusions drawn from it are open to question.

PREFACE
Feather Objects in Culture

Eiseley, Loren
1978 **The Star Throwers**. New York: Times Books.

Kluckhohn, Clyde
1985 **Mirror for Man**. Tuscon: University of Arizona Press.

Mead, Margaret
1972 **Blackberry Winter: My Earlier Years**. New York: William Morrow.

INTRODUCTION
Why Feathers?

Gregor, Thomas
1977 **Mehinaku: The Drama of Daily Life in a Brazilian Indian Village**. Chicago: University of Chicago Press.

Murphy, Robert F.
1989 **Cultural and Social Anthropology: An Overture**, 3rd ed. Englewood Cliffs, N.J.: Prentice Hall.

CHAPTER 1
Ancient Plumage: Featherworking in Precolumbian Peru

Arriaga, Father Pablo Joseph de
1968 [1617] **The Extirpation of Idolatry in Peru**, tr. L. Clark Keating. University of Kentucky Press.

Avila, Francisco de
[1598?] see Salomon and Urioste 1991

Bernedo Malaga, Leonidas
1950 El Descubrimiento de Noventa y Seis Mantos del Arte Plumario de los Antiguos Peruanos. **El Deber** (Arequipa, Peru), February 18, 1950.

Betanzos, Juan de
1987 [1551] **Suma y Narración de los Incas**, ed. Maria del Carmen Martín Rubio. Madrid: Atlas.

Cobo, Bernabe
1979 [1653] **History of the Inca Empire**, tr. Roland Hamilton. Austin: University of Texas Press.

1990 [1653] **Inca Religion and Customs**, tr. Roland Hamilton. Austin: University of Texas Press.

Conrad, Geoffrey, and Arthur A. Demarest
1984 **Religion and Empire: The Dynamics of Aztec and Inca Expansionism**. Cambridge: Cambridge University Press.

Donnan, Christopher B.
1978 **Moche Art of Peru: Pre-Columbian Symbolic Communication**. Los Angeles: University of California Press.

Garcilaso de la Vega, El Inca
1987 [1609] **Royal Commentaries of the Incas and General History of Peru**, tr. Harold V. Livermore. Austin: University of Texas Press.

Gonzalez Holguín, Diego
1952 [1608] **Vocabulario de la Lengua General de Todo el Peru Llamada Lengua Qquichua o del Inca**. Lima: Instituto de Historia Universidad Nacional Mayor de San Marcos.

Guaman Poma de Ayala, Felipe
1980 [1583–1615] **El Primer Nueva Corónica y Buen Gobierno**, ed. John V. Murra and Rolena Adorno. Mexico City: Siglo Veintiuno.

Murra, John V.
1962 Cloth and Its Function in the Inca State. **American Anthropologist** 64(4):710–28.

Paul, Anne, and Solveig A. Turpin
1986 The Ecstatic Shaman Theme of Paracas Textiles. **Archaeology** 39(5):20–27.

Peters, Ann H.
n.d. Syntax and Paradigm in a Visual System: Paracas Necropolis "Block Color" Images. Paper presented at the Northeast Conference on Andean Archaeology and Ethnohistory, Amherst, Mass., November 1988.

Quilter, Jeffrey
1985 Architecture and Chronology at El Paraíso, Peru. **Journal of Field Archaeology** 12:279–97.

Rabineau, Phyllis
1975 Catalogue of the Cashinahua Collection. Pp. 151–235 in **The Cashinahua of Eastern Peru**, by Kenneth M. Kensinger et al. Haffenreffer Museum of Anthropology, Brown University Studies in Anthropology and Material Culture, 1.

Rowe, Ann Pollard
1984 **Costumes and Featherwork of the Lords of Chimor: Textiles from Peru's North Coast**. Washington, D.C.: Textile Museum.

Rowe, John H.
1967 Form and Meaning in Chavin Art. Pp. 72–103 in **Peruvian Archaeology: Selected Readings**, ed. John H. Rowe and Dorothy Menzel. Palo Alto, Cal.: Peek Publications.

Sallnow, Michael J.
1987 **Pilgrims of the Andes: Regional Cults in Cusco**. Washington, D.C.: Smithsonian Press.

Salomon, Frank
1980 Killing the Yumbo. Pp. 162–208 in **Cultural Transformations and Ethnicity in Modern Ecuador**, ed. Norman E. Whitten. Urbana: University of Illinois Press.

Salomon, Frank, and George Urioste
1991 **The Huarochirí Manuscript: A Testament of Ancient and Colonial Andean Religion**. Austin: University of Texas Press.

Santacruz Pachacuti Yamqui Salcamaygua, Joan de
1950 [1613] Relación de Antigüedades deste Reyno del Pirí. Pp. 207–81 in **Tres Relaciones de Antigüedades Peruanas**, ed. M. Jimenez de la Espada. Asunción: Editorial Guaranía.

Sharon, Douglas
1976 The Inca Warachikuy Initiations. Pp. 213–36 in **Enculturation in Latin America: An Anthology**, ed. Johannes Wilbert. Los Angeles: UCLA Latin American Center Publications.

1978 **Wizard of the Four Winds: A Shaman's Story**. New York: Free Press.

Squier, Ephraim George
1967 [1869] A Plain Man's Tomb. Pp. 210–16 in **Peruvian Archaeology: Selected Readings**, ed. John H. Rowe and Dorothy Menzel. Palo Alto, Cal.: Peek Publications.

Zuidema, R. T.
1983 Masks in the Incaic Solstice and Equinoctial Rituals. Pp. 149–56 in **The Power of Symbols: Masks and Masquerade in the Americas**, ed. N. Ross Crumrine and Marjone Halpin. Vancouver: University of British Columbia Press.

1990 **Inca Civilization in Cuzco**. Austin: University of Texas Press.

CHAPTER 2

An Ancient Andean Feathered Headdress

D'Harcourt, Raoul
1962 **Textiles of Ancient Peru and Their Techniques**. Seattle: University of Washington Press.

Mead, Charles W.
1908 Technique of Some South American Feather-Work. **Anthropological Papers of the American Museum of Natural History** 1(1):3–17.

Rowe, Ann Pollard
1980 Textiles from the Burial Platform of Las Avispas at Chan Chan. **Nawpa Pacha** 18:81–148.

1984 **Costumes and Featherwork of the Lords of Chimor: Textiles from Peru's North Coast.**. Washington, D.C.: Textile Museum.

Yacovleff, E.
1933 Arte Plumaria entre los Antiguos Peruanos. **Revista del Museo Nacional** (Lima) 2:137–58.

CHAPTER 3

Social and Spiritual Languages of Feather Art: The Bororo of Central Brazil

Albisetti, César, and Angelo Jayme Venturelli
1962 **Enciclopédia Bororo**. Publicacão no. 1, Museu Regional Dom Bosco. Campo Grande, Mato Grosso: Museu.

Calil Zarur, Elizabeth Netto
1989 Art and Symbolism in Central Brazil: The Bororo Indians of Mato Grosso. Ph.D. dissertation, University of Georgia, Athens.

Petrullo, V. M.
1931 Primitive Peoples of Mato Grosso. **University Museum Journal** 23:81–184.

CHAPTER 4

Feathers Make Us Beautiful: The Meaning of Cashinahua Feather Headdresses

Kensinger, Kenneth M., Phyllis Rabineau, Helen Tanner, Susan G. Ferguson, and Alice Dawson
1975 **The Cashinahua of Eastern Peru**. Haffenreffer Museum of Anthropology, Brown University Studies in Anthropology and Material Culture, 1.

CHAPTER 5

Fragments of the Heavens: Feathers as Ornaments Among the Waiwai

Colson, Audry Butt, and John Morton
1982 Early Missionary Work among the Taruma and Waiwai of Southern Guyana. **Folk** (Copenhagen) 24:203–61.

Farabee, William C.
1918 **The Central Arawaks**. Philadelphia: University Museum, University of Pennsylvania.

1924 **The Central Caribs**. Philadelphia: University Museum, University of Pennsylvania.

Fock, Niels
1963 **Waiwai: Religion and Society of an Amazonian Tribe**. Nationalmuseets Skrifter, Etnografisk Raekke, 8. Copenhagen: National Museum.

Howard, Catherine V.
1988 Trade Beads, Women's Sexuality and Men's Oratory among the Waiwai of Northern Amazonia. Paper presented at the 89th Annual Meetings of the American Anthropological Association, Phoenix, Ariz.

n.d. Mawayana Myths. Ms., University of Chicago.

Kopytoff, Igor
1986 The Cultural Biography of Things: Commoditization as Process. Pp. 64–69 in **The Social Life of Things**, ed. A. Appadurai. Cambridge: Cambridge University Press.

Mauss, Marcel
1967 **The Gift**, tr. I. Cunnison. New York: W. W. Norton.

Munn, Nancy D.
1974 Symbolism in a Ritual Context: Aspects of Symbolic Action. Pp. 579–612 in **Handbook of Social and Cultural Anthropology**, ed. J. J. Honigmann. New York: Rand McNally.

1977 The Spatiotemporal Transformations of Gawa Canoes. **Journal de la Société des Océanistes** 33:39–53.

1986 **The Fame of Gawa: A Symbolic Study of Value Transformation in a Massim (Papua New Guinea) Society**. Cambridge: Cambridge University Press.

Ogilvie, John
n.d. A Factual Account of Indian Life, Pp. 44–408. Unpublished ms., University Museum Archives, University of Pennsylvania.

Pezzati, Alessandro
n.d. Narrative of W. C. Farabee's Amazon Expedition 1913–1916. Unpublished ms., University Museum Archives, University of Pennsylvania.

Roe, Peter G.
1989a The Language of the Plumes: 'Implicit Mythology' in Shipibo, Cashinahua and Waiwai Feather Adornments. Paper presented at the 7th LAILA/AILA International Symposium, Albuquerque, N.M.

1989b Of Rainbow Dragons and the Origins of Designs: The Waiwai *Urufiri* and the Shipibo *Ronin ehua*. **Latin American Indian Literatures Journal** 5:1–67.

1990 Gifts of the Birds: Avian Proto-Cultural Donors and Ogres in Waiwai Mythology. Paper presented at the 8th LAILA/AILA International Symposium, San José, Costa Rica.

Turner, Terence S.
1979 The Gê and Bororo Societies as Dialectical Systems: A General Model. Pp. 147–78 in **Dialectical Societies**, ed. D. Maybury-Lewis. Cambridge, Mass.: Harvard University Press.

1980 The Social Skin. Pp. 112–40 in **Not Work Alone**, ed. J. Cherfas and R. Lewin. Beverly Hills: Sage.

1991 "We Are Parrots," "Twins Are Birds": "Play of Tropes" as Operational Structure. Pp. 121–58 in **Beyond Metaphor: The Theory of Tropes in Anthropology**, ed. J. Fernandes. Stanford: Stanford University Press.

Weiner, Annette
1983 A World of Made Is Not a World of Born: Doing Kula on Kiriwina. Pp. 00–00 in **The Kula: New Perspectives on Massim Exchange**, ed. J. Leach and E. Leach. Cambridge: Cambridge University Press.

Yde, Jens
1965 **Material Culture of the Waiwái**. Nationalmuseets Skrifter, Etnografisk Raekke, 10. Copenhagen: National Museum.

CHAPTER 6

Feathers are for Flying

Albisetti, César, and Angelo Jayme Venturelli
1962 **Enciclopédia Bororo**, Vol. 1. Publicacao no. 1, Museu Regional Dom Bosco. Campo Grande, Mato Grosso: Museu.

Becher, Hans
1960 **Die Surára und Pakidái: Zwei Yanonámi-Stämme in Nordwestbrasilien**. Mitteilungen aus dem Museum für Völkerkunde in Hamburg, 26. Hamburg: Museum.

Biocca, Ettore
1966 **Viaggi tra gli Indi, Alto Rio Negro—Alto Orinoco; Appunti di un**

Biologo. Vol. 2, **Gli Indi Yanoáma**. Rome: Consiglio Nazionale delle Ricerche.

Boglár, Lajos
1965 Anmerkungen zur Jagd bei den Nambikuara-Indianern. **Abhandlungen und Berichte des Staatlichen Museums für Völkerkunde Dresden** (Berlin) 24:37–48.

Dawson, Alice
1975 Graphic Art and Design of the Cashinahua. Pp. 131–49 in **The Cashinahua of Eastern Peru**, by Kenneth M. Kensinger et al. Haffenreffer Museum of Anthropology, Brown University Studies in Anthropology and Material Culture, 1.

Flint, Weston
1891 The Arrow in Modern Archery. **American Anthropologist** 4:63–67.

Guppy, Nicholas
1958 **Wai-wai: Through the Forests North of the Amazon**. London: John Murray.

Heath, E. G., and Vilma Chiara
1977 **Brazilian Indian Archery**. Manchester: Simon Archery Foundation.

Henry, Jules
1964 **Jungle People: A Kaingáng Tribe of the Highlands of Brazil**. New York: Random House.

Holmberg, Allan R.
1969 **Nomads of the Long Bow: The Siriono of Eastern Bolivia**. American Museum Science Books. Garden City, N.Y.: Natural History Press.

Hough, Walter
1891 Arrow Feathering and Pointing. **American Anthropologist** 4:60–63.

Kensinger, Kenneth M.
1989 Hunting and Male Domination in Cashinahua Society. Pp. 18–26 in **Farmers as Hunters: The Implications of Sedentism**, ed. Susan Kent. Cambridge: Cambridge University Press.

Kensinger, Kenneth M., Phyllis Rabineau, Helen Tanner, Susan G. Ferguson, and Alice Dawson
1975 **The Cashinahua of Eastern Peru**. Haffenreffer Museum of Anthropology, Brown University Studies in Anthropology and Material Culture, 1.

Lane, Federico
1959 Arcos e Flechas dos Indios Kaingáng do Estado de São Paulo. **Revista do Museu Paulista** (São Paulo) n.s., 11:71–97.

Lyon, Patricia J.
1987 Language and Style in the Peruvian Montaña. Pp. 101–14 in **Ethnicity and Culture**, ed. Réginald Auger, Margaret F.

Glass, Scott MacEachern, and Peter H. McCartney. Calgary: Archaeological Association, University of Calgary.

Métraux, Alfred
1949 Weapons. Pp. 229–63 in **Handbook of South American Indians**, Vol. 5, ed. Julian Steward. Bureau of American Ethnology, Bulletin 143. Washington, D.C.: U.S. Government Printing Office.

Nimuendajú, Curt
1926 **Die Palikur-Indianer und ihre Nachbarn**. Göteborgs Kungl. Vetenskaps-och Vitterhets-Samhälles Handlingar, Fjärde Följden, 31(2). Göteborg: Elanders Boktryckeri Aktiebolag.

Rabineau, Phyllis
1975 Catalogue of the Cashinahua Collection. Pp. 151–235 in **The Cashinahua of Eastern Peru**, by Kenneth M. Kensinger et al. Haffenreffer Museum of Anthropology, Brown University Studies in Anthropology and Material Culture, 1.

Reina, Ruben E., and Robert M. Hill, II
1978 **The Traditional Pottery of Guatemala**. Austin: University of Texas Press.

Rydén, Stig
1941 **A Study of the Siriono Indians**. Göteborg: Elanders Boktryckeri Aktiebolag.

Siskind, Janet
1973 **To Hunt in the Morning**. New York: Oxford University Press.

Steinen, Karl von den
1894 **Unter den Naturvölkern Zentral-Brasiliens: Reiseschilderung und Ergebnisse der Zweiten Schingú-Expedition, 1887–1888**. Berlin: Dietrich Reimer.

Wilbert, Johannes
1972 **Survivors of Eldorado: Four Indian Cultures of South America**. New York: Praeger Publishers.

Yde, Jens
1965 **Material Culture of the Waiwái**. Nationalmuseets Skrifter, Etnografisk Raekke, 10. Copenhagen: National Museum.

Chapter 7

Feathers of Blood & Fire:
The Mythological Origins of Avian Coloration

Ayensu, Edward S., ed.
1980 **Jungles**. New York: Crown Publishers.

d'Ans, André-Marcel
1975 **La Verdadera Biblia de los Cashinahua**. Lima: Mosca Azul Editores.

Farabee, William C.
1918 **The Central Arawaks**. Philadelphia: The University Museum, University of Pennsylvania.

Fock, Niels
1963 **Waiwai: Religion and Society of an Amazonian Tribe**. Nationalmuseets Skrifter, Etnografisk Raekke 8. Copenhagen: National Museum.

Gregor, Thomas
1985 **Anxious Pleasures**. Chicago: University of Chicago Press.

Hahn, Robert A.
1976 Rikbakca Categories of Social Relations: An Epistemological Analysis. Ph.D. dissertation, Harvard University, Cambridge.

Levi-Strauss, Claude
1969 **The Raw and the Cooked**, tr. John and Dorothy Weightman. New York: Harper and Row Publishers.

Murphy, R. F.
1958 **Mundurucú Religion**. Berkeley: University of California Press.

Roe, Peter G.
1982 **The Cosmic Zygote**. New Brunswick, N.J.: Rutgers University Press.

Von Hagen, Victor Wolfgang
1937 **Off with Their Heads**. New York: Macmillan.

Wagley, Charles
1977 **Welcome of Tears**. New York: Oxford University Press.

Weiss, Gerald
1975 **Campa Cosmology**. Anthropological Papers 52(5). New York: American Museum of Natural History.

Wilbert, Johannes, ed.
1970 **Folk Literature of the Warao Indians**. Los Angeles: UCLA Latin American Center Publications.

Wilbert, Johannes, and Karin Simoneau, eds.
1982a **Folk Literature of the Mataco Indians**. Los Angeles: UCLA Latin American Center Publications.

1982b **Folk Literature of the Toba Indians**. Los Angeles: UCLA Latin American Center Publications.

1983 **Folk Literature of the Bororo Indians**. Los Angeles: UCLA Latin American Center Publications.

1985 **Folk Literature of the Chorote Indians**. Los Angeles: UCLA Latin American Center Publications.

1986 **Folk Literature of the Guajiro Indians**, Vols. 1 and 2. Los Angeles: UCLA Latin American Center Publications.

1987a **Folk Literature of the Chamacoco Indians**. Los Angeles: UCLA Latin American Center Publications.

1987b **Folk Literature of the Nivakle Indians**. Los Angeles: UCLA Latin American Center Publications.

1988 **Folk Literature of the Mocovi Indians**. Los Angeles: UCLA Latin American Center Publications.

1989 **Folk Literature of the Toba Indians**, Vol. 2. Los Angeles: UCLA Latin American Center Publications.

CHAPTER 8

Crowns of Power: Bird and Feather Symbolism in Amazonian Shamanism

Alexander, Michael, ed.
1976 **Discovering the New World, Based on the Works of Theodore de Bry**. New York: Harper and Row.

Brown, Leslie
1976 **Eagles of the World**. New York: Universe Books.

Crévaux, Jules Nicolas
1883 **Voyages dans l'Amérique du Sud**... Paris: Hachette.

Donnan, Christopher B.
1976 **Moche Art and Iconography**. Los Angeles: UCLA Latin American Center Publications.

Furst, Peter T.
1968 The Olmec Were-Jaguar Motif in the Light of Ethnographic Reality. Pp. 132–74 in **Dumbarton Oaks Conference on the Olmec**, ed. Elizabeth P. Benson. Washington, D.C.: Dumbarton Oaks Research Library and Collections.
1974 Archaeological Evidence for Snuffing in Prehispanic Mesoamerica. **Botanical Museum Leaflets** 24(1):1–28.
1976 **Hallucinogens and Culture**. San Francisco: Chandler and Sharp.

Goeje, C. H. de
1943 Philosophy, Initiation and Myths of the Indians of Guiana and Adjacent Countries. **Internationales Archiv für Ethnographie** (Leiden) 45.

Goldman, Irving
1963 **The Cubeo: Indians of the Northwest Amazon**. Illinois Studies in Anthropology, 2. Urbana: University of Illinois Press.

Hissink, Karin, and Albert Hahn
1961 **Die Tacana**, Vol. 1. Stuttgart: W. Kohlhammer.

Koch-Grünberg, Theodor
1916 **Vom Roroima zum Orinoco**, Vol. 2. Stuttgart: Schrecker und Schroder.

Métraux, Alfred
1945 The Tupinambá. Pp. 95–133 in **Handbook of South American Indians**, Vol. 3, ed. . Bureau of American Ethnology, Bulletin 143. Washington, D.C.: U.S. Government Printing Office.

Nimuendajú, Curt
1914 Die Sagen von der Erschaffung und Vernichtung der Welt als Grundlagen der Religion der Apapocuva-Guaraní. **Zeitschrift für Ethnologie** 46.

Preuss, Konrad Theodor
1921 **Religion und Mythologie der Uitoto**, Vol. 1. Göttingen: .

Reichel-Dolmatoff, Gerardo
1967 Rock Paintings of the Vaupés: An Essay of Interpretation. **Folklore Américas** 26(2):107–13.

1971 **Amazonian Cosmos**. Chicago: University of Chicago Press.

1975 **The Shaman and the Jaguar**. Philadelphia: Temple University Press.

Roth, Walter E.
1915 An Inquiry into the Animism and Folklore of the Guiana Indians. **Thirtieth Annual Report of the Bureau of American Ethnology**. Washington, D.C.: U.S. Government Printing Office.

Wagley, Charles
1959 Tapirapé Shamanism. Pp. 405–23 in **Readings in Anthropology**, Vol. 2, ed. Morton H. Fried. New York: Thomas Y. Crowell.

Wassén, S. Henry
1965 **The Use of Some Specific Kinds of South American Snuff and Related Paraphernalia**. Etnologiska Studier 28. Göteborg: Ethnographical Museum.

Wilbert, Johannes
1974 The Calabash of the Ruffled Feathers. **Stones, Bones and Skin: Ritual and Shamanic Art**. Artscanada 184–87:90–93.

1985 The House of the Swallow-tailed Kite. Pp. 145–82 in **Animal Myths and Metaphors in South America**, ed. Gary Urton. Salt Lake City: University of Utah Press.

1987 **Tobacco and Shamanism in South America**. New Haven: Yale University Press.

Zerries, Otto
1962 Die Vorstellung vom Zweiten Ich und die Rolle der Harpye in der Kultur Naturvölker Süd-amerikas. **Anthropos** 57:889–914.

1977 Die Bedeutung des Federschmuckes des Südamerikanischen Schamanen und dessen Beziehung zur Vogelwelt. **Paideuma** 23:277–312.

CHAPTER 9

Harvesting Feathers

Blomberg, R.
1961 **Chavante**, tr. R. Spink. New York: Taplinger.

Harner, Michael
1973 **The Jivaro**. Garden City, N.Y.: Anchor Press/Doubleday.

Karsten, Raphael
1935 **The Head-hunters of the Western Amazonas**. Helsinki: Societas Scientiarum Fennica.

Métraux, Alfred
1928 **La Civilisation Matérielle des Tribus Tupi-Guarani**. Paris: P. Geuthner.

Roquette-Pinto, E.
1938 **The Nambicuara Indians of Central Brazil**. São Paulo: Companhia Editora National.

Stern, Jane, and Michael Stern
1990 A Reporter at Large (Parrots). **The New Yorker** (July 30).

Steward, Julian, ed.
1949 **Handbook of South American Indians**, Vol. 5. Bureau of American Ethnology, Bulletin 143. Washington, D.C.: U.S. Government Printing Office.

CHAPTER 10

The Sources of Feathers

Delacour, J., and D. Amadon
1973 **Curassows and Related Birds**. New York: American Museum of Natural History.

Hilty, S. L., and W. L. Brown
1986 **A Guide to the Birds of Colombia**. Princeton: Princeton University Press.

Isler, M. L., and P. R. Isler
1987 **The Tanagers: Natural History, Distribution, and Identification**. Washington, D.C.: Smithsonian Institution Press.

Meyer de Schauensee, R.
1970 **A Guide to the Birds of South America**. Wynnewood, Pa.: Livingston.

Ridgely, R. S., and G. Tudor
1989 **The Birds of South America**. Vol. 1, **The Oscine Passerines**. Austin: University of Texas Press.

Snow, D.
1982 **The Cotingas**. New York: Cornell University Press.

CREDITS

ILLUSTRATIONS	EXCERPTS

ILLUSTRATIONS

Figures 1.16 and 1.17: Copyright held by the photographer, Dinorah Marquez.

Figures 1.23 and 1.27: Reprinted with permission of the publisher, Institut d'Ethnologie (Paris), from *El Primer Nueva Coronica y Buen Gobierno* by Felipe Guaman Poma, pages 132 and 256 respectively.

Figures 3.2–3.22: Copyright held by Elizabeth Netto Calil Zarur.

Figures 4.2, 4.3, 4.8, 4.11, 4.12: Copyright held by Kenneth M. Kensinger.

Figures 5.1–5.3, 5.5, 5.6, 5.11, 5.15–5.21: Copyright held by Catherine Howard.

Figures 6.2–6.9: Permission for reproduction must be obtained from Patricia J. Lyon.

Figures 8.4, 8.13, 8.14: Copyright held by the photographer, Richard Evans Schultes.

Figure 9.3: Copyright held by the photographer, James A. Yost.

Figures 10.1–10.46: Please see page 127 for credits.

EXCERPTS

Introduction:
Permission to reprint the excerpt on page xxi has been granted by the publisher, the University of Chicago Press. Please see References for details of specific citation.

Chapter 1:
Permission to reprint excerpts on pages 5, 9, 11–15 has been granted by the University of Texas Press at Austin. Please see References for details of specific citations.

Chapter 7:
Permission has been granted by the American Museum of Natural History to reprint the excerpt on page 80. Please see References for details of specific citation.

Permission has been granted by The Regents of the University of California to reprint excerpts from several volumes of *Folk Literature of South American Indians* published by the Latin American Center of the University of California at Los Angeles. These appear on pages 81, 85, 86, 88–91. Please see References for details of specific citations.

Permission has been granted by the Rutgers University Press to reprint the excerpts on pages 83 and 88. Please see References for details of specific citations.

Permission has been granted by the University of California Press to reprint the excerpt on page 84. Please see References for details of specific citation.

Elizabeth Netto Calil Zarur
received her Ph.D. in the history of art from the University of Georgia at Athens in 1989, concentrating on the Pre- and Post-columbian periods in the Americas, and has done fieldwork among the Bororo Indians of Brazil. The title of her dissertation is "Art and Symbolism in Central Brazil: The Bororo Indians of Mato Grosso." As a consultant to the project, she identified the clan and subclan for the pieces in the exhibit and explained how the Bororo use certain colors, species, and patterns to mark identity in their featherwork. Dr. Calil Zarur also holds an M.F.A. in the history of textiles and fabric design from the University of Georgia, Athens, and has exhibited her own artwork. She is currently a member of the Art Department at Wheaton College, Norton, Massachusetts.

Kay L. Candler
is a research associate at The University Museum, University of Pennsylvania, a doctoral candidate in anthropology at the University of Illinois, Urbana-Champaign, and the assistant curator of "The Gift of Birds." Ms. Candler's area of specialization is the southern highlands of Peru, where she has conducted two and a half years of ethnographic fieldwork. This is reflected in her dissertation, "Place and Thought in a Quechua Household Ritual." She served the University Museum Featherwork Project as consultant on the archaeological feather ornamentation from coastal Peru.

Peter T. Furst
is a research associate in the American Section of The University Museum, University of Pennsylvania, and an emeritus professor of anthropology and Latin American studies at the State University of New York at Albany. Dr. Furst earned his Ph.D. from the University of California at Los Angeles in 1966, and has conducted extensive fieldwork in Mesoamerica, specifically among the Huichol Indians. He has published widely on such topics as iconography, shamanism, and hallucinogens.

Virginia Greene
is the senior conservator at The University Museum, University of Pennsylvania. Ms. Greene received her M.A. in anthropology from the University of Pennsylvania in 1968 and her diploma in conservation from the University of London in 1971. She has done field conservation in Israel, Ireland, and England, and has recently completed a study of the pottery figurines found at the Mayan site of Tikal, Guatemala.

Catherine V. Howard
is a doctoral candidate in anthropology at the University of Chicago and has completed two years of fieldwork among the Waiwai of northern Amazonia. Among Ms. Howard's areas of research are intervillage gathering festivals and the indigenous conception of beauty. Her dissertation, "Wrought Identities: The Waiwai Indians' search for the 'Hidden Tribes' of Northern Amazonia," is a study of the expeditions conducted by the Waiwai to contact and assimilate remote groups in the region. She served as consultant on the Waiwai for the University Museum Featherwork Project.

Kenneth M. Kensinger
is a professor of anthropology at Bennington College and the coeditor of this catalogue. His extensive knowledge of Cashinahua culture and language is reflected in numerous publications, and he is responsible for the Museum's collection of Cashinahua artifacts, gathered on many trips to the group's home in Peru. His scholarly interests focus on all facets of Cashinahua life, ranging from hunting and the cultivation of manioc to language and craft production.

Patricia J. Lyon
is a research associate at the University of California, Berkeley, and has done extensive anthropological, archaeological, and ethnohistorical work in Peru. Dr. Lyon received her Ph.D. in anthropology from the University of California, Berkeley, in 1967; the title of her dissertation was "Singing as Social Interaction among the Wachipaeri of Eastern Peru." She has edited a volume of articles on South American ethnology, Native South Americans, and her most recent publication deals with change in Wachipaeri marriage patterns. The pottery and arrows of Peru are among her scholarly interests.

Jon F. Pressman
is a graduate student in Anthropology at the University of Pennsylvania, a research assistant for "The Gift of Birds," and a junior fellow in the Kolb Foundation of The University Museum, University of Pennsylvania.

Ruben E. Reina
is an emeritus professor of anthropology at the University of Pennsylvania, curator of the American Section at The University Museum and of "The Gift of Birds", and coeditor of this catalogue. Dr. Reina received his Ph.D. from the University of North Carolina in 1957 and has done extensive fieldwork in Guatemala, Argentina, Spain, and Puerto Rico. He has taught at the University of Pennsylvania since 1957 and continues to teach and conduct research on South American and Mayan cultures. He has published widely on such topics as community culture, cultural change and continuity, and urbanization.

Mark B. Robbins
received his M.S. in zoology from Louisiana State University in 1982, and is the ornithological collections manager at the Academy of Natural Sciences, Philadelphia. As a specialist in the birds of South America, Mr. Robbins was able to identify the various avian species represented in the feathered objects of the exhibit and to provide the necessary background information on these birds. He has done extensive fieldwork in Colombia, Ecuador, and Peru. His scholarly interests include feeding, display and mating habits of South American avifauna.

DATE DUE

APR 1 2 2004